RETRIEVAL & RENEWAL

IN CATHOLIC THOUGHT

The middle years of this century marked a particularly intense time of crisis and change in European society. During this period (1930-1950), a broad intellectual and spiritual movement arose within the European Catholic community, largely in response to the secularism that lay at the core of the crisis. The movement drew inspiration from earlier theologians and philosophers such as Möhler, Newman, Gardeil, Rousselot, and Blondel, as well as from men of letters like Charles Péguy and Paul Claudel.

The group of academic theologians included in the movement extended into Belgium and Germany, in the work of men like Emile Mersch, Dom Odo Casel, Romano Guardini, and Karl Adam. But above all the theological activity during this period centered in France. Led principally by the Jesuits at Fourviére and the Dominicans at Le Saulchoir, the French revival included many of the greatest names in twentieth-century Catholic thought: Henri de Lubac, Jean Daniélou, Yves Congar, Marie-Dominique Chenu, Louis Bouyer, and, in association, Hans'Urs von Balthasar.

It is not true — as subsequent folklore has it — that those theologians represented any sort of self-conscious "school": indeed, the differences among them were important. At the same time, they were united in the double conviction that theology had to speak to the present situation, and that the condition for doing so faithfully lay in a recovery of the Church's past. In other words, they all saw clearly that the first step in what later came to be known as *aggiornamento* had to be *ressourcement* — a rediscovery of the riches of the whole of the Church's two thousand year tradition. According to de Lubac, for example, all of his own works as well as the entire *Sources chrétiennes* collection are based on the presupposition that "the renewal of Christian vitality is linked at least partially to a renewed exploration of the periods and of the works where the Christian tradition is expressed with particular intensity."

In sum, for the *ressourcement* theologians theology involved a "return to the sources" of Christian faith, for the purpose of drawing out the meaning and significance of these sources for the critical questions of our time. What these theologians sought was a spiritual and intellectual communion with Christianity in its most vital moments as transmitted to us in its classic texts, a communion which would nourish, invigorate, and rejuvenate twentieth-century Catholicism.

The *ressourcement* movement bore great fruit in the documents of the Second Vatican Council and has deeply influenced the work of Pope John Paul II and Cardinal Joseph Ratzinger, Prefect of the Sacred Congregation of the Doctrine of the Faith.

The present series is rooted in this twentieth-century renewal of theology, above all as the renewal is carried in the spirit of de Lubac and von Balthasar. In keeping with that spirit, the series understands *ressourcement* as revitalization: a return to the sources, for the purpose of developing a theology that will truly meet the challenges of our time. Some of the features of the series, then, will be:

- a return to classical (patristic-mediaeval) sources;
- a renewed interpretation of St. Thomas;
- a dialogue with the major movements and thinkers of the twentieth century, with particular attention to problems associated with the Enlightenment, modernity, liberalism.

The series will publish out-of-print or as yet untranslated studies by earlier authors associated with the *ressourcement* movement. The series also plans to publish works by contemporary authors sharing in the aim and spirit of this earlier movement. This will include interpretations of de Lubac and von Balthasar and, more generally, any works in theology, philosophy, history, and literature which give renewed expression to a classic Catholic sensibility.

The editor of the Ressourcement series, David L. Schindler, is Gagnon Professor of Fundamental Theology at the John Paul II Institute in Washington, D.C., and editor of the North American edition of *Communio: International Catholic Review,* a federation of journals in thirteen countries founded in Europe in 1972 by Hans Urs von Balthasar, Jean Daniélou, Henri de Lubac, Joseph Ratzinger, and others.

MAURICE BLONDEL

The Letter on Apologetics

AND

History and Dogma

Texts presented and translated by

ALEXANDER DRU

and

ILLTYD TRETHOWAN

WILLIAM B. EERDMANS PUBLISHING COMPANY
GRAND RAPIDS, MICHIGAN

To Henri de Lubac, S.J.

The Letter on Apologetics first published as *Lettre sur les exigences de la pensée contemporaine en matière d'apologétique et sur le méthode de la philosophie dans l'étude du problème religieux* (in *Annales de Philosophie Chrétienne*, Jan.-July 1896).

Text copyright © 1956 by Presses Universitaires de France.

History and Dogma first published as *Histoire et Dogme. Les lacunes philosophiques de l'exégèse moderne* (in *La Quinzaine*, 1904).

Text copyright © 1956 by Presses Universitaires de France.

English translation copyright © 1964 by Harvill Press.
Original text by Alexander Dru and Illtyd Trethowan copyright © 1964
by Alexander Dru and Illtyd Trethowan.
This edition published 1994 by
Wm. B. Eerdmans Publishing Co.
255 Jefferson Ave. S.E., Grand Rapids, Michigan 49503
All rights reserved
Printed in the United States of America

00 99 98 97 96 95 94   7 6 5 4 3 2 1

Nihil obstat: Joannes M. T. Barton, S.T.D., L.S.S., Censor deputatus
Imprimatur: Georgius L. Craven, Epus Sebastopolis,
Vic. Gen. Westmonasterii, dei 26a Feb., 1964
Cum permissu Superiorum, O.S.B.

Library of Congress Cataloging-in-Publication Data

Blondel, Maurice, 1861-1949.
[Lettre sur les exigences de la pensée contemporaine en matière d'apologétique
et sur le méthode de la philosophie dans l'étude du problème religiuex. English]
The letter on apologetics, and, History and dogma / Maurice Blondel;
texts presented and translated by Alexander Dru and Illtyd Trethowan.
p.   cm. — (Ressourcement)
Translation of: Lettre sur les exigences de la pensée contemporaine en matière
d'apologétique et sur le méthode de la philosophie dans l'étude du problème religieux; and of:
Histoire et dogme.
Includes bibliographical references and index.
ISBN 0-8028-0819-0 (paper)
1. Apologetics — Methodology. 2. Catholic Church — Apologetic works. 3. Catholic
Church and philosophy. 4. Dogma. 5. History (Theology) 6. Catholic church — Doctrines.
I. Dru, Alexander   II. Trethowan, Illtyd, 1907-   . III. Blondel, Maurice, 1861-1949.
Histoire et dogme. English.   IV. Title.   V. Title: Letter on apologetics.   VI. Title: History
and dogma.   VII. Series: Ressourcement (Grand Rapids, Mich.)
B2430.B583L4713   1994
230'.2 — dc20
94-29496
CIP

CONTENTS

Foreword   6

Preface   9

PART ONE

INTRODUCTION   11

Historical and Biographical *by Alexander Dru*

    I. The relevance of Blondel   13

    II. Blondel's life and work   34

Philosophical and Theological *by Illtyd Trethowan*

    III. Some principles of Blondel's thought   80

    IV. Disputed questions   98

PART TWO
presented and translated by Illtyd Trethowan

Prefatory Note   119

THE LETTER ON APOLOGETICS   125

PART THREE
presented and translated by Alexander Dru

Prefatory Note   211

HISTORY AND DOGMA   219

Bibliography and Abbreviations   291

Index   295

FOREWORD

It is a bold thesis that Blondel advanced a century ago. Not that it has lost its audacity since then. The past century has not been immune to the influence of his thought, but the influence has been quietly general. It has consisted in the wide, though by no means unanimous, acceptance of a distinctive approach to age-old issues. His thought engages the tension between philosophical reason and the Catholic faith. It is not too much to hold that, along with the work of patristic scholars, his thought was a principal current leading up to the Second Vatican Council. For his "method of immanence" met both the philosopher's demand for legitimate autonomy and the Christian claim to strictly supernatural revelation and the order of grace.

No doubt, his thought helped prepare for the more positive approach to the modern world that characterizes the spirit of the Second Vatican Council. But if his thought has played a part in the updating of the church *(aggiornamento)*, it was also his intention to reanimate the sense of Christian tradition. For that reason the coupling of the two essays, the *Letter on Apologetics* and *History and Dogma*, provides the easiest and most complete general introduction to this difficult philosopher. Careful reading yields a rich harvest of reflection upon the aspiration for the infinite which was the driving and unifying élan of his thought. In Blondel, philosophy retained its relative autonomy, even while reason was obliged to confront its radical insufficiency in the face of supernatural revelation.

The present reissue of the two essays makes available the still timely and — for those unfamiliar with Blondel's thought — indispensable introduction co-authored by Alexander Dru and Dom

Illtyd Trethowan. Together they provide the historical context and the thematic schema of a philosophy whose trajectory continues to animate the thought of others. Trethowan's thematic essay touches upon questions that are still under discussion. The work of Henri de Lubac, which owes much to Blondel, has provided a new level for the discussion of nature and grace; a massive three-volume collection of essays on *Christliche Philosophie* (Verlag Styria, 1987-90) has appeared that shows the variety and continuing vitality of the notion so central in thought (if not in name) to Blondel's project; and finally, although interpretation of Blondel's thought is gradually receiving more definitive understanding, the implications of his thought are far from being exhausted.

The historical introduction by Alexander Dru contains information to which the educated English language reader does not have easy access even today: the tribulations of turn-of-the-century Roman Catholicism, and specifically the Modernist crisis and *Action française,* but also the remarkable riches of what is rightly called a Catholic renaissance. The sketch of Blondel's career is helpful in providing the general context of his work and in briefly indicating the further development of his thought in his later writings.

The present translation originally appeared in 1964, and Alexander Dru's section of the Introduction, while valuable in its historical information, still bristles with a certain *parti pris.* The angry and justified refutation of the charge of modernist tendencies made against Blondel is understandable, given the controversies of pre–Vatican Two Catholicism. The near contempt for Scholasticism would have been understood by readers of a generation or two ago as an attack upon certain circles of Neo-scholastic thought, and Blondel himself in his later years looked more kindly upon the work of St. Thomas Aquinas. Nevertheless, one ought not to relegate Blondel's lack of sympathy in this regard to merely historical circumstances. That would diminish the importance of his challenge, which is directed as much toward Catholics and other Christians as it is toward today's secular humanists. The issue of the relation of reason to faith, of nature to grace, and of philosophy to theology is an ever-open issue which requires of each generation that it rethink that relation, if only to preserve its true character. As philosophy changes its colors, so must Christianity find new ways of relating to it, and to all the enterprises of reason.

Today's critique of modernity is largely the product of a secular reason. At the hands of the deconstructionists and under the icon of Nietzsche's thought, the critique seems to claim for itself an overweening and open-ended autonomy, if not of reason, then of language or of liberty. But even if not all secular thinkers profess the end or the death of humankind, the movement seems more apt at negative critique than at establishing the grounds for a determinate freedom — for a freedom that liberates us beyond ourselves. The seeds of a more positive resolution of our liberty are to be found in Blondel's tortuous thought, seeds of promise that make the labor of thinking along with him an adventurous journey into a still open future.

KENNETH L. SCHMITZ

PREFACE

In France, and to some degree in both Germany and Italy, Maurice Blondel is recognized as one of the outstanding figures in the Catholic revival which began at the turn of the century and which culminated after many vicissitudes in the Second Vatican Council. Blondel, it is now clear, was one of the fathers of the movement; and if some knowledge of his aims and ideas is necessary for a balanced view of the movement, so too a general, overall view of the movement in which he worked is necessary if the importance and relevance of his work is to be appreciated. The reason why Blondel is still completely ignored in English-speaking countries, and if mentioned is usually misrepresented, is that Catholicism in these countries has been little affected by these intellectual trends. The Modernist Controversy, though it involved von Hügel and Tyrrel and Maud Petre, appears as a defunct episode. The *Action française* affair is regarded as a purely local deviation. And subsequent developments, if noticed at all, are treated as the manifestations of over-zealous and often misguided reformers. A coherent general picture of the history of the Church during these years is still wanting, with the result that Blondel seems at best a specialist whose work is irrelevant to larger, plainer issues, and at worst a philosopher of dubious orthodoxy.

It is this situation which has dictated the form which this introduction has taken. It is not an introduction to the *œuvre* and metaphysic of Blondel, which, supposing that the authors were competent to undertake it, would require his ideas to be transposed into the existing climate of thought. The introductory matter is simply designed to facilitate the reading of two short but capital texts. These texts have been chosen because, more than any others,

9

they reveal Blondel's historical importance and position. The texts, even more than the preliminary matter, precisely because they are limited in their scope, are, we believe, the best introduction to Blondel's thought. Moreover, this approach enables us to avoid the questions of detailed interpretation which arise when the work as a whole is taken into account. Whether the first version of his most important work, *L'Action* (1893), or the second version (1936) is to be preferred, or even if neither is regarded as wholly satisfactory, the problems raised in the *Letter on Apologetics* and *History and Dogma* lose none of their relevance.

The introductory matter has tried to do two things: first to enable the reader to understand the situation in which Blondel wrote as he understood it; and secondly to explain the problems in which he was engaged as clearly as possible. Some repetition was unavoidable; but it is hoped that where the same matter recurs the different context will justify its inclusion.

The references given will indicate the extent of our debt to French works on Blondel. A special acknowledgment is, however, due to Père Henri de Lubac and to Père Henri Bouillard, not only for the use made of their studies and commentaries, but for the interest which they have shown in the preparation of this book; and we must thank Père Bouillard's publishers, Les Éditions du Sêuil, for allowing us to quote extensively from his *Blondel et le Christianisme*. We should also like to take this opportunity of thanking the heirs of Maurice Blondel, in particular M. Charles Blondel, for facilitating the work, and Mlle. N. Panis, in charge of the Blondel Archives at Aix-en-Provence, for the loan and gift of editions which could not otherwise have been obtained.

PART ONE

INTRODUCTION

His influence

There is nothing in the work of Maurice Blondel to catch the eye; he does not dazzle, like a Pascal, nor does he hypnotize by the movement of his dialectic, like Hegel. His work is sober, and addressed to the academic world. But though it shocked the official philosophers and theologians of the time it never brought him into the limelight or aroused interest outside the prescribed circle for which it was intended in the first place. Until his death in 1949 at the age of eighty-eight, he remained a somewhat remote and inaccessible figure. His influence, he had rightly foreseen, was to be 'subterranean': *peu apparente, peu rapide, peu étendue d'abord;* and he believed that his thought 'while not appealing to superficial or docile minds' would be disseminated by a professional *élite*. Towards the end of his long life, however, when he published his major works—and no doubt as a result of the change in the ethos of Catholicism which he had helped to bring about—he received a modest degree of recognition. Since his death his achievement has been more and more fully acknowledged, his work more fully understood, and the originality of his thought more widely recognized.

In 1926, for example, M. Maritain spoke of 'the extremely improbable hypothesis' that Blondel's philosophy would give rise to a new school of theology.[1] A little more than thirty years later, in 1961, Père Henri Bouillard could virtually reverse this opinion and point to the paramount influence of *L'Action* and the works which followed. 'These theologians,' he writes, naming some of Blondel's contemporaries, 'and others we cannot enumerate here, did not restrict themselves to explaining Blondel's thought. They drew inspiration from it and allowed it to fertilize their own works. Through them it penetrated into apologetics and theology.

[1] *Réflexions sur l'intelligence*, Nouvelle Librairie Nationale, 1926, p. 108.

But that influence soon overflowed the circle of those who were called *blondeliens.* It reached men whose thought was fundamentally thomist.'[1]

But it was not only among the theologians, Père Bouillard continues, that Blondel's influence was felt. The presence of his work, if not a direct dependence, can be felt in one form or another in the thought of many of the Catholic philosophers who came after him—from his friend Victor Delbos to Le Senne and Lavelle and M. Gabriel Marcel, and among a younger generation, Jean Lacroix, Étienne Borne, Père Albert Cartier, and Père Gaston Fessard who owes to Blondel the initial impulse of his thought. The name of Père Henri de Lubac, whose work has done so much to extend the influence of Blondel, should be recalled at this point.

'It is above all in methods of apologetics and theology, and in the theology of the act of faith, that the influence of *L'Action* and the *Letter on Apologetics* was felt during the first years. In this field it has profoundly modified the theology of the twentieth century by making it rediscover and steep itself in traditional themes.'[2]

To this it should be added that *History and Dogma* remains the classical treatment of the problem of tradition and, as Père René Marlé writes:

It is not only the most forceful answer, perhaps, to *L'Évangile et l'Église,* it constitutes the most powerful systematic essay written up to the present time on the question which preoccupies theologians above all others . . . the question of the nature and role of tradition.[3]

The purpose of underlining Blondel's influence is not to enhance his prestige, but to set him firmly in his context. For a long time it was 'subterranean' and his work never aroused any curiosity outside the circle of his co-religionists—apart from the isolated instances of William James in Boston, and Adolf Lasson in Berlin with whom he exchanged a few letters. This was partly due to the fact

[1] Henri Bouillard, *Blondel et le Christianism* (Ed. du Seuil, 1961), p. 41. Among the latter, the names of Rousselot and, in a different context, Maréchal are mentioned.

[2] Bouillard, p. 42.

[3] René Marlé, in *Au Cœur de la Crise Moderniste* (Aubier, 1960), p. 351.

that Blondel was at once plunged into the theological controversies of the day. His aim, it is true, was 'to answer the reproach that Catholic thought was sterile', but this could not have been done by an isolated, freelance thinker. And this explains why, though he always thought in terms of addressing sincere unbelievers 'by speaking their language', his first task was to preach to the converted, to rejuvenate Catholic thought, and to make theology (and Catholic philosophy) 'rediscover and steep itself in traditional themes', so that what he had to say should be said as a member of the Church.

This first phase can now reasonably be said to be completed, for, as Père Bouillard says, 'even those who remain alien to his ideas no longer speak as though his work had not existed',[1] though of course this may not be apparent to those judging solely from the situation in English-speaking countries. Nevertheless, the Catholic renewal abroad which led to the present Council will be extended by the Council to those parts of the Church where its influence is still only slight, and it will then be seen that Blondel performed the task which he set himself and presented a precise formulation of the Catholic position not only in a language addressed to sincere unbelievers, but in a key sympathetic to other Christian Churches still inclined more often than not, in English-speaking countries, to identify Catholicism with an older apologetic and theology deriving from a period when they were in many respects coloured by opposition to an equally dated Protestantism.

Blondel's thought made its way slowly and without any of those aids to reflection which launch or promote a reputation: he had neither the persuasive grace of Bergson nor the powerful, incantatory force of Péguy. His close friend and admirer, André Pérové, made no attempt to gloss over the obscurities of his involuted way of expressing his thought—*affreux Maurice, trop compliqué!* Cardinal Mercier tried in vain to wean him from attempting to forestall every conceivable misunderstanding and, as a result of his crab-like flanking movements and search for all-round protection, only adding to them. He was, he admitted, 'entirely foreign to the ways of thought of the autodidact' and became increasingly concerned with 'the technical organization' of his thought.

[1] Bouillard, p. 16.

I have little taste or aptitude for exercising influence through persuasion [Bergson] and authority [Péguy], but I have a strong desire to address, whether by teaching or with my pen, those who, being placed at the source of the movement of ideas, contribute to form the current of opinion.[1]

But this minute preoccupation with technical precision, even at the cost of accessibility, conceals a boldness of vision at first sight incompatible with its form of expression.

I dreamed insanely of gathering together all the waters of the truth, all the flowing waters of knowledge into a sort of philosophical ocean, a Pacific Ocean in which innumerable systems and controversies would be reconciled.[2]

The insane dream was there from the beginning, as the ambition to renew Catholic thought, and to the end, as the inspiration of his last works, the Trilogy (*La Pensée, l'Être et les êtres, L'Action*). 'Up till now,' he wrote in 1886, 'little more has been done than to appropriate a pagan philosophy', so that 'there is still no such thing as a genuinely Christian philosophy, issuing from the Gospels'.[3] It is this vision which prompts M. Tresmontant to describe Blondel's work as characterized by 'an extraordinary audacity', and leads M. Borne to say that 'it would be difficult to solve the problem of Christian philosophy with greater elegance, humility and audacity'. Père Bouillard, the most restrained of writers, makes a revealing comparison when he says 'that to describe the universally concrete and to wish only to find the truth in totality surely recalls the project of Hegel'.[4] That the comparison is not a rhetorical flourish may be seen from Peter Henrici's study *Hegel und Blondel*. Nor was Blondel disconcerted by the parallel. Père Gaston Fessard recalls that when he first read the *Phenomenology of Spirit* he was 'won over by the resemblance between its plan and that of Blondel. When I told Maurice Blondel of my impression a few years before his death, he replied: That is exactly what my friend Victor Delbos said to me.

[1] *Carnets Intimes* [*C.I.*], 1894, p. 550.

[2] Quoted from an unpublished *Cahier* by Albert Cartier, *Existence et Vérité*, p. 6.

[3] *C.I.*, p. 85.   [4] Bouillard, p. 26.

When he read my thesis for the first time he said: You have re-done the *Phenomenology of Spirit*.'[1]

The mention of Hegel's name is not of course intended to suggest any general similarity, though it can be helpful in suggesting the dialectical character of Blondel's thought and emphasizing his sense of its historical situation. Unlike other Catholic philosophers, Blondel was conscious not merely of his historical situation **as of** something extrinsic and detachable, but of his necessary place in the movement of thought in which he was engaged. As a Christian he could not be content merely to understand that situation, but had to enter into it and fulfil his mission. The existential character of his thinking demands a more than formal attention to the context from which it sprang.

The Catholic Renaissance

Blondel was born in 1861 and belonged to a very gifted generation, the generation of Proust, Péguy, Claudel and Gide, of Debussy and Ravel, of Matisse and Rouault, of Bergson, Duchesne and Loisy. The decades astride of 1900 have, it is true, a *fin de siècle* air about them, but the decadence of *la belle époque* was simply the negative side, as it were, of a renaissance in all the intellectual and cultural spheres. Much the same thing is true of the political sphere: the frivolous fanaticism of the Dreyfus Affair conceals a profound change, *la révolution dreyfusienne;* just as in the religious sphere the fanatical controversies and authoritarian condemnations obscure the fact that Catholicism was renewing itself from within. Indeed, one of the most striking aspects of the cultural renaissance was that it embraced a number of Catholics—no longer in the familiar role of eccentrics and reactionaries, but as contributors to the general ferment of ideas and forms, men whose work was not only brilliant and arresting, but fertile for the future.

In the history of the Church it was a grand turning-point: a revolution more far-reaching than the Dreyfus revolution, a renaissance as vigorous as the cultural renewal. But it was so unforeseen

[1] Fessard, *La Dialectique des Exercices de Saint Ignace de Loyola*, p. 29, note. Cf. the same author's *La méthode de réflexion chez Maine de Biran* (1938), p. 183.

that it was not at first recognized for what it was; so contrary to conventional ways of thinking that it aroused more opposition than enthusiasm; so foreign to the 'tradition' established that its most seminal mind was not understood for another quarter of a century: Péguy, whose influence was to extend over the whole field of Catholic thought and activity, was hardly read till the thirties, ten to twenty years after his death in the first battle of the Marne.[1] The first and obvious reason for this delay, and for the array of misunderstandings against which Blondel, like Péguy, had to struggle, was the preliminary examination of conscience demanded, the *mea culpa* which Catholics were called upon to make, the acknowledgment of errors, mistakes and shortcomings without which they could not understand the historical situation in which they had to act. But the graver the political situation of the Church became, the less palatable were the admissions required. This obstinate resistance has had the effect of concealing the Catholic revival and emphazising its inevitable obverse, the crisis in the life of the Church. In English-speaking countries particularly the period is still regarded, more often than not, as a series of false starts resolved by authoritative condemnations: of Americanism (1892), Modernism (1907), the Sillon (1910), the *Action française* (1926); and seen in that light it holds little interest except to the historian of the past. It is as though only the negative features of the period were visible, and as though the renaissance had never happened because it was superfluous: a view of the period that effectively obscures the importance of Blondel or of Péguy, for to see them it is necessary to see the movement which they inaugurated as a whole and as they saw it.

The revolution[2] which occurred within the Church can best be seen as a double event: as the renewal of Catholic life and thought, the re-establishment of links with the culture of the time, but con-

---

[1] See Alexander Dru, *Péguy* (Harvill Press, 1959).

[2] The term revolution is not chosen idly or for the sake of its rhetorical reverberations. It is used because it accurately describes the importance of the turning-point, the creative element in the movement as well as the violence of the opposition which it met with. For the crisis—perhaps unprecedented—was at the same time the *dénouement* of a long-standing and hitherto intractable problem: the situation of the Church in the modern world.

ditioned by the profound division within the Church on the problems which this rejuvenation raised. Blondel, it will be seen, was alive to the fundamental character of the crisis from very early on, and for the first thirty years of his life he was deeply involved in all its aspects, philosophical, exegetical, political and social. With remarkable prescience he foresaw the main lines of the outcome because he was already in possession of an articulate philosophy which, demanding 'action' and 'engagement', was embedded in history. He never lost sight of the positive element nor allowed himself to be misled for a moment by the negative, that is by the errors of opposing factions which threatened the renewal of Catholic thought, art and scholarship, whether the errors were, to use his own words, Modernist or Veterist errors.

Blondel's attitude to the crisis is given in three essays: in the *Letter on Apologetics*, where he deals with the philosophical issues; in *History and Dogma*, where he gave his solution to the problems raised by historicism and biblical criticism; and in *La Semaine Sociale de Bordeaux et le Monophorisme*, where he deals with the political and social aspects of the crisis as it crystallized round the *Action française* movement. The first two essays speak for themselves, and are given here in full with such comments as seemed necessary. The last of the three will be touched on when we have considered the events which led up to it.

The origins and developments of the religious crisis

'We in France and in Catholic countries have assisted for centuries at the strange spectacle of "the whole duty of man" being divorced from honest scholarship, genuine art and living thought.'[1]

The need to escape from that situation divided Catholics into two camps—in spite of the superficial uniformity achieved in the nineteenth century. Blondel remarks:

> With every day that passes, the conflict which sets Catholic against Catholic in every order—social, political, philosophical—is revealed as sharper and more general. One could almost say that there are now two quite incompatible Catholic

[1] Maurice Blondel, *Letter on Apologetics*, p. 187 below.

mentalities, particularly in France. And that is manifestly abnormal, since there cannot be two Catholicisms.[1]

The conflict which became acute during the last ten years of the Pontificate of Leo XIII (1893-1903), the conflict 'which set Catholic against Catholic in every order', was the consequence of the *malaise* produced by the centuries of sterility and maladjustment to which Blondel refers: it was a painful awakening to the real situation of the Church obscured for so long by political interests and philosophical myopia—though the example of the Catholic revival in Germany during the first quarter of the nineteenth century was enough to show that the condition of the Church in Latin countries was not unavoidable.[2]

The origins of the conflict must be sought, not in the immediate past, but much further back. The decisive moment can in fact be defined with some precision and occurred at the end of the seventeenth century, when the sclerosis which finished by paralysing the monarchy began to spread to the State Church which relied increasingly upon it. The Revocation of the Edict of Nantes and the Jansenist controversy had already weakened the Church. The consequences of these two episodes might not have been lasting had it not been for the paradigmatic conflict between Bossuet and Fénelon which followed. Quietism was the ostensible occasion of their quarrel; but since their disagreement centred on the very heart of the Christian life it necessarily extended, whether by implication or explicitly, to every aspect of it.

The rapidity of the decline which followed is striking. The Church of Pascal and Malebranche, Bérulle and Condren, of Vincent de Paul and Francis of Sales, of Mabillon, Richard Simon and Fénelon, was reduced to impotence in face of the rationalistic critique of Bayle and his imitators. But the languid support provided by the monarchy during the eighteenth century made it possible for the Church to ignore the effects and deny the causes of the splendid isolation into which it had withdrawn. Blondel's generation

[1] Maurice Blondel, *History and Dogma*, 1904, p. 221 below.

[2] I would refer the reader to my short essay in the Faith and Facts series published by Burns and Oates: *The Church in the XIXth century: Germany 1800-1918* (1963).

was the first to emerge from the ghetto, to understand the reasons which had made it possible, and to open their eyes to the consequences.

For the first time since Christianity formed souls and societies, we find ourselves faced by a public and social apostasy which is no longer merely the schism of a nation or a king, nor the heresy of a doctor or a sect, nor a political and moral revolt, but which is a whole civilization cutting itself off completely from Christianity.[1]

But if Blondel was ahead of most of his contemporaries in grasping the causes of the weakness of the Church and its dwindling membership, others came to confirm, expand and add to what he had said.

It is perhaps [Claudel wrote] because those great truths were forgotten under the influence of Jansenism, never to be sufficiently deplored, and because it held one part of God's work in contempt, the noble faculties of imagination and sensibility, to which certain lunatics would have added reason itself, that religion has just been through a long crisis, from which it is barely beginning to emerge. The crisis, which reached its most acute phase in the nineteenth century, was not primarily an intellectual crisis . . . I would prefer to say it was the tragedy of a starved imagination.[2]

Claudel, too, recognized that the 'crisis' was not of yesterday. He saw that it had been most acute in the nineteenth century, and that what is commonly looked upon as 'the crisis' was, at the same time, its *dénouement*. Writing as a poet—in an essay on Dante—Claudel diagnosed the collapse of Catholicism as a failure of imagination and sensibility; he stressed the resulting divorce between Catholicism and genuine art. The quotation can be misleading in isolation. What Claudel meant was that the intellectual crisis would not have arisen as it did if reason and sensibility (that is, feeling) had

[1] Maurice Blondel, *La Semaine Sociale de Bordeaux et le Monophorisme* (Paris: Bloud, 1910), p. 25. This was being said at the same time, and with incomparable force, by Péguy. See *Temporal and Eternal*, by Charles Péguy, translated by Alexander Dru (Harvill Press, 1958).

[2] Paul Claudel, *Positions et Propositions* (Gallimard, 1926), I, p. 175.

not been separated so that imagination was held in contempt. Blondel was the first Catholic thinker in France methodically to harmonize *l'esprit de géométrie* and *l'esprit de finesse*, to recall Pascal's terms.

But it was Henri Bremond, Blondel's lifelong friend and correspondent, who traced the failure of imagination and the divorce between reason and feeling to its source. Bremond was not a philosopher but a man of great sensibility and penetrating intuition. He introduced the ideas of Newman into France, and elaborated Claudel's *Parabole d'Animus et d'Anima* in *Prière et Poésie* (1926), where he gave his own romantic theory of poetry. His lasting work is *L'Histoire littéraire du sentiment religieux en France*[1] interrupted by his untimely death. In it Bremond tells the story of the rise of the great school of spirituality after the Wars of Religion, and of the source of the revival which lasted to the end of the fourteenth century. But the movement which began with *L'humanisme chrétien* was brought to a halt a hundred years later, by the disastrous quarrel between Bossuet and Fénelon. Bremond died before completing his account of the ravages of 'anti-quietism', but it can easily enough be supplemented from his *Apologie pour Fénelon* and above all from the Preface to his edition of Caussade's work: *Bossuet, Maître d'oraison*. By the middle of the eighteenth century the condemnation of Quietism had produced a situation in which Caussade could not contemplate publishing his views except by subterfuge, and was obliged to call his attack on Bossuet by a title implying nothing but praise. Bremond summarizes Caussade's findings under three headings:

1. The spiritual revival had been succeeded by 'the rout of the mystics', and the magnificent development which had occurred earlier was halted.

2. The 'rout' of the mystics was caused by the numerous works of Bossuet against Fénelon, and it had been so effective that even today (1741) no open attempt to reverse the trend could be made.

3. Bossuet's influence had been *néfaste*. One of his chief objec-

[1] Called, most inaccurately, in English *The History of Religious Thought*—as though to demonstrate the fear and contempt in which feeling was held.

tions to Fénelon was that he was a follower of St Francis of Sales.[1]

The condemnation of Quietism (1699) was followed by the extinction of the spiritual, mystical tradition, which was ridiculed and equated with 'enthusiasm'.[2] The rapidity of the decline of religion must be attributed to what Péguy calls 'a mysticism in reverse', to the self-centred Christianity of the nineteenth century, a Christianity which had largely forgotten its spiritual or mystical heritage. The isolation of Catholicism was begun by the Revocation of the Edict of Nantes and was completed by its externalization—for as a result of the fear of Quietism spirituality itself was externalized into 'devotions' and the emphasis was placed on outward expressions of religion. And if, as Claudel says, the influence of Jansenism persisted—surviving a persecution which did not stop at desecrating the graves of Port-Royal—and if its spirit pervaded the theological manuals of the nineteenth century, this was because, once the true spiritual tradition had been driven underground and silenced, the choice lay between an official religion, *l'hypocrisie majestueuse* (Maritain) of the Gallican Church, relying on the secular arm, and, on the other hand, a private, puritanical, and anti-mystical religion reacting against it—the religion of the Jansenists, the declared enemies of Fénelon.[3]

In philosophy, the victory of Bossuet (who was no philosopher, as Bremond points out) led to what Blondel calls Extrinsicism, to an utter contempt for *le fait intérieur*, to a fear and suspicion of

[1] Bremond had found Caussade's book among a heap of volumes that were to be destroyed. He gave it to an admirer of Caussade to edit in 1895. It is one of the source-books for the history of 'religious sentiment' in France.

[2] Bossuet's *protégé*, La Bruyère, joined in the hunt for Quietists, and his *Dialogues sur le Quiétisme* (there seems to be little doubt that they are genuine) began a tradition which came to an end with Knox's *Enthusiasm*.

[3] The proportions of the caricature of Catholicism given by Stendhal in *Le Rouge et le Noir* (1831) are correct and his terms are accurate: either the political religion of a secret society, 'Les Chevaliers de la Foi', and the ridiculous affectation of Mgr d'Affre (in real life the Cardinal-Duc de Rohan, Archbishop of Besançon), or the ridiculous inhuman austerity of the head of the Seminary, M. Picard, the Jansenist. It is true that Stendhal would have found a personal religion quite as ridiculous, though not all his clerical figures are hypocrites.

Pascal himself, to the divorce between thought and feeling and will which explains the impotent rationalism of nineteenth-century scholasticism: the scholasticism Blondel rightly regarded as the *lingua franca* of official theology. The Quietist controversy, in the course of which Bossuet wrote that he had 'God, the King and Madame de Maintenon on his side', marks the great caesura and is at the origin of the divorce between Catholicism and living thought, genuine art and honest scholarship which Blondel and his generation (who rediscovered the spiritual tradition) were the first to recognize, understand and reverse.[1]

It will now, perhaps, be more easily understood why the Church in Latin countries reacted to the Revolution like the Bourbons, learning nothing but forgetting nothing. The policy of Pius VI and Hercules Consalvi was to restore the alliance between the Throne and the Altar in the belief that the only possible situation for the Church was that which it had enjoyed, in theory at least, in the Middle Ages. This policy, equivocal under the Empire, artificial under the Bourbons, became politically disastrous under Napoleon III, greeted as the new Charlemagne if not the new Constantine. As Blondel observed, the *compelle intrare* so fatally reintroduced by the Revocation of Nantes ended in a *compelle exire.*

The 'two incompatible mentalities' Blondel speaks of were implied in the conflict between Fénelon and Bossuet, but owing to the power of the dominant party the conflict did not become open until the Bourbon Restoration when it was crystallized by the emergence of the modern world. The two parties make their first appearance in the struggle between the theocrats and classicists (Bonald, Maistre) and the romantic liberals (Chateaubriand, Ballanche), the former harking back to Bossuet, the latter to Fénelon; but they soon narrowed and hardened into the Ultramontane party (Veuillot) and the liberal Catholics (Acton, Montalembert). As long as the intellectual life of Catholicism was dormant, the conflict was

---

[1] The extent of the change brought about by Péguy, Blondel, Bremond, von Hügel (*The Mystical Element in Religion* dates from 1908) and others is illustrated in *Introduction to Spirituality* (1961) by Louis Bouyer, in the Preface to which Quietism, which had been the *crux theologorum* for two hundred years, is dismissed in one sentence as a pseudo-problem.

insoluble because it remained superficial and appeared to be a matter of *policy*—the participants were as yet unconscious of the philosophical and theological problems it concealed. By the end of the reign of Leo XIII, however, roughly speaking from the date of *L'Action* (1893), the conflict spread to every sphere and led to a crisis without precedent—or, as Claudel would have said, the most acute phase of the crisis was over and it had reached its final stage, the period of *dénouement*. The 'diplomacy' of Leo XIII had been as ineffectual in dealing with the situation as the intransigence of Pio Nono, and he left the 'crisis' to explode in the inexperienced hands of his successor, Pius X.

⋅ The conflict which followed occurred in two phases: the Modernist Controversy (1902-1907); and the Veterist Controversy (1907-1926), the conflict centring round the *Action française* which remained in power until its condemnation in 1926. This long struggle had, it is true, been signalled by the disturbances created by 'Americanism'—a mare's nest, like Quietism—which served to shatter the illusions fostered by Leo XIII's 'liberal' policy and to prepare a reaction. From 1893 to 1902 Blondel, as a result of *L'Action* and the *Letter on Apologetics* (1896), was enemy No. 1. But in 1902 Loisy published *L'Évangile et l'Église* in answer to Harnack's *Spirit of Christianity*, and was deprived of his Chair at the Institut Catholique in Paris. A year later Blondel replied to Loisy in *History and Dogma*, dissociating himself from both Modernists and Veterists (extrinsicists) and defining the third way: Tradition.[1] Four years later it seemed as though the Modernist Controversy had been ended by a ukase, the Decree *Lamentabili* and the Encyclical *Pascendi* condemning Modernism. But Loisy's exit was only the end of the prologue, and prepared a change of scene. The controversy which had hitherto turned on exegetical problems, and which called for a theology of history, moves on to a different plane, down to the level of politics and social questions—in one sense further from the intellectual centre of the storm, but at the same time nearer to the heart of the matter: the situation of the Church in the modern world.

Since *Graves de communi* (1901) the encouragement given to the

[1] See below, Prefatory Note to *History and Dogma*, p. 213.

Christian democrats and the social Catholics had been muted, and *Rerum Novarum* was played down. With the accession of Pius X the reversal of policy was completed and until the accession of Benedict XV the Vatican policy was unambiguously reactionary.[1] Three years after the condemnation of Modernism, the most active group of Christian democrats was silenced by the condemnation of their paper *Le Sillon* (1910), and the injunctions of Leo XIII recommending co-operation with the Third Republic (the *ralliement*) were lifted in the following year. It was this change in Vatican policy, the immediate consequence of the difficulties of the Church in France and the anti-clerical *régime* of Combes, and of the danger presented by Modernism, which favoured the rise of the *Action française* movement in which all the hitherto heterogeneous elements of political Catholicism were forged into a coherent ideology. The movement became so strongly entrenched that it survived the 1914 War to enjoy a second spring in the post-war years, until it was pole-axed by an utterly unforeseen condemnation in 1926— a decisive date when the ideas of Blondel and his friends, of Péguy and others, began to reach a wider public and to liberate Catholicism and convert the uniformity of the nineteenth century into an organic unity within which freedom was once again possible.

The brief quotations from the *Letter on Apologetics* and *History and Dogma* will have shown how directly Blondel was involved in the crisis. In both these essays, however, he had been primarily concerned with the underlying philosophical and theological themes. Modernism, in his view, was not the cause, but the effect of the crisis: 'a recoil from Veterism', from a philosophy incapable of dealing with new questions. The essence of the crisis was now coming to light: a conflict between two incompatible mentalities, between the *policy* of the Veterists, and the philosophy behind it, and a return to tradition which seemed novel and even modernist to those who had forgotten it or never known it. *La Semaine Sociale de Bordeaux et le Monophorisme* (1910) is still the most

[1] See, for example, Merry del Val's letter to Count Albert de Mun. Blondel pointed out that the Ultramontanes had adopted the economics of liberalism. Merry del Val's letter is printed in *Études*, 1913.

penetrating analysis of *intégrisme* and the final stage of the long crisis.[1]

The gravity of the situation is stated uncompromisingly:

One must even say that, in so far as monophorism (*intégrisme*) triumphed, the Catholic apostolate would be sterilized, the religious sense perverted, Christian piety falsified: how essential, therefore, to describe, if only schematically, and following an artificially rigorous logic, the itinerary taken by such a speculative deviation to its practical conclusions, (*Semaine*, p. 93)

Blondel wished to show that the doctrines openly taught by the *Action française* were those which unconsciously dictated the *policy* of the dominant party in the Church, and to expose its inconsistencies and its unchristian character.

The Action française

The *Action française* movement, founded by Vaugeois and Maurras in the early days of the Dreyfus Affair, was at first without a precise ideology. It was something of the order of Déroulèdes's *Ligue des Patriotes*, and was influenced by Barrès. It was neither Catholic nor royalist, but a political and moral reaction to the decadence of public life, to the scandals and 'affairs' which threatened the stability of the Third Republic. As the Dreyfus Affair grew into the Dreyfus Revolution, however, the balance of the political parties was unsettled by the emergence of socialist and marxist parties under Jaurès and Guesde, while the incrimination of the General Staff and the army favoured the rise of a conservative nationalism. This realignment of the parties gave Maurras his opportunity, and the *Action française* became the rallying point for a rejuvenated conservatism, hitherto divided on the royalist issue and the 'religious question'. This change on the Right had already been prepared by the *débâcle* of 1870 and the excesses of the Radicals during the eighties. The way for a new conservatism had been smoothed

[1] Originally published as a series of nine articles in *Annales de philosophie*, and subsequently in book form by Bloud et Gay under the pseudonym Testis. I have given a brief account of the argument in *The Downside Review* (July 1963).

intellectually by a reaction against liberal, anti-clerical ideas. The reaction is typified by Taine's critique of the Revolution myth: *Les Origines de la France contemporaine*, and in particular by the last volume, *L'Église et l'École*, acknowledging the rights of a traditional religion and morality. Out of that promising situation Maurras created the first consistent and successful reactionary movement which France had known since the Restoration.

Born in Martigues in 1871, Charles Maurras could well be described in the manner of his master Taine as a product of his time and place and *milieu*. He came of an impoverished family of the small bourgeoisie, rooted in the soil of Provence, with its clear skies, its classical ruins, its Latin feeling. Steeped in the literature of Greece and Rome, he found himself at an early age without faith, with an ardent admiration for the Latin Catholicism of his country and a firm belief in the positivist philosophy of Comte. Unlike the men of previous generations, he had left the Church of Bossuet with a feeling of sadness, and his admiration for the outward aspects of Catholicism survived, preserved as part of the classical landscape which he loved. This was the new aesthetic factor which he was to exploit so brilliantly. Frustrated from an early age by deafness, he projected his inner world of dreams in terms of a positivist sociology and reconciled the contradictions between his feeling for the past and his scientific ideas with persuasive literary skill.

When Maurras first went to Paris—with a letter of introduction to Maurice Blondel—he was not a royalist. His conversion to royalism came after the founding of the *Action française*, at a time when it seemed to all but the faithful few that royalism had been finally discredited as a result of its opportunist alliance with a farcical dictator, Boulanger, and by its clerical affiliations. His conversion was a stroke of genius, his 18th Brumaire. Under the cloak of royalism Maurras succeeded in uniting the heirs of Comte and Taine with the disciples of Bonald and Maistre, combining the positivist sociology of the former with the royalism and Catholicism of the latter. The *Action française* presented itself as the living continuation of the French classical tradition, of the *grand siècle*: the one myth capable of opposing the myth of the Revolution and the principles of '89. For although the slogan of the movement was *la politique d'abord*, and while its strength lay in an implacable logic, its appeal lay in its literary *panache*, in the aesthetic glamour of a traditionalism which, reinforced by the positivist and historical arguments of Comte, could meet the arguments of Marx on their own ground.

The essence of the *Action française*, as Blondel pointed out, was the alliance between Positivism and Catholicism—a programme which Maurras first put forward in *Trois Idées politiques* (1898), where he gave his source. In 1856 Comte had reached the conclusion that the European Tradition could only be saved if the Church accepted his offer of a formal alliance. He despatched an emissary, Alfred Sabatier, to Rome and hoped to conduct preliminary negotiations with the General of the Jesuits. He accepted the rebuff which his proposals met with patiently, but never abandoned the idea. Maurras, in more favourable circumstances, was able to put Comte's proposal into practice. He could not have succeeded if there had not been a natural affinity between the ideology of Bonald and that of Comte—who regarded Bonald as the founder of modern sociology.[1] The rapidly worsening position of the Church in France placed Maurras in a uniquely favourable light: he came forward as the champion of Catholicism, all the better armed for being unencumbered by faith. The abrogation of the Concordat, the withdrawal of financial assistance by the State, the expulsion of the religious orders, the danger to the schools, cruelly embarrassed the authorities of Catholicism and emphasized the need for the confident and organized resistance ('by every means, even legal') offered by the *Action française* movement, whose membership was not restricted to those who believed.

In 1903 Maurras sent Louis Dimier to Rome, as Comte had sent Alfred Sabatier, in order to establish relations with the Vatican. Dimier, it is interesting to note, found the greatest difficulty in obtaining an audience with the new Pope, Pius X: the *Action française* was unknown. A year or two later the alliance was well-cemented and Maurras's position was impregnable. He made no attempt to conceal his atheism, and little to hide his loathing of Christianity. But he spoke with admiration of the Roman Church

[1] Cf. Robert Spaemann: *Der Ursprung der Soziologie aus der Geist der Restauration*, Kösel-verlag 1959.

which had created 'Catholicism' by eliminating almost all the mystical and semitic elements of the Gospels. His anti-semitism was pleasing to the opponents of Dreyfus and the Dreyfusards. He made great play with an unrepentant and extreme Ultramontanism and founded a Chair for the Syllabus of 1864 in the *Action française* Institute. No one opposed the 'protestant' views of the Modernists more roundly, or encouraged authoritarianism so frankly. The Christian democrats of the *Sillon* and the social Catholics of the *Semaines Sociales* were denounced as modernists and even as mystics (i.e. Quietists). To Pius X Maurras appeared as *un bel defensore della fede*; the Cardinal Secretary of State, Merry del Val, selected the *Action française* representative in Rome to ensure a fruitful collaboration; the French Hierarchy, traditionally conservative, welcomed the *Action française*, and they were followed in this by the Religious Orders.

Maurras's success is partly explained by the fact that the *Action française* provided a well-fortified bastion into which the conservative elements in the Church could retreat, and owing to the low intellectual level of the majority of the clergy and laity the alliance between Positivism and Catholicism aroused no suspicions. All the old ideas governing the policy of the authorities of Catholicism seemed merely to have been fused into a majestic whole: the anti-mystical current dating from the seventeenth century, the conservative sociology of Bonald, the static and 'classical' conception of the Church and Tradition of Maistre, the militant political Catholicism of Veuillot, the authoritarianism of Pio Nono, and the emotional opposition to the 'modern world' of *l'émigration intérieure*, of those who would never compound with the Revolution. But where these component factors had, in the past, been *policies*, often unconscious of the philosophy they implied, they became, in the eminently articulate mind of Maurras, an ideology. The principal regulating ideas of the *Action française*—royalist in politics, classical in taste and outlook, Ultramontane in religion—were not severally or individually incompatible with Christianity, but in the organized form they now received they engendered as well as expressed a mentality or atmosphere which was unchristian and uncatholic. This ambiguity accounts for the fact that when Pius X was asked in 1907 to publish the findings of the Holy Office and to condemn the works of Maurras he refused to do so; and explains why, twenty years later, when Pius XI condemned the *Action française* he refused to particularize his reasons for the condemnation and contented himself with saying that it was not so much the doctrines of the movement that were false as 'the atmosphere'—the 'mentality' Blondel had said—that was reprehensible. And for the same reason, no doubt, this essentially French movement was not without influence in other countries, in England for example, where it was echoed by a jingoistic Catholicism asserting its claim to be 'the European tradition'—defended by Comte and Maurras.

All these facts taken together would not, however, have conferred upon the movement an aura of hyper-orthodoxy. This was supplied by the unqualified support given to Maurras and his movement by the leading neo-thomist theologians whose influence in Rome and in France was paramount: Cardinal Billot, Maurice de la Taille, s.j., Père Clérissac, o.p., Dom Besse, Père Janvier, Père Le Floch, Director of the French Seminary in Rome, Père Rolland-Gosselin, o.p. The greatest neo-thomist theologian of the day, Père Garrigou-Lagrange, o.p., advertised his enthusiasm for the work of Maurras by publishing one of his theological works with the *Action française* publishing house.[1] To these names should be added the gifted laymen who wrote in *L'Action française*, or independently, in favour of the movement: Léon Daudet, Henri Massis, Jacques Maritain. It was this theological supporting force which underlined the connection between theory and practice and which determined Blondel to intervene. But for that theological and intellectual support the final form of political Catholicism would not have lasted so long nor have died so hard; and owing to it Catholicism accepted a declared atheist as its intellectual leader for twenty-five years.

The crisis had opened with the Modernist controversy, and was to end in the conflict over Veterism. No one, however, doubted that religion in general and Christianity in particular were passing

---

[1] I have only named the writers whose work must be taken seriously, not the army of popularizers and clerical journalists and Bishops who gave their support to Maurras.

through an unprecedented crisis. The only question seemed to be whether it involved the dissolution or the evolution of religion; whether it should be met by a stern resistance to change or a willingness 'to move with the times' by Veterism or Modernism. Of the small group of men who did not think in these antithetical terms, Blondel was the first to provide a consistent answer to the whole problem. The shortest statement of his attitude in the crisis is given in his answer to an *enquête* conducted by the *Mercure de France* in 1907.[1]

The present crisis, perhaps unprecedented in depth and extent—for it is simultaneously scientific, metaphysical, moral, social and political—is not a dissolution (for the spirit of faith does not die) nor even an evolution (for the spirit of faith does not change), it is a *purification* of the religious sense and an *integration* of Catholic truth.

A purification, because what succumbs or dissolves in the present struggles, the decaying institutions, the petrified forms, are either dying or dead ... It is useless for party to be aligned against party: those who, in order to defend the Church, immure themselves in a fortress of resistance only hasten the spread of change. There are some, no doubt, who with the intransigence of 'men of olden times' hope that without changing themselves they can succeed in changing others; but no, they can only succeed by being more profoundly modified themselves, by being stripped of 'the old man'—it is only when they have been brought back to the conditions of the Gospel that they will once again attract the hearts of men ...

... And by those means, as a result of an apparent levelling and destruction a fuller integration of the thought and life of Christianity is being prepared. No form of religion other than the Catholic will profit from the radical effort of criticism and philosophy: the laborious parturition of modern consciousness will not end in some sort of symbolism [Modernism] detached from dogma, or in literal, mechanical

[1] Among the contributors were Georges Goyau, Bremond, Edmund Gosse, Pareto, Humperdinck and Saint-Saëns.

practice [Veterism]; but with a more precise definition of dogmatic facts and truths. And it is this precision, though in appearance restrictive, which will allow its universal application and its wonderful equilibrium to be seen better: a religion of supernatural authority, but also of inward freedom.

But Blondel had not waited for the crisis to burst in order to discover his task. He had seen and felt the essential problem ever since his student days, and one of the earliest entries in his *Carnets Intimes* reveals the extent of his foresight and the hope with which he faced the crushing difficulties he was the last to minimize.

I want to speak of the contemporary state of mind. A great renewal is taking place at the present time: it will be apparent that it is a question of adopting a whole moral attitude, that it is not only in the domain of thought that our salvation is decided, but above all in the secret recesses of the heart, that the time of heresies and even of schisms is over, that not to be entirely for the Church is to be against it. Passing through pantheism, one tires of its beautiful, comfortable, vacillating indifference; it is impossible to live in that aesthetic atmosphere any longer. The old logic, no doubt, was very narrow and it has burst. Truth is no longer *adequatio rei et intellectus* and no one lives on 'clear ideas' any longer. But there remains the truth, and the truth which remains is living and active; it is *adequatio mentis et vitae*.   11.x.86.

The one unexpected thing about Maurice Blondel is the rapidity, the sureness and the completeness of his original vision or intuition, though it was to take him sixty years to find the adequate technical expression for his metaphysical experience.

'I propose,' he wrote in his *Carnet* in October 1886, when he was twenty-five, 'to study action, because it seems to me that the Gospel attributes to action alone the power to manifest love and to attain God! Action is the abundance of the heart.'

II. BLONDEL'S LIFE AND WORK

Early years

Maurice Blondel was born in Dijon on the 2nd of November 1861.
He came of a family which had owned land in Burgundy since the
middle of the thirteenth century and could trace its name to the
generation which first assumed the patronymic. Lawyers and
doctors, occasionally entering the Church, they were a solid race,
exceptionally long-lived—Claude Blondel (1745-1847) and Blondel's
sister Thérèse (1849-1950) both lived into their hundredth years.
And as his father Henri Blondel could write with some reason, 'the
best heritage one can leave is the moral capital which is handed down
in the blood and informs the secret depths of body and soul'.

Henri Blondel, a lawyer like his brother Hyppolite, lived in easy
circumstances with a town house in Dijon and a country house
at Quincy, as well as a smaller house at Saint-Seine-sur-Vingeanne.
Material cares were never to trouble Maurice Blondel.

Maurice was the fourth child, small, slight, sinewy, with quick,
deft movements and very prompt reactions. From the first he was
reflective and *presque trop sage*, with a precocious sense of the family
ties which bound and protected him, of the obligations they
entailed and the comforts they ensured. He had an enlivening sense
of the beauty of the winter as he trotted through the streets, in
gloves and muffler, to the Lycée, of the summers at Saint-Seine, of
the restful atmosphere of his home. He had, too, a vivid sense of
the unquestioned tradition of Catholicism within the family circle
and of the gulf which therefore separated him from a material and
sceptical civilization. In this sheltered, shuttered world Blondel
grew up retiring, excessively shy, fussy in matters of health, circumspect, conscientious in the extreme; but the very excess of his
prudence developed in him an anxious, disturbing, questioning
spirituality that ventilated his world and called for action. Perhaps
it was this inner tension which first suggested the dialectics of
L'Action, the dynamism and interplay of reflection and action, of

34

thought and existence, which one finds fully present, though as yet undefined, in the earliest pages of the *Cahiers Intimes* which begin, when he was twenty-one, with the words:

> *Je veux*
> *Que toute ma vie réponde et définisse:*
> *Je veux*

When the question of a career came up for discussion Blondel, though anything but adventurous, announced his wish to attend the École Normale and prepare himself to become Professor of Philosophy in one of the State universities—a suggestion that somewhat disturbed his parents, though his brother Georges had studied law in Paris.

> In the milieu in which I lived, with few ties with the university world, shy as I was, very attached to family life, delicate in health, fearful to excess of anything unknown, I should never have even conceived the project if I had not been driven by an idea which pressed secretly upon me. Without perceiving the strangeness of the means, it seemed to me that the École (I only knew of it by name), which inspired awe in all those around me and in myself, was the path which I should have to take in order to attain my end, to arm myself against those whom I longed to make hear the truth, to acquire a more direct and profound knowledge of those who were mistaken, sincere unbelievers whose prejudice it was the dream of my youth to dissipate by talking to them in their language.

Forewarned that the École was a danger to faith and morals, alarmed as much as surprised by his success in the examination and the interview, Blondel left Dijon in November 1881. The picture which had been drawn was not altogether misleading: living in college was very different from the comfortable, cushioned existence at home. The bad, inadequate food, the boisterous company, the lack of privacy, the extremely exacting curriculum, affected his health and he became something of a valetudinarian. Yet in some respects Blondel was singularly fortunate. He had Émile Boutroux for his Professor of Philosophy, and a Catholic, Léon Ollé-Laprune for his Director of Studies, both of whom recognized his talent and sympathized with his way of philosophizing. And among his class-mates he found lifelong friends—Victor Delbos, the philosopher, André Pérate, who died Custodian of Versailles, Johannes Wehrlé, of Saint-Phillipe du Roule who supported him through all his controversies and the difficulties which were about to begin.

Blondel sat three times for the *agrégation* before being admitted, so that it was only in 1886 that he began teaching, while preparing his doctorate thesis. 'How much I suffered,' he afterwards wrote, 'during the last part of my university career from the rationalistic scholasticism [which he had learnt in Dijon], which cost me a serious illness at the École Normale, caused me to be refused the *agrégation* twice and which prompted M. Lachelier to advise me, if not to give up philosophy, at least to limit myself for a long time to the study of Royer-Collard.'

But Blondel's difficulties had only begun. When he proposed the subject of his thesis, *action*, it was rejected out of hand, and he was informed that thought, not action, was the sphere of philosophy. After he had explained his intention in some detail, however, his choice of subject was allowed, and he was encouraged to follow his inspiration by no less a figure than Lucien Herr, Librarian to the Ecole Normale Superiéure, a big, large-hearted man, always ready with a helping hand, who a few years later was to play a consider-able part in the early life of Charles Péguy.

Mon petit Blondel, Herr said to him, *tu devrais ne point faire figurer un seul nom propre dans cette thèse-là, qui mérite d'être traitée en plein drap; c'est du neuf!*

Such was Blondel's intention.

The reflections, or rather meditations, which gradually shaped his inspiration into a thesis and his thesis into a book are to be found in the *Carnets Intimes* (1883-1894), where one can follow day by day the gradual clarification of his vocation and his work down to the year of his marriage and his appointment as Professor of Philosophy in Aix-en-Provence. They do not systematically exclude the ordin-ary everyday affairs of life—we hear occasionally of his travels abroad, usually in the company of his brother, to Scandinavia, Germany, Belgium or Italy, of the shoots at Saint-Seine, and the family reunions at Quincy—but these are asides, and entirely sub-

sidiary to the examination of conscience in which he followed out
the resolution of the first entry, to become transparent to himself,
through action, to its last consequences.

15th December 1883. To devote oneself to others and to act,
misereor super turbam, that is the great saying, but how? Intellectual needs, moral needs, social needs, everything cries out
for help. Christ is there, but who are we to give him to and
where are we to take him? To devote oneself to others is the
rule common to all men, just as Christianity is the universal
remedy—but how? Is it to be in intellectual conflicts, in the
mêlée of ideas? Then I shall end by becoming a priest. Or in
hand-to-hand fights, in the political and social fray? There
the cassock is a scarecrow. It compromises one and one compromises it. One's personal action is incommoded and
restricted.

. . . It is true that I am speculative rather than active: I
have some ideas of my own; but will they ever acquire the
semi-scientific precision needed to make them efficacious?
And especially where I am concerned, who have not the gift
of defining an ideal, would not an intellectual life tend to
become a moving phantasmagoria of interlinked forms whose
indefinite contours overlap and penetrate one another? Is it
not action alone which defines ideas?

There are three human ways of serving the supernatural:
either by making room for it in the intellectual order, which
invades it and seems to force it back, by preparing room for
it with the help of healthy, clearly defined, really scientific
ideas in philosophy and in the theory of the human mind; or
by making room for it in social and political action, by introducing it by example, by means of discussions and
personal influence, into the traditions of the people, the
customs of the countryside, through legislation and practical
reason; or by calling upon it to reanimate the generosity
of feelings, the dry or withering heart, the enthusiasm that is
dulled by the abuse of material things, of positive, scientific
things—by becoming a Christian Rousseau. In a word
one must restore either the object, or the practice or the

feeling of religion and moral things. It goes without saying that each of these means only supplements the supernatural action upon any Christian, and upon others through the communion of saints. That is the common, impersonal source of the power for good; great thoughts, noble resolutions, striking and influential devotion to others, spring from the inchoate prayer and austerities of the humble and the ignorant.

In the very next entry, Blondel recognizes that *le Rousseau chrétien, ce ne sera jamais moi;* but the phrase is arresting enough to bring home the intensity and precision of his meditations. He felt the almost insuperable difficulty of 'vaccinating passion', of producing, as Kierkegaard had tried to do, 'a beneficent gust of feeling' so that Christianity should not just be something applied from outside like a brake, but so that faith should be set in motion. His task, he realized, was to be in the intellectual order, but perhaps it could be said that the precision and breadth of view which he brought to his task enabled him to contribute to all three spheres, and not merely directly in specific articles but by unfolding in his work and through action the meaning of the integration of Catholic truth.

> Abstract work tires and depresses me: it is contrary to our nature, to all nature. One must act in order to know oneself.
> To compose an intellectual work, to write a thesis applying only one's mind to it, developing it logically, is sometimes culpable folly. The examination of conscience and firm resolution are the only efficacious methods in the order of thought as in the moral order. There can only be doctrinal unity where there is a common discipline and conformity in life.[1]

The shortest and simplest statement of his ideal recalls the work of Friederich von Hügel: 'To combine a very great and very generous feeling with the very great exigencies of science: mystic and scholar'.

Blondel passed the *agrégation* in 1886, his name coming last in the class. A month or two later he was appointed to the Lycée at Montauban, and after a few weeks was transferred to Aix, where he

[1] *C.I.*, pp. 23-4.

was appointed as Professor at the University in 1894 to remain there for the rest of his life. In 1889 Blondel asked for a year's leave during which he hoped to write his thesis, and returned with that intention to Saint-Seine. Early in the following year, however, he was recalled for a few months to fill a vacancy at the Collège Stanislas, where, for the first time, he entered into close touch with a group of Catholics interested in social questions, who were to become the founders of the *Sillon* movement—the paper was founded by Renaudin, though Marc Sangnier was the creator of the movement. 'It was my pupils at Stanislas,' Blondel wrote much later, in 1924, to Paul Archambault, 'who after consulting me about their plans, their programme and their title, founded *le Sillon*. Quite a correspondence passed between us [after his return to Saint-Seine, that is] before the first number of that elegant review appeared. The first collaborators belonged to my philosophy class of 1890-91.'[1]

Blondel's support of the social Catholics never wavered. His wife's brother-in-law, Adéodat Boissard, was one of the founders of the *Semaines Sociales* (a sort of perambulating, yearly university for the study of social questions), and its most active supporter and at one time President, Henri Lorin, was greatly interested in Blondel's thought. It was as a result of these ties that Blondel's criticism of Veterism, the *Action française* and the neo-thomist reactionaries, took the form and the name of *La Semaine Sociale de Bordeaux*, which was written at the request of Henri Lorin. It would give a very false idea of Blondel's philosophy to overlook his permanent concern for the social aspect of the Catholic revival or to conceal his horror of the bourgeois philosophy preached by the authorities of Cath-

[1] *Maurice Blondel and Auguste Valensin, 1899-1912*, 2 vols. [Bl-Val Corr.] (Aubier, 1957), vol ii, p. 177. Renaudin, Augustin Léger, Albert Lamy, are mentioned among others. The group was first of all called *la Crypte* and it was only when Renaudin fell ill that Sangnier took over. As soon as Sangnier began to exert his powerful personal influence Blondel began to have his doubts. 'Un premier tort à mon sens, ce fut au début du *tournant* politique et social, de trop solliciter les bénédictions, l'appui, la tutelle des autorités religieuses.' When the reaction under Pius X came the movement was trapped, and could not revive. As late as 1913 Merry del Val was explaining that charity was made impossible by socialism.

olicism. Engagement, for him, was not a concept but a fact, and for all his prudence he was always ready, when once he was sure of his ground, to commit himself. His main task lay, certainly, in the intellectual order, but though he realized that he was not cut out to be *le Rousseau chrétien* he did not hesitate, when the time came, to make a frontal attack on the *Action française* and on its leader. '*Toucher à Maurras*' Auguste Valensin wrote to him at the time, '*c'est grave*'. He would have found Péguy's attack on the bourgeois Catholicism of the period most sympathetic.

Blondel returned to Saint-Seine in the autumn of 1891 to settle down to the seventh and last version of *L'Action*. '*14th November 1891:* Today I began the definitive version of my thesis.' It was printed and presented to the Sorbonne a year and a half later, in 1893, and it was then that his difficulties began in earnest.

Even before the work was on sale, Blondel was made to feel the violence of the opposition which his ideas were to arouse, and the lack of comprehension which he would have to meet. The prejudice and lack of imagination which the mere subject of his thesis had already revealed were again manifested when he presented it in its finished form, and Émile Boutroux considered the opposition among the examiners so serious that he advised Blondel to call on his more unrelenting critics so that they could let off steam in a private conversation before attending the public oral examination, the *soutenance de thèse*, at the Sorbonne. But although *L'Action* was in the end accepted unanimously, and the examiners conceded its 'noble inspiration', Boutroux was sharply criticized for giving it his unqualified support and Blondel had a rough passage. Paul Janet opened the offensive bluntly.

> Your thought is obscure; your way of writing obscures it still more. It takes me an hour to read one of your pages and then I fail to understand it; I calculated that it would take me forty-five days to read your thesis. Our French school had a different way of thinking and writing: but nowadays no one is content to write in the ordinary way; as long as I tried to follow you, I took great pains and achieved no result. As soon as I gave up the attempt and began turning the pages of your book, I found a number of interesting things and some charm-

ing reflections: it is like the *Parerga* of Schopenhauer, which are far superior to the work itself.[1]

Blondel's reply is worth quoting, not only because there is some truth in Janet's complaints, but because it explains certain things about his aims and method.

It is indeed the honour of the French school to have been clear: not to cite contemporaries, Descartes is clear, Malebranche is clear, Condillac is clear, Laromiguière, Cousin and Jouffroy are clear. But there is a certain clarity, as Descartes himself remarks, which is often deceitful and dangerous, because it leaves those who have not understood under the illusion of having understood, and because, by veiling the real complexity of things from them, it tempts them to reduce everything to a sort of lazy *simplisme*: a full understanding of Cartesian thought is no doubt as laborious to acquire as a full understanding of Hegelian thought. Style should be a precision instrument which renders the whole feeling and nothing but the feeling of the inevitable difficulty of things. Whatever one does, one can never make certain meditations easily accessible; they require an initiation analogous to that of higher mathematics. It is also true that one can never hope to succeed in preventing impatient and presumptuous minds from wanting to grasp and believing they have penetrated everything without competence ... If I wrote certain parts of my work six or seven times, it was not for the pleasure of remaining obscure: I sincerely tried to diminish the difficulties which arise from the imperfection of the expression, and I am distressed not to have succeeded better. And yet I did not hope and did not wish to make all the obstacles disappear. Style is not only a passage open to others, giving them access to our thought, it is also a protection against hasty judgments. The right thing would be to be understood neither too soon nor too late. Perhaps one should regret the pleasure derived

[1] This and the following quotations are taken from *Une Soutenance de thèse*, attributed to the Abbé Wehrlé, but in fact written by Blondel immediately after the ordeal. It has been re-published in the first volume of *Études Blondéliennes*, p. 88.

from turning the pages of the book the moment one has given up hope of following the argument. To glance through a book is to look for what one knows already.

What Janet could not believe was what Herr had seen at once: *c'est du neuf*. But there was also a deeper meaning concealed in Blondel's desire to be understood neither too soon nor too late, which Kierkegaard had put forward in an ironic form in the *Unscientific Postscript* as an excuse for the obscurity of his books. The rationalist philosophers, he said, had gone on making everything easy until everyone thought they could understand everything: his task was to make things difficult once again, and give them something more to do. If existence or action were left out of consideration things became all too easy. But there were moments when Blondel forgot his answer to Janet and, tiring of the perpetual misunderstandings (whether of Janet or Père Schwalm and the Abbé Gayraud), longed to be understood. It was on such an occasion that von Hügel recalled him to his own ideas: ' "Make no mistake about it, he (von Hügel) said to me, many people would remain hostile to what requires an effort of inward renewal of them, and to what saps their human ideal of theocratic power. We shall always have to struggle against judaism." '[1] Tyrrell saw the practical advantages of the complexity of Blondel's style: 'Now I am pleased he is obscure, since that will protect his doctrine with an envelope until the season of germination comes.'[2] Perhaps it was this obscurity in Blondel's work which saved him from the denunciations of Maurras—to whom he had sent a copy of *L'Action*—who would certainly have answered Blondel's criticism of his 'human ideal of theocratic power' if it could have been done simply.

The acceptance of Blondel's thesis would normally have given him the right to a professorship. The temper of the times, and more particularly of the University and those whom Péguy called 'les intellectuels', prevented this, and when Blondel called on the Director of Education he was kept standing while the Director informed him curtly that in view of the religious and improperly

[1] Quoted by Blondel in a letter to Johannes Wehrlé.

[2] Quoted by E. Poulat, *Histoire, Dogme et critique dans la Crise moderniste* (Casterman, 1962), p. 538.

philosophical character of his thought his candidature could not be considered. A subsequent appeal was no more successful, except that he was offered a Chair of History, which he declined on grounds of incompetence. Boutroux felt the injustice of the official attitude, and shortly afterwards appealed directly to the Minister of Education, Raymond Poincaré, his cousin by marriage, sending him a copy of the offending book. Blondel was recalled to the Ministry. This time he was politely asked to sit down (*Oh! l'espoir d'une chaire*) and was given the Chair of Philosophy at Aix-en-Provence. Henri Lorin completes the story, quoting from the letter of a friend: 'Just back from Poincaré. On one of the shelves of the bookcase a magnificently bound copy of *L'Action* . . . I asked: "Do you know it?" "Yes, it's very remarkable." Rare praise.'[1]

Until the end of 1893 Blondel's future had seemed uncertain. For the past ten years the idea of becoming a priest had never quite deserted him, and in his state of uncertainty he re-examined his position. He consulted the Abbé Huvelin, who meant so much in the lives of Charles de Foucauld and von Hügel, and he wrote in detail to another friend, a priest at Saint-Sulpice. His doubts were finally resolved in a negative sense, but for the time being this only made him feel more frustrated than ever.

5th December 1893. Frustrated on all sides! I had hoped to be called to your priesthood; but no. I longed passionately to be appointed to some teaching post, and to the apostolate; but no. I had thought that a proposal which had been put to me might be possible, and was already decking it out in imagination; but no, always no. I have only to abstain, instead of advancing, and remain in suspense. How painful it is not to be able to fix one's life, one's mind or one's heart: to reach the age of manhood without even being a child with an allotted task and place.[2]

Two months in Belgium, Holland and Scandinavia did little to restore his spirits, and on his return to Saint-Seine the *Cahiers* begin again in the same black mood.

17th July 1894. You allow me a very vivid and very painful sense of the obscurity of your ways, of the difficulty of your

[1] *Bl-Val Corr.*, vol. II, p. 141.   [2] *C.I.*, p. 496.

faith, and, if I dare say so, of the uncertainty of your very existence and revelation. That suffering must prevent me from remaining either in darkness or in a false light, must join me to other souls, themselves in the dark, and teach me to bring them out of the darkness; I must even encounter that distressing obscurity in the hearts of those consecrated to you. Where, then, shall I recognize your presence and your action and your charity, O terribly hidden God? In the very security of faith, therefore, I feel the doubts, the anxiety of the search, the difficulties which the affirmation of Christianity involves ... I feel the full force of modern prejudices and the dreams of a new humanity in my very bones; I can intimately imagine the state of mind of numerous men, learned, penetrating minds, who move with joy and pride in philosophical speculation; I think, full of fear, of all those, of everything which is without you; and my thought and my heart are mortally troubled.[1]

That entry in the *Cahiers Intimes* was certainly written at a moment when the difficulties of life were pressing upon him. But the strength of his faith, of the whole traditional heritage behind him, of his reasoned conviction, never allowed him to forget the difficulties and obscurities surrounding it, or the exigencies of reason. On the contrary—and this is where he differed most obviously from the brash controversialists of the neo-thomist school—it was that intimate sense of the complexity of things which helped him to define his task.

Like every man, I have a role, a mission to fulfil, a vocation. And I feel more and more drawn to the project of showing, in thought as in my life, the natural necessity of the supernatural and the supernatural reality of the natural ... I must show the actual paths of reason towards God incarnate and crucified; I must conciliate the claims of modern thought; I must move science and philosophy by the methods which are dear to them and which they are right to love; I must remain natural as long as anyone and longer than anyone in order to show more singly, more peremptorily, more

[1] *C.I.*, p. 496.

pacifically, more broadly, more impersonally, the inevitable need for the supernatural. How few men are disposed to follow along those laborious paths, to open up a scientific road among so many obstacles, to understand equally the legitimate exigencies of the modern mind and the redoubtable intransigencies of Christian truth, to fill in the intervening space, and to throw into the abyss between them, so as to fill it, one's life, one's heart, one's thought, one's reason, one's faith, one's future in time and eternity, the whole of oneself? It is to that task that I must consecrate myself. There lies my duty.[1]

His failures had taught him where his task lay. Then, shortly after his appointment to Aix, in the autumn of 1894, the key changes. On a visit to Quincy-le-Vicomte he met his future wife, Rose Royer. '*4th November 1894. Sunday. I never dreamed that someone could love me. A wonderful discovery . . .*'

The context of 'L'Action'

Everything [Blondel writes in the Preface to *L'Action*] is then called in question, even the question as to whether there is a question. The motive power of the whole investigation must therefore be furnished by the investigation itself; and the movement of thought will then maintain itself without any external help. What is this internal mechanism? Here it is. For it is well to indicate the motivating thought in advance, not for the validity of but for the clarity of the exposition, and, by calling in question the very reality of being and together with it the value of life, to mark the knot which unites science, morals and metaphysics. There is no contradiction between them; because where incompatible realities have been thought to be perceived there are only heterogeneous and interdependent phenomena. If this has led to inextricable difficulties that is simply from failing to see where the one and only question lies. It is the whole man who is in question; so that it is not thought alone which must look

[1] *C.I.*, p. 526.

for him. The centre of philosophy must therefore be transposed into action, because it is there that the centre of life is found.[1]

This transposition, which shocked and confused the academic philosophers and the neo-thomist theologians, was Blondel's central inspiration, the motivating thought behind *L'Action*. 'I did not choose it,' he wrote to Boutroux in 1886,[2] discussing the subject of his thesis, 'it presented itself, and it still frightens me.' In another letter, to Victor Delbos, he explains how such thoughts come to one. In philosophy, he says, ideas are propagated like strawberries, 'one begins by taking root in someone else's thought, feeding on his substance; then one sends out a runner which strikes some way off, and one ends by detaching oneself completely from the original plant'.[3] Blondel had been fascinated by the theme of Leibnitz's correspondence with Père Des Bosses, and the title of his Latin thesis, *De vinculo substantiali*, was taken from it. Out of it, though in another sense quite independently of it, sprang the guiding intuition, the seminal idea of his philosophy, the conception of action as the link between thought and being. He could point to the precise source and moment of his inspiration, which was itself, as Herr had said, *du neuf*.

In fact [he wrote to Professor Lasson in Berlin in October 1894] I have as yet read very little; I had hardly left the École Normale, in a state of health which remained precarious for a long time, than I was taken up by the fatiguing task of secondary school teaching at a Lycée; then, obliged to care for my health, and desirous of composing a book in which I could freely express my most cherished thoughts, I asked for leave which I spent in solitude and consecrated to work with no other master than the interior Master whose voice you know. There you have the history of *l'Action*.[4]

[1] *L'Action*, p. xxii-iii.
[2] *Lettres Philosophiques de Maurice Blondel* [*L.P.*] (Aubier, 1961), p. 10.
[3] *L.P.*, p. 17.
[4] *L.P.*, p. 70. Adolf Lasson had written an appreciative review of *L'Action* in the *Zeitschrift für Philosophie*. Unlike the French critics, the editor of Hegel observed that it was 'more dialectical than psychological'.

All this does not, of course, mean that Blondel ignored or was ignorant of the historical context in which he wrote—the opposite was the case. The earliest letters, in which he defends his attitude against his critics of the right and the left, make this abundantly clear, and though the fact hardly needs emphasizing what he there says helps to define his intention.

> Between Aristotelianism, which depreciates and subordinates practice to thought, and Kantianism, which separates them and exalts the practical order to the detriment of the other, there is something to define, and it is in a very concrete manner, through the analysis of action, that I propose to define it.[1]

Far from his being, as his Catholic critics continued monotonously to reiterate, a Kantian, an immanentist, it should be clear from this statement that the aim of his 'insane dream' was not to sacrifice thought or the practical order but to save both by marrying them. This project, so incomprehensible in the context of the French tradition, except for the isolated instances of Pascal and Maine de Biran of whom Blondel always spoke with respect, necessarily made him speak of German thought as the context in which his intuition would be more readily intelligible.

> I have tried to do for the Catholic form of thought what Germany has long since done for and continues to do for the Protestant form, although its philosophy, it is true, was easier to disengage.[2]

If there is anything surprising about this claim, it is that he made it so early. For Blondel could hardly have known at the time that there had been a less complete and important, but nevertheless parallel, attempt by the romantic Catholics at the beginning of the nineteenth century. This movement, which reached its fullest development among the theologians of Tübingen (Drey, Möhler, Staudenmaier, Kuhn and Hefele) had been interrupted in the middle of the century by the aggressive Ultramontanism of the Mainz school, and the moribund scholasticism imported from Italy.

[1] *L.P.*, p. 10. This was written in order to explain and justify his choice of subject.
[2] *L.P.*, p. 34. 20.x.93.

Blondel only came to know of this school about ten years later through his friends Bremond and, more particularly, Georges Goyau, whose study of Möhler and whose history of German Catholicism must have made many things clear to him which he had only vaguely known or suspected. He could then see that the romantic tradition, which he had had to unearth for himself, had been partially discovered a hundred years earlier by the German Catholic romantic school which had finally been overwhelmed by the legalistic classicism that came from France.

Strangely enough, this very obvious affiliation was brilliantly illustrated not long after, though it was paradoxically interpreted, by M. Edmond Vermeil in his fascinating account: *Jean Adam Möhler et l'école de Tubingue* (1913). Vermeil put forward the thesis that the Modernists, among whom he allows a very minor place to Blondel, were continuing the work of the Tübingen school and giving substance to their half-hearted innovations. The mistake in perspective was inevitable at the time, and, once realized, does nothing to dim the excellence of M. Vermeil's study. But if the thesis is inverted, it demonstrates plainly enough that Blondel's claim was fully justified. Blondel, Laberthonnière, Bremond and Goyau—among others—were neither Modernists nor Veterists, but were carrying on (unbeknown, at first, to themselves) the tradition of Tübingen (and in some respects therefore of Newman) and digging down to the foundations, in the depths of which Blondel was quarrying. The Tübingen school had learned from Schelling, Hegel and Schleiermacher, to such good purpose that they were accused by Bauer of stealing the latter's thunder, in order to answer the rationalism of the enlightenment and the critical philosophy of Kant, and more particularly to recover a full doctrine of the Church and tradition (as opposed to the legalistic conception current since the Counter-Reformation). Blondel had seen, like Kierkegaard before him, that the situation of philosophy demanded a more radical transposition of questions and needed to be plunged back into existence and revitalized by action.

But with some notable exceptions the existential tradition in French thought as represented by Pascal and Maine de Biran was held in small esteem at that date, and the *Action française* party took its

cue from Maurras who spoke of *le funeste Pascal*. Blondel was therefore almost forced to look abroad for the context in which to make
his position intelligible, and when he wanted to speak of Pascal—
so wrongly understood, as he thought, in France—he illustrated
what he had to say with reference to 'tendencies among the German
mystics who, through a sort of presentiment of modern pantheistic
(i.e. idealistic) doctrines, had been able to find the secret of the moral
life in the practical reconciliation of opposites.'[1] Blondel's many
references to German thought and the importance which he
accorded it may not have been based on a detailed and scholarly
knowledge of German philosophy, but he had in Victor Delbos an
authority on whom he could safely rely and whom he trusted.
From the few letters published it can be seen that their discussions
must often have revolved on precisely this point—Blondel's affiliation with the romantic philosophers as the precursors of existentialism as it emerged in the work of Kierkegaard some thirty years
later.

> Instead of juxtaposing the philosophy of essence and the
> philosophy of existence, as you would like to do, in the foot-
> steps of Schelling, I try to show that they are coincident and
> interpenetrate everywhere, without ever being confused or
> replacing one another. Note that in this I am logically con-
> sistent with what you want: for if one restricts oneself to
> juxtaposing dialectic and practice, one leaves an irreducible
> and irrational element outside metaphysics, which is contrary
> to the hypothesis; the only way of saving an integral meta-
> physic—which is precisely what you want to save without
> sacrificing practical life—is to understand that it penetrates it
> and does not replace it.
>
> . . . The trinitarian rhythm of Hegel delights me; but
> however high thesis and antithesis may reach, the Christian
> idea, better understood and further developed, always
> furnishes a higher synthesis. People always try to invent a
> better and more beautiful ideal, a larger truth. But as human-
> ity grows, Christ rises above the horizon. And the perma-
> nent task of philosophy and apologetics (which, for me, you

[1] *L.P.*, p. 155. 3.x.92.

see, are at bottom one) is to discover that he is greater, incomparable.[1]

Seen as a deliberate attempt to do for Catholicism what had been done to some extent for Protestantism in Germany, there can be no doubt that Blondel's intention was from the first metaphysical, though, as he says, philosophy and apologetics were for him ultimately one. The subsequent modifications in his work, made during the last part of his life, in no way affect that original intention. *L'Action* (1893) was, from the first, part of a whole, and it was this which left the final sections open to misunderstandings. It was the root sent out by his meditation on Leibnitz, and action remained the *vinculum*, the link between thought and being, between reflection and experience. The subject of the Leibnitz-Des Bosses correspondence is the Eucharist, and it was the Leibnitz correspondence which, as he says, supplied him with the solution to the problem of immanence and transcendence and suggested to him the place which incarnation and the Incarnation were to take in his thought. The importance which this idea came to assume for him is brought out in the first of two memoranda which he wrote at, the request of his friend and former pupil, Auguste Valensin, on some of the early essays of Père Teilhard de Chardin in 1919.[2]

The problem of the Incarnation seemed to me (perhaps even antecedently to any other philosophical question) to be the touchstone of a genuine cosmology. I share the ideas and the feelings of Père Teilhard de Chardin in face of the Christological problem. Faced by the horizons widened by the natural and human sciences, one cannot, without betraying Catholicism, rest satisfied with mediocre explanations and with limited views which make Christ into an historical accident, which isolate him from the cosmos like an extrinsic episode, and which seem to make him into an intruder or an exile, *dépaysé* in the crushing and hostile immensity of the universe. Long before the *Loisysme* of the 'little red books'

---

[1] *L.P.*, pp. 69ff. 1.x.94. See also Delbos's article in *Cahiers de la Nouvelle Journée III*, 'Le mysticisme allemand'.

[2] Published by Père de Lubac in *Archives de Philosophie*, Jan.-Mar. 1961. Extracts were given in the *Bl-Val Corr.* See also below, p. 89.

[Loisy's polemical works] I had an intensely clear consciousness of this alternative: either withdrawal towards a fatal
symbolism or advance to a realism that was consistent to the
very end, towards an integral realism which harmonized
the metaphysics of Christianity with mysticism as lived by
the saints, by the faithful themselves . . . We are led to the
instauratio tota in Christo . . . Let us therefore go forward
without hesitation in a sense in which, as the world and man
grow in the eyes of man, Christ grows still more in our eyes
and our hearts.

It would be easy to multiply Blondel's earlier references to
Panchristisme[1] and to show how early his views on the problem were
formed. In a letter to Bremond (4.1.03), criticizing Loisy's Christo-
logy, he writes: 'and it seems to me infinitely dangerous, to say
no more, and you know how deeply my *Panchistisme* revolts
against it'—and he returns to the same point at the end of *History
and Dogma*. It was this sense of a dynamic Christianity which led
Blondel to say that the *Génie du Christianisme* was the 'musical
prelude' to the Catholic renewal and that 'it is time to begin an
integral work of criticism and apologetics, opening up more fully
"the spirit of catholicism" '.[2] The reference to Chateaubriand was
not misplaced and shows once again how fully Blondel realized that
he was taking up the argument first sketched out by the romantics.
Chateaubriand's 'musical prelude' was certainly not a scientific
argument, but with his breadth of view and his poetic sensibility
and imagination he saw that the static notion of tradition defended
by his adversary Bonald must lead to disaster. 'Catholicism,' he
wrote, 'is not the closed circle of Bossuet, but a circle which
expands with society.' The definition of what Chateaubriand called
an expanding circle, tradition, is given in *History and Dogma*.

The context of *L'Action* is further defined dialectically, and without reference to individual thinkers, in the third part of the *Letter on
Apologetics*, under the heading: 'The mutual renewal of philosophical and religious perspectives as a result of a fully consistent

---

[1] e.g. *Au Cœur*, pp. 51, 53, 60, 68, which date from 1902 and 1903. See also
the *Letter on Apologetics*, p. 203, below.

[2] *Au cœur*, p. 80, n. 26, 1.

development of modern thought'. Here Blondel goes beyond the romantic writers and foresees the convergence of philosophical and religious thought on the same or similar questions which was to culminate in the discovery of Kierkegaard's work and the various contemporary forms of existentialism. Bergson, no doubt, remains the great liberator, but his philosophy belongs in a sense to the past: it was a philosophy of nature, modern in form, particularly as regards its feeling for time and duration. Blondel, on the contrary, in spite of the old-fashioned form of his work, is fundamentally the more modern of the two.

> One may say, in a sense, [Père Cartier writes] that he is the first existentialist, though one can also speak with M. Paliard of his 'anti-existentialism', meaning that his philosophy of action, by breaking the circle of immanence, at the same time broke the circle of subjectivity and of a solitary liberty. It must be admitted that, in order to draw Blondel's thought on to a deeper level than that on which he explicitly took up his position, some degree of transposition is necessary, though it only makes Blondel more consistent with his central inspiration.[1]

Blondel, like Bergson, was writing for a generation which had grown up under the influence of Taine and of positivism (hence the appeal of Maurras's positivist Catholicism) and was faced by a 'separated philosophy' which dismissed the whole problem of transcendence as incommensurable with a consistent immanentism and rationalism. But Blondel saw that this confident positivism must inevitably criticize itself, and that it could not rest satisfied with such artificially drawn frontiers. This was in fact already becoming apparent as the work of Nietzsche percolated into France. 'Thus, far from drawing up an indictment against the tendencies of modern philosophy, we must rather reproach it for not having

---

[1] Albert Cartier, *Existence et Vérité* (Presses Universitaires de France, 1955), p. 41. Père Cartier's study can usefully be read as complementary to Père Bouillard's interpretation. The latter is conceived in the context of Catholic thought and theology; the former examines Blondel in the context of contemporary existentialist philosophy. Both are necessary if full justice is to be done to Blondel's work as a whole.

worked them out completely; we have only to ask it to be faithful to its principles so that it will find in its fully developed conclusions a grand conformity with the Christian spirit.'[1] In the same way that the hiatus between thought and action established by Kant led to the existentialism of Kierkegaard, so the inner inconsistencies and the limitations of a 'separated philosophy' prepared the way for the answer of the philosophy of action. But there is this difference, among many others, between Blondel and Kierkegaard, that while Kierkegaard—in opposition to Hegel and writing as he always did as a 'corrective'—makes the 'choice' appear as the end of dialectics (so that all he has to say of the second form of reflection is often overlooked), Blondel tends to reverse the procedure and to make the existential moment, *l'option religieuse*, the starting point of his dialectic. 'If the good option, on the *level of existence*,' Père Cartier writes, 'is the point of departure beyond dialectics, which cannot again be called in doubt, on the *level of reflection* it must enter into the dialectic and be justified by it.'[2] Kierkegaard's polemical style, the wish and the need to disabuse his generation of the errors of a metaphysical religion, led him to give his work as a whole so sharp an anti-Hegelian turn and bias that he often seems to forget one half of his thought and therefore brings everything back to 'the level of existence'. Blondel, on the contrary, always conciliatory, and moreover faced by an anti-metaphysical positivism, leans to the opposite side, and this makes it possible to speak of his 'anti-existentialism'. The relationship between them is often complementary; and this explains why Blondel, perhaps surprisingly at first sight, since he was after all the philosopher of *action*, has more often been compared to Hegel than to Hegel's great critic. But it should not be forgotten that Kierkegaard was not joking when he said that if Hegel had only described his logic as an experiment in thought he would have been the greatest thinker who had ever lived.[3]

It is in this perspective that the 'audacity' of Blondel's metaphysic appears as an attempt not merely to juxtapose, but to unite, as he says to Delbos, the philosophy of essence and the philosophy of existence. It was this guiding thought, and the audacity of his

[1] *Letter on Apologetics*, p. 184 below.   [2] Cartier, *Existence et Vérité*, p. 40.
[3] *Journals*, 497, p. 134.

undertaking, which led Blondel to make concessions and alterations in his later work (whether rightly or wrongly is not here in question), and not simply a desire to escape from controversy and to avoid censure. There is, for this reason, justice in M. Tresmontant's contention that *L'Action* cannot be taken as the whole of Blondel's work.

The opening chapters of *L'Action* could be said to be symmetrical with the opening phase of Kierkegaard's work. Blondel begins with a criticism of the attitudes which claim to evade the 'choice' and to avoid action. What Kierkegaard calls the aesthetic stage or sphere Blondel examines under the name of dilettantism (Renan and Barrès, in fact) or scepticism and nihilism on the level of existence. Both these opening phases have been read as psychological analyses, though both form part of the dialectic, as Lasson rightly saw. Were they only descriptive they would lead nowhere except by implication. But Kierkegaard, like Blondel, believed that 'ethics is the trap in which to catch a man'. Ultimately there is no evading the choice. But in other respects Blondel's investigation proceeds along different lines. He accepts the rationalism of the immanentists for whom everything is drawn from the human mind, and he adopts their method so as to involve them in the dialogue. This consists and 'can only consist in nothing else than in trying to equate in our consciousness what we appear to think and to will and to do with what we do and will and think in actual fact: so that behind the factitious negations and ends which are not genuinely willed may be discovered our innermost affirmation and the implacable needs which they imply'.[1] This should not be read as an appeal from conscious to unconscious desire or will and their conflict, but to *thought* clarified in action and action clarified by reflection. The terms in which the dialectic is worked out—*la volonté voulante* and *la volonté voulue*—have the disadvantage of suggesting a purely superficial contrast between conscious and unconscious when Blondel's intention is to investigate the dynamism of the whole man, the unity which is composed of intelligence, feeling and deliberate will, and to examine not an ethical conflict but the meaning of existence as revealed to us in our need to harmonize our nature and our exist-

[1] *Letter on Apologetics*, p. 157 below.

ence so as to discover our destiny—invoked in the first sentence of *L'Action* and revealed in the final 'option'.

This investigation, it should be noted, is not confined to the inner world, for man only discovers himself through action, that is, in all the relationships of life, of family, society, nation and humanity. Reflection alone is always insufficient, because thought and action are ultimately one. A closed system is therefore one which, being complete, excludes the further possibility of action (and so of thought) and is superstitious in character. Here again Blondel speaks in terms which recall Kierkegaard, for whom a system of existence was impossible and superstition was, like scepticism, the opposite of faith in which 'man begins to exist'. The choice or option, on the other hand, is the opening on to and the possibility of transcendence so that at the culminating point the alternative presented is between the death of action or its continued life: either the self-sufficiency of a closed world, or a philosophy open to the transcendent *as yet undefined*. A Christian philosophy would, in this sense, be one which is becoming Christian.[1]

Blondel's philosophy was his answer to the indifference of those who thought in terms of a separated philosophy, to the comment made to him by one of his fellow-students at the École: 'Why should I be obliged to inquire into and take account of a casual event which occurred 1900 years ago in an obscure corner of the Roman Empire?' The problem to him was: 'How should one envisage the philosophical problem in the light of religion, so that religion should not simply be a philosophy and so that philosophy should not be absorbed in any way into religion?' He in no way minimizes the difficulty, and the expressions which he uses to characterize it have, since his time, become familiar: 'the scandal of the reason', 'a leap of generosity', 'a deep wound'. For all his faith, or rather because of it, he had no desire to oversimplify or to claim for polemical reasons that faith was easy and could be attained by logical reasoning alone. 'I will confess to you that it seems to me that one should never sacrifice certainty to disquiet (*inquiétude*), nor disquiet to certainty: that arid, crude way of thinking one has "arrived" and of being in brutal possession of the object of one's faith is no doubt idolatry; but

[1] See below, p. 107.

55

equally so that susceptibility of the conscience which takes pleasure in never finding, as though its aim and its object were in fact not to have any. A genuine and merited moral certainty only exists where there is first of all, and simultaneously, disquiet: disquiet, consistent with the laws of its own perpetual renewal, only exists on condition of a perpetual progress in the sum total of certitudes.'[1] Perhaps the first and most elementary difficulty in understanding Blondel lies in the dialectical movement of his thought, which seems to have confused Paul Janet so that he could only find a number of interesting things and 'some charming reflections'. Janet's fault was not lack of intelligence, but, as Blondel gently reminded him, a common error, that of looking for what one already knew.

L'Action, however, had not only been coldly received by Janet and the University; Léon Brunschwicg, the future editor of Pascal, had announced 'a courteous but firm opposition, in the interests of reason'. Only William James, as has been said, Lasson, and Rudolf Eucken (Max Scheler's teacher) showed any interest in the book. Among Catholics the position was the same: widespread official opposition and one or two independent thinkers who saw its importance. The only difference was that the Catholic opposition was not troubled by courtesy, and Père Schwalm, for example, lectured Blondel as he must have done his first-year students, letting him off with a warning.[2] It would be difficult to convey the degree of misrepresentation except by saying that it was informed by a malicious party spirit. Blondel was consistently referred to as a Kantian, an immanentist, a subjectivist, was denounced to Rome and, as soon as the word gained currency, labelled a Modernist. But *L'Action* deeply impressed his friends, Delbos and Wehrlé, and won him two new admirers, Friederich von Hügel and Lucien Laberthonnière—the latter's relations with Blondel will be discussed in the following section.

Von Hügel first met Blondel in Rome in the spring of 1895, and

[1] *L.P.*, p. 28.

[2] The details of the controversies which ensued need not be gone into here, instructive though they are for the history of the period and the intellectual background of the religious crisis. The real points at issue between Blondel and the thomists are dealt with in the philosophical sections of the introduction.

was won over by *L'Action* and its author. His letters began to pour in with requests for more copies of *L'Action* to send to his friends, for off-prints of the latest article, for a photograph to place next to Eucken's and with offers of help and some excellent advice, as when he wrote that his enemies would only dislike him more if they understood him better. Tyrrell was made to read *L'Action*; but it is a question how much either of them understood of Blondel's intention. There is nothing in von Hügel's later works or letters to suggest that the first rapturous enthusiasm was based on a solid understanding of Blondel's philosophy. Von Hügel, it is true, resented Blondel's criticism of Loisy, but it seems improbable that had he understood *L'Action* he could have forgotten it so completely. They were temperamentally poles apart, and a week at Aix had not been enough to break down Blondel's reserve. Nor was the difference wholly or even mainly temperamental. Von Hügel, in spite of his learning, his culture, his philosophical interests, was entirely lacking in technique. 'I think the clarifying business (of which we are so immensely proud),' he wrote to Maud Petre, 'misleads and impoverishes us.' That it could do so is obvious enough; but the lack of it could also be a disadvantage. Blondel, on the other hand, was 'entirely foreign to the habits of mind of the autodidact' and became increasingly concerned with the clarifying business, with 'the technical organization of his thought'. In the end that difference of approach made communication very difficult even to two minds which basically had and held so much in common, and not least the desire to unite thought and feeling, honest scholarship and mysticism. Von Hügel remains a somewhat isolated figure, not on account of his ideas which, on the contrary, are still very pertinent, but because his lack of technique prevented him from giving them a sufficiently personal expression and condemned him to eccentricity. Blondel's technical mastery, though it may seem at first to dehydrate his style, enabled him to give his very personal thought a form which, in the long run, could neither be ignored nor circumvented. Von Hügel was no hare; but there is something of the tortoise about Blondel.

The Correspondence with Laberthonnière: 1919-1926

There is a danger of dismissing 'the terrible years' of the Modernist crisis as an interruption in Blondel's work, but enough has been said of his attitude in the controversies to show that his interventions were of decisive importance. If he refused to reprint *L'Action* it was not so much because it had given rise to controversy, as because he was dissatisfied with certain aspects of it, some of which are discussed below. Nothing von Hügel or other friends could say made him budge: copies might change hands at fr. 2,000, and typed copies circulate as the demand increased; but this only confirmed Blondel in his decision: *L'Action* should only reappear as part of the metaphysical work to which it belonged. This final 'organization of his thought' was not completed until fifty years later, and was published between 1936 and 1949. The intervening years had certainly provided obstacles enough to its conclusion: the years of controversy (1893 to 1913), the War (1914 to 1918), the renewal of the fight against the *Action française* (1914 to 1926), and then the loss of his sight, the necessity of adapting himself painfully to dictation.[1]

One name dominates the whole period down to 1926: that of Père Lucien Laberthonnière. The voluminous correspondence begins in 1894, when Laberthonnière wrote to express his enthusiasm and gratitude on reading *L'Action*, and it ends thirty-two years later when their disagreements had lasted so long that there seemed nothing further to say.

Laberthonnière was born in 1860. On completing his studies at the Grand Séminaire at Bourges he joined the Oratorians and in

---

[1] For the period after 1913 there is still a dearth of material—apart from his published works. The documents and correspondence published from the Blondel Archives stop in 1913. There is, however, the valuable selection from the letters of Laberthonnière and Blondel, which is due to the initiative and ability of M. Claude Tresmontant, and this enables one to guess at some of the immediate causes of the modifications in his thought between 1913 and 1926. But the selection omits all private matters—the personal disagreements which arose between Blondel and his correspondent.

1887 began teaching at their school at Juilly, where Lamennais had once lived. He was transferred for a time to Paris and continued his studies under Boutroux, and, as dissatisfied as Blondel with the arid scholasticism he had been fed upon at Bourges, he began to formulate his own point of view, inspired by the two thinkers who meant so much in Blondel's early years, Pascal and Maine de Biran. In 1896 he went back as superior to Juilly, and when the religious orders were expelled by Combes in 1902 he returned to Paris where he remained for the rest of his life living in the rue Las Cases. In 1905 Blondel bought a long established periodical, *Annales de Philosophie Chrétienne*, and installed Laberthonnière as editor. Laberthonnière was by then a respected figure among the French clergy, though as a priest he was infinitely more exposed to the intrigues of the *Action française* neo-thomists than Blondel. When he published *Catholicisme et Positivisme* in 1911, a more direct and unguarded attack than Blondel's *La Semaine Sociale*, he signed his own death warrant. Three years later *Le dogmatisme moral* and *L'idéalisme grec et le réalisme chrétien* were put on the Index, and their author was refused all further permission to publish for the rest of his life. The injustice of this harsh, relentless measure has since been recognized and was regretted by some at the time; but the life-sentence was never lifted. Yet when the French Bishops replied to the German episcopate's pronouncements on the War, the answer was drafted by Laberthonnière; and the only preacher to repeat Lacordaire's success in the yearly Lenten Sermons in Notre Dame, Père Sanson, read from a text written by his brother Oratorian.

Until the 1914 War Laberthonnière and Blondel worked in perfect harmony, meeting regularly and spending part of the summer together. But while they were at one in their opposition to Modernism and to Veterism in all its forms, their ways of thinking and writing were very different. Laberthonnière was a fighter, impatient of the slowness of his adversaries and infinitely less cautious than Blondel. He united a fine gift for the exposition of ideas to speed in the cut and thrust of controversy, and, by no means averse to a sally, he would have found life dull if he had to weigh every adjective and forestall all the misunderstandings of a man as unpredictable as the notorious Mgr Turinaz, Bishop of Nancy. He did not endear himself to the authorities by singling out their statements for tart comment, and Blondel always felt that his polemical talents were not sufficiently under control. Their collaboration was nevertheless happy; as a result of their complementary gifts—though the work was mostly done by Laberthonnière—*Annales de Philosophie Chrétienne* played an important part in the controversies of the period, and provided a platform for writers sympathetic to Blondel's ideas. Among the contributors whose names have not been forgotten are Henri Bremond, Georges Goyau, Étienne Gilson. Occasionally there would be an article by some heavy-weight such as Brunetière (once shortly before his death) or Archbishop Mignot (though the latter did not sign his name: Blondel, for similar reasons, often wrote under pseudonyms or under the signature of a friend).

The first number of the review edited by Laberthonnière set the tone and, as though to establish the tradition in which it worked, pointed to the need to break away from the narrow Latin, Roman and Mediterranean conception of Catholicism by pointing to the relevance of the German Catholic writers of the romantic period. It contained reviews of Georges Goyau's *Jean Adam Möhler*, of Bremond's first study of Newman, and of a German life of Staudenmaier by Bremond. On this point, as on so much else, Blondel and Laberthonnière were at one: 'Like you, *mon révérend Père*, I think there is great profit to be drawn from German philosophy . . . It seems to me that up to now all that has been done is to adapt ancient philosophy to Christianity, and that everything remains to be done.'[1]

Bremond was one of the most regular contributors. It was in *Annales* that he published the articles which formed the basis of his *Apologie pour Fénelon*, and several of the essays introducing Newman to French readers. Under Laberthonnière, in fact, *Annales* became the foremost periodical of its kind. 'You have struck a magnificent note in *Annales*,' William James wrote, 'I have copied whole pages of your work.' 'I still recall,' Blondel wrote years later, 'with admiration and gratitude your courage in *Annales* both to say and to let others have their say; and for my part I owe you an infinite obligation. But that method did not enlighten men's minds as much

[1] *Correspondance Philosophique, Maurice Blondel—Lucien Laberthonnière* [*Corr-Phil.*] (Editions du Seuil, 1961), p. 80. 2.x.94.

as might have been desired.' Probably nothing which could have been done at that time would have satisfied Blondel, who only felt the difficulties and the seeming hopelessness of the position. But *Annales* had the punch of the *Rambler*, and exerted a long-term influence of the kind which Blondel in fact expected. At a time when it seemed that Newman might well be condemned with the Modernists an immediate effect was inconceivable.

Blondel certainly felt that Laberthonnière was inclined to overstate his case and that he laid himself open to criticism, but as long as 'the heroic battles' against Veterism lasted the disagreements between them were muted by the force of the opposition their ideas encountered. After the War these differences very soon came to the surface, magnified by their very different temperaments, by the crystallization of their thought, and by the fact that Laberthonnière, condemned to an unnatural silence, was obliged to assist as spectator at the gradual recognition of Blondel, while his own very considerable and valuable part in their collaboration was passed over in silence. If, as Blondel had written, the crisis called for a double labour of purification and integration, perhaps it would not give an altogether false picture of their roles to say that the work of purification came easily to Laberthonnière, while the work of integration came naturally to Blondel. In the letters of the post-war years it almost seems as though the two inseparable and complementary tasks were being isolated and even turned against one another, as the ardent temperament of Laberthonnière and the conciliatory temperament of Blondel drove them, against their deeper feelings, against one another. Laberthonnière, confined to an *in pace*, could only feel the need to oppose the 'system' root and branch. Blondel, still relentlessly pursued by the *Action française* neo-thomists, but in changing circumstances which were to lead to its unexpected condemnation in 1926, was more inclined than ever to continue the work of integration, to embrace, not to exclude, all that was valuable and true in thomism. This did not of course mean that he became insensitive to the injustice done to Laberthonnière, and, ten years after the censure condemning him to perpetual silence, Blondel wrote to Cardinal Mercier expressing his indignation at the treatment of Laberthonnière and asking Mercier to intervene. Nothing further has been published about Blondel's request; but in *Dialogues avec les précurseurs*[1] M. Jean Guitton describes how, on one of the Cardinal's last visits to Paris, he arranged to see Laberthonnière. The fact that Mercier, who had done so much to revive the study of St Thomas in Louvain, should have shown his sympathy for the sharpest critic of neo-thomism is not as paradoxical as it may appear. The thomists of Louvain, Maréchal and his friends, had been among the earliest to recognize Blondel. 'They were won over,' Maréchal had written to him in 1912, 'by the vigour and fullness of a thought which has known how to rejoin the great metaphysical tradition without ignoring any of the exigencies of the critique of knowledge ... Convinced thomists and devoted sons of the Church, they beg him to believe in their profound and respectful sympathy not only for the man but for the philosopher.'[2]

Now that 'the heroic battles' seemed to Blondel a thing of the past, he would have liked to avoid controversy as far as possible; but for Laberthonnière they were not over, and there was nothing to blunt his sense of the ugliness of the current notion of authority.

The notion of authority and the notion of obedience [he wrote in November 1919] are more falsified than they have ever been. St Francis, St Bernard, St Catherine, were faced with churchmen *as they were*. We find ourselves faced *with what they claim to be*. The result is that we are in untruth, in a lie which takes every kind of form. You say: we must just put up with it and become martyrs. But in what sense do you bear witness if your silence and your attitude are such that while suffering inwardly you allow nothing of the protest that springs from your conscience to appear?[3]

Blondel was certainly not insensitive to the evils which Laberthonnière referred to. He had been bowled over by *Pascendi* in 1907, in spite of the fact that he welcomed a clear condemnation of Modernism as an attempt to evacuate the transcendence of God whether by philosophical or exegetical methods.

I have read the Encyclical and am still stupefied. Is it possible? What inward or outward attitude should one adopt? And above all how can one prevent so many souls from fall-

[1] P. 89. [2] *Bl-Val Corr.* II. p. 266. [3] *Corr. Phil.*, p. 251, x. ii. 20.

ing into the temptation to doubt the *goodness* of the Church?
How fortunate are those who have fallen asleep in the Lord.'[1]

But at the same time he refused to see the history of the Church
simply as 'a succession of Bismarcks and Machiavellis' and claimed
that Laberthonnière's attitude meant resisting evil through evil
'when there is only one form of Christian victory, that which is
won through patience and the good', since that was the only way of
'giving the redemptive and creative efficacity of grace its field of
action'. He does not discount intellectual action, only it must be
'more positive than negative and critical, prudent and long-term
rather than controversial and immediate'.[2]

Laberthonnière's position made it doubly difficult for him to
acknowledge the change which was taking place, though from time
to time it was brought home to him. On one occasion, for example,
a young student from Louvain called on him on the recommenda-
tion of Père Maréchal 'to express his gratitude *for all he owed me*' and
seemed 'well informed about all we have done'. On another
occasion he was told that, the last time Père Rousselot[3] spoke to
Père Huby, Rousselot had said that he felt closer to Laberthonnière
than to St Thomas.

The disagreement began on what might appear to be a matter of
policy, but as the endless letters passed between the rue Las Cases
and the rue Roux-Alphéran in Aix, the extent to which they had
drifted apart could no longer be concealed. Authority, Laberthonnière wrote, had been transformed from a Christian into a pagan
concept, from the idea given in the Gospels into an idea identical
with that of Rome and the law (fully illustrated by the *Action
française*). As in everything, Laberthonnière saw the influence of
Aristotelianism behind the deleterious change, and, as the argument
began to wind down deeper, he reproached Blondel with changing
his ground. 'You must not,' the victim of the criticism replied,
'imagine that in speaking of Aristotle I intended or even dreamed

---

[1] *Bl-Val Corr.* I, p. 357.   [2] *Corr. Phil.*, p. 225, 12. iii. 20.

[3] Killed in 1915. Author of *L'Intellectualisme de St Thomas* and of an important
essay *Les yeux de la foi* (1910), Rousselot was an admirer of Blondel and Laberthonnière; he had crossed swords with them in *Annales*, but their discussions,
whether in public or in private, had always been friendly.

of making the smallest concession or any advance to the neo-peripateticians and the neo-thomists.'[1] He would have liked Laber-thonnière to be less severe on what he called Blondel's 'intellectual-ism', and to resist the temptation to go to extremes. 'Conversely, you tend to be too severe on thought in your advocacy of "moralism", to use the expression with which you characterize the inspiration you believe to be at the back of L'Action: well, no; that interpretation, which Delbos knew to be yours, was one which worried him profoundly and against which he adjured me to resist, in order to preserve the equilibrium of a doctrine which is an *integral realism* and which does not sacrifice either of the aspects of being, either thought or life, nor any of the persons of the Trinity!'[2]

From Aristotle the discussion moved on to thomism, and there again the distance between them seemed unbridgeable, for, since Rousselot's books had appeared, Blondel had begun to study St Thomas more closely and, unlike Laberthonnière, was so little prejudiced that he was the first to arrange that St Thomas should be among the set books in the University examinations. But Blondel's conciliatory attitude had done nothing to mollify Père Garrigou-Lagrange or Maritain[3], and since the *Action française* was then at the height of its power Laberthonnière felt that Blondel was modifying his expressions to no purpose. To this Blondel replied that Laber-thonnière's refusal to see any good in thomism, like his refusal to see anything but Machiavellism in the government of the Church, only weakened his case: 'Well, while being perhaps more severe on St Thomas than you are, I must add that in my opinion your criticism misses the mark, so that you leave the thomists an easy answer.'[4] Blondel was thinking more and more in terms of the integration of Catholic truth, Laberthonnière more and more in terms of purifying Catholicism of the materialism and positivism of the *Action française*. This comes out clearly enough in a letter from Blondel dated 19th August 1921, in which the argument moved on

[1] *Corr. Phil.*, p. 268; 3.xi.21.   [2] *Corr. Phil.*, 269-270; 13.xi.21.
[3] M. Maritain's criticisms were published in *Réflexions sur l'Intelligence* (1926) and in *Les Degrés du Savoir*, 1932, pp. 869-878.
[4] *Corr. Phil.*, p. 319; 26.viii.24.

to the relation between real and notional knowledge—a point on which Blondel did change his views:

You rebel, and with reason, against the physicist and ultimately materialist interpretation which has been extracted more and more from thomist aristotelianism; and you have underlined more strongly than has ever been done before the coherence with which its links unfold in doctrine and history. From the point of view of notional knowledge on which the 'system' takes its stand, that passivism (i.e. a purely receptive idea of knowledge) is false and fatal. You see all that . . . to the point of seeing nothing else; it is indeed 'the system', but what is false and bad about the notional knowledge and the physicism of that pseudo-metaphysic does not alter the fact that where real knowledge is concerned there is an essential moral and supernatural truth in the idea of the *pati divina et omnia*. In studying the reasonable and even rational realism of the mystics I have come to understand the danger of an exclusive philosophy of action better, the danger of a sort of moral Fichteism, and of spiritual egotism, the need to make oneself permeable, not materially or notionally, but voluntarily, lovingly, to the universal and infinite action of 'what is not us' though 'we have become all that'. For a long time I resisted the idea of a *passion* so onerous to the premature autonomy of the human will and action; but in coming closer and closer to it I had the feeling of remaining more and more faithful to our first inspiration, of being at the very antipodes of a naked and brutal obediential power, of realizing *l'Action* to its maximum. Is that to fall into 'deleterious confusions'? Let me have your opinion on this question of conscience, on the debate in which I have been involved and not with my understanding alone.

. . . As a result of a sort of inverted symmetry or illegitimate transference, the scholastics did not perceive that discursive thought and notional knowledge is constructive activity, and applied words to it that are twisted out of their natural meaning and that only apply to real knowledge, with all the mortification and the unitive life it presupposes. But if

this counterfeit has all the philosophical, political and theological disadvantages which you see with such terrible clarity,
there would, on the other hand, be an immense danger for
our spiritual life in overlooking the passive methods of illum-
ination and union. It is with the object of obtaining more
attention and adhesion for that aspect, so unknown to philosophers, that I have used any argument which came to hand,
borrowing expressions, formulae of which I could not find
the equivalent elsewhere. That too is what St John of the
Cross did, who is certainly the least materializing of men,
and who would have the same horror as you of your Mon-
ster: he relies continually on the theology of the School, but
breathes a 'transposed' spirit into it. After these explanations,
however succinct they may be, I hope I shall no longer irri-
tate you if I say (as you said at Fribourg, after assisting at the
fight between Portalié and Gardeil) that there is not one
thomism, but a hundred . . . that there is not a *system* but a
summa, a compilation, a juxtaposition.[1]

But nothing could any longer bridge the gulf which separated
them. Sometimes in his exasperation Laberthonnière would pour
out all his pent-up ideas, and one of these attempts at a complete
reply to Blondel ran to four hundred pages—parts of which have
been published in book form.[2] But before the correspondence
which had lasted for thirty years stopped, before the friendship
which had meant so much to both of them faded out, Blondel was
given a last opportunity of expressing his old admiration. Laberthonnière, who had promised to help Père Sanson with the sermons
he was to preach in Notre Dame, found that he was obliged to
compose the whole series, which Sanson then read. The resounding
success with which they met pleased Blondel, especially as he could
join in the general praise.[3]

The fourth *conférence*, so central, so essential, seems to me

[1] *Corr. Phil.*, pp. 298-9.

[2] Published by Louis Canet along with other posthumous volumes [Vrin,
Paris.]

[3] Sanson was later attacked by the *Action française* neo-thomists, and his second
course of sermons suspended.

marvellously well done, and what I have read of it fills me to overflowing with joy.[1]

This was the last moment when they forgot their disagreements.

The last period: the Trilogy: 1926–1949

The Blondel-Laberthonnière correspondence covers a transitional period in Blondel's life during which he was not only amassing notes for 'the technical organization of his thought', but was modifying his expressions and sometimes his thought not only in response to criticism but as he turned successively and in detail to particular problems: *Le procès de l'intelligence* (1922), *Le problème de la mystique* (1925), *Le problème de la philosophie catholique* (1932). There are no letters for the period subsequent to his breach with Laberthonnière, but there is a short autobiographical work which not only recounts the past but explains his attitude at the time, 1928, and his plans for the future. *L'Itinéraire philosophique de Maurice Blondel*, dedicated to Henri Bremond, though attributed to Frédéric Lefèvre, was written by Blondel. Lefèvre, who published 'literary portraits' in *Les Nouvelles Littéraires* week by week over a number of years, had persuaded Blondel to be interviewed. '*Une heure avec . . .*', as the articles were called, was not, however, enough for Blondel, and after discussing the matter with Lefèvre he completed the dialogue himself, noting that instead of an hour it would have occupied several. It was published, after some extracts had appeared, in book form, and although the specialist may not find it of great interest the ordinary reader may well think it Blondel's most successful literary work; it not only gives a reasonably short and clear account of his philosophical aims but conveys something of the author's personality, tastes and sympathies. And if, as Péguy held, a philosophy worthy of the name is always a 'voyage of discovery', Blondel's 'itinerary' conveys precisely that element, the unfolding of his work, the sources of his inspiration, the part played by his friends, the movement, or to use another of Péguy's expressions, the *approfondissement*, the deepening process, which began with *L'Action* and ended with the Trilogy (*La Pensée*, *L'Être et les êtres*, *l'Action*), and

[1] *Corr Phil.*, p. 335; 19. viii. 21.

L'Esprit chrétien. The dialogue begins in the library of the former Hôtel Gallifet, Blondel's house in the rue Roux-Alphéran, where he takes a backward glance at his life and the starting point of his thought; it continues in his summer house, the Bastidon outside Aix, where he and his interlocutor discuss theories of art; and it ends as they climb the Mont Saint-Victoire, on to which the Bastidon looks across the plain, and discuss the Trilogy.

Since 1926 Blondel had been unable to read and had had to give up his work at the University. That 'brutal warning' not to go on indefinitely poring over the notes for his *opus magnum*, the Trilogy, had been accepted, and he had 'painfully apprenticed himself' to a new method of composition and had begun to dictate. 'It would be better not to speak of my interior distress,' he wrote to Laberthonnière, 'of my obnubilation and the agonizing deformation of objects. Dictating exasperates me; and being read to is useless, since I hear badly, and it gives me a headache almost at once. But I am forcing myself nevertheless to a few pages a day, *va comme je te pousse*, and so add four or five pages a day to my elucidations, and since November last I have dictated (parts of) *L'Esprit chrétien, La pensée, L'Être et les êtres* and a number of other things. But it's dreadful.' He had begun, as he says in the *Itinéraire*, 'to bind up the little sheaf one calls a doctrine, and to catch a little of the universal truth in the perspective of a limited personal point of view.'[1] Between November and June he dictated 600 pages, and without blinding himself to the difficulties ahead he hoped to complete his work. Though the Trilogy was not published for another six years, by which time he had made further modifications in his thought, the rough sketch which he gives of it is in its main lines correct.

The account of the Trilogy follows the three books (the first and last in two volumes) into which it is divided. Instead of beginning with the *Cogito, à la* Descartes, or with the fact of consciousness, Blondel begins, he says, using a method of analysis which is neither that of Condillac nor of Maine de Biran, but of Lavoisier—in order to show, or at least to suggest, 'a new field to be explored'. For even if the solution were imperfect, at least the problem would have been

[1] *L'Itinéraire philosophique de Maurice Blondel* (Paris: Spes, 1928), p. 123.

indicated. So, leaving aside the question (to be discussed in *La Pensée*) of the cosmic and biological preparations for thought, and omitting the material supplied by psychoanalysis—for example in the valuable but tendentious work of Freud—Blondel begins in the *Itinéraire* by considering the dynamic nature of thought which he sees revealed even by the etymology of the word in different languages—by the linguistic studies of Marcel Jousse (*Études de psychologie linguistique*) or by such works as de Tizac's *L'Art classique chinois* with its study of the history of ideographs.[1] *Thought is not an isolated function.*

'Thought, like the generation of life itself, passes through the lowest and most carnal functions' but in addition to that fundamental truth there is a corresponding one: 'while thought becomes incarnate at the deepest level, it is so *dépaysée*, so lost, that it at once goes beyond that sphere in order to dominate it and in doing so escapes into an invisible, ideal world which seems to it to be reason and reality itself.'[2] This is what makes Lévy-Bruhl and the sociologists—we should say anthropologists—say that primitive thought is alogical or pre-logical; but that is only true if one presupposes a derived or canalized idea of the workings of the mind which, though it may look purer and richer, is in fact poorer, petrified and notionalized. For there 'is a logic of the moral and even of the mystical life which, passing through and utilizing discursive logic', realizes a unitive logic. This must not be understood as an attack on the 'intellectuals', however. 'If abstract and discursive logic is preceded by a more concrete thought and a *régime de participation*, that is because it must be followed by a more intimate knowledge, by a life of conscious and willed communion, just as a primitive and an oral style must be integrated in and survive the test of a learned culture so as to reappear more beautiful than before'.

These two forms of thought must both be preserved, and in *La Pensée*[3] Blondel considers the manner in which Pascal and Newman attempted to do this. Pascal, he writes, had not shown clearly enough the extent of their co-operation; Newman 'perhaps stressed the antithesis abstractly considered too onesidedly, without really coming to grips with the strange marriage of these conjoined

[1] Ibid, p. 144.   [2] Ibid, p. 140.
[3] *La Pensée*, 2 vols (Alcan, 1934), vol II, pp. 25 ff.

thoughts and the fertility of a union which seems at first sight to be lacking in love'. This was one of the points at which Blondel approaches Kierkegaard, where everything turns on the question of communication: 'The task is not to annul the one [form of communication] at the expense of the other, but to preserve, on the contrary, their equilibrium, their simultaneity, and the place where they are united is existence.' Though where Kierkegaard tends to return to the level of existence, Blondel wished to remain simultaneously on the level of reflection. For 'without the secret unity of concrete thought, abstract, analytic and discursive knowledge would never find either its origin, its consistency or its end'.

The example which Blondel takes to show the fertile union of the two aspects of thought is art, and in particular the romantic theory of Claudel already referred to. Paul Claudel, he writes, is 'too intelligent to be an intellectual and too much of a poet to be unreasonable; he is reasonable as a poet in verse as in prose, in verse which is neither ratiocination nor sensation, in a prose which is made of words and action and intuition'.[1] In the *Parable of Animus and Anima* Claudel celebrates the epithalamium of the two indissoluble yet irreducible aspects of thought. But the myth which Henri Bremond had elaborated in *Prière et poésie* is incomplete and inexact. It is not enough to recognize two sorts of thought: one must explain and regulate their co-habitation and define the nature of the material which links them together. They cannot become one; and for this reason: Animus (the discursive reason) is not the husband of Anima. Animus is only an ambassador, a messenger of the Gods, of the Royal Spouse, and Anima is indeed Queen. It is Anima who knows Being (Kierkegaard would have said existence, and this marks once again the difference in approach). Animus is only charged with announcing and presenting the real Spouse— which is why Animus so often suspects the poets and still more the mystics who warn Anima of his tricks and his adulterous intention. Though if Animus remains true to his function his task is great and indispensable.

In the place of the parable of Animus and Anima, Blondel suggests another comparison, altogether more 'crude' and 'anthro-

[1] *L'Itinéraire*, p. 178.

pomorphic': the myth of *inflation*. In order to make our natural wealth fruitful we need a fiduciary value. The authentic riches of gold need a fiduciary, paper currency in order to circulate freely and facilitate exchange; but these signs can be multiplied at will and given a fictitious value, in fact 'inflated'. Notional knowledge divorced from real knowledge proliferates and creates an artificial world. But so long as the signs correspond to real values, they are sane, fertile, and indispensable in mobilizing and even anticipating real values. The essential thing is therefore to preserve their 'equilibrium'.

These considerations lead on to Being—to *L'Être et les êtres*—to the most difficult part of the work, and the dialectical movement involves the examination of two problems usually separated: the first problem is to attain to Being and to fulfil our destiny; the second to realize being in us and constitute a concrete ontology.[1] This is the subject of the dialogue which takes place during the ascent of Mont Saint-Victoire, which at one point is compared to the ascent of Mount Carmel, to the work of St John of the Cross.

Ontology, Blondel begins by saying, is not simply a chapter, the most abstract of all, of a general theory . . . and it is essential if we are to continue our ascent to escape from that difficulty, from that crevasse. The domain of being is illuminated by our two kinds of knowledge, and it lies as it were between our analytical, representative knowledge and our vital, intellectual certitudes, which *l'esprit de finesse* and a unitive contemplation can increase without limit. The domain of being is therefore doubly accessible, both to the vision and the grasp of the mind. The real is knowable; but what we know is not all the real. The first thing to save is therefore the aspect of being which notional knowledge does not attain.[2]

Just as in the first section of the dialogue Blondel explains his ideas with reference to Claudel, so now he develops his idea with reference to Valéry whose *sévérités si intelligentes*, though he considers them unjust, he nevertheless sympathises with to the full. Valéry, in fact, declares that metaphysics (the metaphysics which imagines it lives off notions, though it dies of them) is simply a form

[1] Ibid, p. 190.   [2] *Ibid.*, p. 199.

of *trompe l'œil*, and that it consists 'in pretending to think A when one is thinking B'[1], since 'the real can only be expressed by the absurd'. To him, therefore, the real sage is the dancer (*Eupalinos et la Danse*), whose vain ubiquity triumphs over every form of dogmatism in the process of perpetually sinking to the ground. Yet no one in fact resigns himself to an intelligence so hostile to intelligence. Despairing of finding reality in reality, Valéry thus constructs it in the ideal. 'There is no real knowledge, he tells us, except that which can transmute itself into being', which realizes itself in the substance of being which is act, and which 'creates a transcendent order, a transcendent which did not exist, which will no longer exist the moment we turn back to look at it, like Lot's wife, and salt it away in our mummifying knowledge' (a view, Blondel adds, which is similar to that of the Italian *attualisme* of Gentile). But though it was right to oppose those who baptized a false 'intelligible' real, there is no reason to call what is purely immanent by the name of transcendent.

'Why does modern idealism rebel against the idea of a being external or transcendent to our minds?'[2] The explanation, Blondel suggests, is the wrong application of a thesis legitimate in its original context. The positive sense of this thesis is that to be is essentially to act. To pretend to know this real being passively would be to claim to represent it as it is—which is utterly false and implies identifying a passivity with an activity. Real being can only be known by an acting thought which assimilates itself to it, not by reflecting, by mirroring it, but by a thought which restores it in itself. The error lies in supposing that because we cannot know the real except *through* an active thought, we only know it *as* a subjective action (here again the parallel between Blondel and Kierkegaard emerges), as an immanent creation or as an ideal product. This is, according to Blondel, Heidegger's error.

The authentic transcendent is neither a notional, mummified transcendent, nor an irrational influx, nor an obscure, affective connaturality, nor a simple projection of our immanent life. On the contrary, our intelligent and active life little by little restores within us, *ad modum recipientis*, the reality which it is its function to com-

[1] *Ibid.*, p. 211. [2] *Ibid.*, p. 219.

municate and assimilate itself to. Anima was not misled by the promises of Being; for action is the mode of our communication with Being.[1]

In Italy, where some of Blondel's works had appeared in unauthorized translations, his ideas had been associated with the philosophical movement of Croce and Gentile. The falsity of this identification is revealed, he points out, by his conception of the ultimate metaphysical problem, 'the crux of the philosophical and religious drama': how precisely does a concrete, integral realism *restore* and not construct or *create*, a reality which remains distinct from it?[2] To envisage this metaphysical problem solely from the point of view of notional knowledge is to act as though, having developed a linear and a plane geometry, one were to stop short—not suspecting the existence of solid or three-dimensional geometry. The Trilogy is not an accidental assemblage of books: it claims to translate an essential, real trinity: thought, action and being.

The conflict and solidarity of notional and concrete knowledge led Blondel to restore the function of the third term—too often only implied or mentioned for form's sake. And here Blondel can be said to have adopted and developed the tripartite division of Pascal: the order of reason, the order of the heart, the order of charity. The two forms of knowledge are always inadequate, but they reveal the need for a completion, just as the two sides of an arch require the key-stone which, though it appears to be supported by them, in fact supports them. If one wishes to give the word *being* meaning (in the same way that one has tried to give a 'real' and coherent meaning to the word *thought*) one cannot stop at the crude affirmation of an opaque real, unknown to itself and others; nor at the cold and evanescent conception of a reflection, a pure narcissism, a sort of egoism *à deux*. For reality to be clearly intelligible and for truth to be plainly real, it must either be lovable or loving. 'The problem of being is also the problem of the spirit, of charity, of socialization and personalization simultaneously.' This is expressed in the account of the creation in Genesis: *et vidit quod esset bonum*.[3]

The last pages of the *Itinerary*, then, move on to *L'Esprit chrétien*, which Blondel declares to have been *primum in intentione* but

[1] *Ibid.*, p. 222.   [2] *Ibid.*, p. 224.   [3] *Ibid.*, p. 234.

ultimum in executione, the work on which he had been engaged ever since the publication of *L'Action* (1893), finally to become the coping-stone of his *œuvre*, the Christian conclusion to his work as a philosopher. It had not lost all its original characteristics; it was still directed, he says, against all forms of separated philosophy or natural religion, against extrinsicism and the immanentist doctrines of the Modernists: it is, he says, the *pars purificans* of his work, corresponding to the need for a 'purification' of religion which he had seen in 1907 growing out of the crisis. But it was not, in spite of its early origin, the first thing aimed at, nor was it in the first place sought after: it *resulted* spontaneously from the positive task (the integration of Catholic truth) which consisted in confronting the gifts or dowry of faith with the gifts of reason and consciousness, and in examining how they meet, see one another and embrace. The 'enigmas' of philosophy are compared and contrasted with the 'mysteries' of religion, and the task is to make them embrace—a dream, he adds, which others will realize—the 'insane dream' which had haunted him from his youth. Two names, however, might indicate what he saw in his dream.

Étienne Gilson had recently shown that the doctrine of St Bonaventure reaches as far and is as consistent as that of St Thomas, and he had concluded that the two syntheses, while incompatible, were both legitimate, were two aspects of a larger truth—'the one tending to stabilize rational philosophy so that the supernatural life seems impotent to intervene except by supervening as an intruder; the other tending to approach human wisdom in the light of revelation and grace to such a degree that the consistent knowledge and reality of reason and nature seem evanescent.' To Blondel that double attitude is unacceptable, and the final aim of his work was to bring about a 'transmutation' thanks to a more 'histological' union. For the two heterogeneous forms of thought do not involve a sort of double-entry accountancy in the concrete homogeneity of our one and inescapable destiny. Yet the expression 'metaphysic of charity' (Laberthonnière's expression, which Lefèvre is made to put into Blondel's mouth) is too ambiguous to serve as a description of the synthesis. It unites an originally Aristotelian term with one which is purely Christian and does not therefore adequately describe the 'living equilibrium' of elements too often opposed or sacrificed one to another, even in Catholic consciences. It is only in the full Christian tradition of the saints and mystics that that conflict is stilled. Elsewhere it is always present, and from a critical point of view it can be regarded as the consequence of one of three conceptions, all of which claim to be Christian.

According to the first conception God, imperiously required by the religious sense, is a mysterious power and transcendency, the absolute subject, hostile to any form of anthropomorphism (as for example in the Old Testament). The second conception sees God as the Object *par excellence*, the perfect 'intelligible', the principle of essences and existences, to be served and feared. But there is also a third conception, that of the Good News, the conception expressed by St John and in the words *Deus caritas est*. In practice these conceptions are always mixed, but unequally and so that one or other gains the upper hand. And therein lies the difficulty. For if the God of Charity is allowed to conceal the God of Fear and the God of Truth, then humanity responds fully to God by a reciprocal generosity. To avoid extremes, however, one must not introduce the *duc in altum* either too soon or too late. The exacting love of God does not wish to deify us metaphorically, or anthropomorphically, but inflexibly, 'insanely'. To magnify the goodness of God by eliminating the idea of mortification from the human vocation is to debase and mutilate the gift and the idea of God.

At this point Blondel rejoins Kierkegaard and parts company with Laberthonnière and ultimately, no doubt, with Teilhard de Chardin; and it was at this point that the correspondence with Laberthonnière was finally interrupted.

> I cannot admit [the latter had written] that there should be supernaturalization artificially added to naturalization. I am unable to distinguish as between a creative God and a supernaturalizing God. We are not first of all an eternal essence which God then contrives to turn into an existence by individualizing it and multiplying it by some matter or other ...
> In saying I cannot distinguish between a creative God and a supernaturalizing God, I mean to say that I cannot distinguish and separate the incarnation from the creation. All this would

of course need to be explained and developed and made more precise.[1]

You conclude [Blondel replied] that there is no need to distinguish between 'the gifts of the Creator' and the 'gifts of the Incarnation and redemption', that there is continuity, not to say unity between the natural and supernatural order, orders which abstraction alone discerns artificially. Well, for my part I believe that there is an abyss to cross, and in order not to see it one must not *realize in concreto what God is*. I believe that the divine love has found the means of *communicating the incommunicable*, not in order to oppress and brutalize man, but on the contrary in order to join him in the intimacy of a union which cares nothing for differences and essences ... Because advantage has been taken of all this, by translating it into a fallacious ideology, you do not admit the realist and mystical sense of this divine participation. . . .

You persist in only wanting to see in it the instrument of a 'brutal stultification of our being', you speak of circles having to be squared; well, in this instance it is you who are stumbling over the play of concepts and images instead of looking for the secret of divine love; and when you say you cannot conceive of this *mortification* except as a deterioration of our being, of our being under the pressure of a monstrous thing which reduces us to being less than human, I say that that is a complete misunderstanding, blindness to the unitive life, the sin against the Christian spirit, to the deepest and highest aspect of *vivere mihi Christus est*, the concrete experience and the speculative intelligence of which must be indissolubly bound up with one another. The whole meaning and future of our Christian and philosophical effort is at stake, our inward attitude to God and to the Church and perhaps the eternal fate of our souls.[2]

The continuity of natural and supernatural which Blondel had begun by emphasizing in opposition to the extrinsicists, the neo-thomists, and those who thought in notional terms, he ends by

[1] *Corr. Phil.*, p. 309.   [2] *Ibid.*, p. 310.

modifying when it is presented to him in real terms, in the perspective of asceticism. Either extreme is false.

People are afraid of confusing (them); one should be afraid of not uniting them enough, of making Christianity into an extrinsic addition, of not making the very obvious barriers and mortifications appear in reality to be merely very secret means of realizing a more beatifying union; and it is in fact when one does not know how to unite properly that one is afraid of confusing. If nowadays the life of humanity all too often withdraws from Christianity, it is perhaps because it has too often been uprooted from the viscera of man.[1]

Everything, it is true, appears to come from below, and everything comes down from above: the key-stone holds the arch, and it is action which opens us to the real, to the supernatural. 'To think of God is our action,' he concludes, quoting Joubert.

Between 1913 and 1928 Blondel's thought underwent further modifications, some of which have been illustrated from his correspondence with Laberthonnière. In some instances his meditations led him into blind alleys from which he withdrew—for example this distinction between notional and real knowledge which he later modified in a sense more critical of Newman. But though the *Itinerary* could obviously not allow of his expressing all the *nuances* of his thought, and though in some respects he modified his views still further, it at least indicates the breadth and scope of the work which occupied him until his death in 1949. Only a full-length study could do justice to the changes and developments in his thought over a period of sixty-five years. Perhaps it could be said rather crudely that 'how' Blondel saw things did not change, while 'what' he saw was sometimes modified, and this corresponds to some extent to the two groups into which his interpreters fall. Some, perhaps the majority, would say with Père Cartier that 'what constitutes the originality of the philosophy of action is less the truth affirmed or the solutions proposed than the aim and the method; less the problems than the problematic. Blondel's permanent contribution appears to us to lie—beyond the particular problems

[1] *L'Itinéraire*, p. 261.

which, if not dated, are already transposed—in his vigorous elucidation of the *situation of philosophy*'.[1] M. Tresmontant, on the other
hand, regrets the tendency to concentrate on the first *Action* and to
forget the Trilogy. 'It is permissible to prefer the first *Action* and the
Letter on Apologetics to the mature work, the properly metaphysical
work. But what is inadmissible, from the objective point of view
of the history of thought, is to claim to present or expose the thought
of Blondel while restricting oneself to the *œuvre de jeunesse*, while
relegating the Cathedral to the shadows with a few polite expressions
and a totally inadequate summary'.[2]

But the disagreement is, as M. Tresmontant allows, to some
extent one of temperament and fashion, and M. Étienne Borne
provides an example of how the two elements in Blondel's work
can and perhaps should be held in equilibrium. At one time restricting himself to *L'Action* (1893), M. Borne came under the influence
of Paul Archambault, one of Blondel's closest disciples, and came
to recognize the value of the later works more fully. The first
Action then seemed to him to recall the inspiration of Pascal; the last
period that of Leibnitz; and indeed Blondel himself learned from
both. But there will always be those who, like Laberthonnière, felt
uncomfortable as Blondel developed his metaphysic: 'I still find
you too Leibnitzian,' he wrote, 'in your desire to conciliate the
philosophy of *actuation* (the metaphysic of creation) with the philosophy of action.'[3] And yet to M. Borne that is the real achievement
of Blondel.

The question really is whether, in order to understand action,
reason ought not to reform itself and, from having been
analytic as it habitually is, bringing back the other to the
same, the multiple to the one and the dynamic to the static,
become dialectical by surpassing itself in a movement which
is the very opposite of a denial, and which would make it
capable of explaining change and the new. The analytic
method, as Bergson was discovering at the same time, only

[1] 'Le Philosophe de L'Action' in *Archives de Philosophie*, Jan.-March,
1961, p. 20.
[2] *La Métaphysique de Maurice Blondel*, p. 14.
[3] *Corr. Phil.*, p. 302.

leads to idealism or materialism; it leads us to confuse action either with an objective, material process or with 'the idea of action, which is not action', to use an expression of Blondel's which must never be forgotten. The dialectical method, on the contrary, means a return to the real, an effort to adjust oneself to a living logic which is not the logic of identity but the logic of *dépassement* (going further), and which has an intelligible meaning. Blondel had the right to claim that he proposed a true and relatively new 'science of action'. Method and doctrine, thought and reality, at last correspond with one another rationally: the dialectic being in the mind but also in the articulations and structures, simultaneously defined and moving, of that privileged object of philosophy which, to both our recent existentialists and Blondelianism, is man, man entering the world and at grips with it; for action is nothing but the living link between man and man in the world, which it is the classical purpose of philosophy to transpose into an intelligible register.[1]

Blondel had started with the question: 'Has human life or has it not a meaning, and has man a destiny?' He answered in a form which antedated existentialism by thirty years or more. His work is at the source of the purification and integration of Catholic truth inaugurated by the religious crisis at the beginning of the century. In spite of, or, from another point of view, because of his concern for technique, Blondel's thought is as relevant now as it was in 1900 to the religious problems of the time: to the *aggiornamento* which he called for and which since the last Pontificate has been officially recognized as necessary, and no less to the movement for reunion which necessarily follows from it.

The *Letter on Apologetics* and *History and Dogma* will, it is hoped, serve as an introduction both to Blondel's work and to the movement of Catholic thought in which he played so significant a part.

---

[1] Etienne Borne, *Passion de la Vérité*, pp. 75-6.

III. SOME PRINCIPLES OF BLONDEL'S THOUGHT

The Importance of Blondel

At this point it is necessary, even in so very general an account of Blondel's place in history, to indicate his attitudes of mind in more detail. This is particularly necessary for an understanding of the *Letter on Apologetics.*

Blondel was, not only first and foremost but all the time, a philosopher of religion. And one has to face the fact that this kind of philosopher is, for the English-speaking world as a whole, the hardest to understand. This is not to be explained simply by the fact that most people nowadays have lost touch with religion, or perhaps think that they have lost touch with it because they are ignorant of what it really is (coming across no genuinely religious persons). There is also the peculiar (but connected) difficulty that the academic conception of philosophy itself has undergone a marked change in England, and in countries under English influence in philosophy, since the first World War.

For there has been a revolution in philosophy in this sense that philosophy in these countries has largely abandoned its ancient claim to seek 'wisdom', to seek for *meaning* in human existence. In the not so distant past it has made sweeping and unjustified claims of this kind, and, as a result, we are still faced by widespread indifference to all such claims, enhanced by the peculiar prestige which is enjoyed today by 'pure' scholarship, *Wissenschaft.* In the general preoccupation with the special sciences, philosophers have even attempted to secure a place for philosophy among these sciences. This attempt may seem to be going out of favour; but there has been, as yet, no general move in a more promising direction. Interest is still concentrated on semantic problems of a remote and intricate kind, and the tendency remains to identify philosophy with the technicalities of logic. Metaphysics, although no longer a hissing and a by-word, is still generally disregarded.

But it is becoming gradually more and more recognized, by

those who have an interest in religion, that the lack of a sane philosophy of religion is at the heart of our distresses. A certain revival of religion among the educated classes has not gone hand-in-hand with a revival of religious philosophy. There are very many religious people who regard philosophy either as a neutral subject in regard to religion or as a profane science which must simply abdicate its claims in face of religion. But it would be possible to show that natural theology is being taken seriously by an increasing number of influential theologians. It is from them, in the first place, perhaps, that the work of Blondel may be expected to receive a welcome.

Even on the face of it, before there is any understanding of his thought (there seems to be no other book devoted to it available in this country), his claims can be seen to be outstanding. For it is hardly possible that the revival of metaphysics in France during the past fifty years (that it has in fact occurred is a commonplace of French philosophical writing) can be overlooked for much longer in this country, even by our philosophers. And the body of literature which has resulted from the centenary of Blondel's birth in 1961 has made it clear that his influence on this revival has been predominant. Mr Reardon has pointed out, in an article which is apparently the only attempt in recent times to obtain *droit de cité* for Blondel's thought in England,[1] that 'in France, at the time of his death in 1949, his reputation among academic thinkers was unexcelled'. 'As an instance of what can be achieved by "the Christian in philosophy",' Mr Reardon continues, 'his work is, I venture to think, the most brilliant of this century.' This opinion is shared by an impressive number of thinkers in France and elsewhere, and the signs are that it will become more and more widespread.

It is becoming increasingly recognized, for instance, that Blondel was an existentialist 'before the letter', in the sense that he anticipated the existentialist insistence upon 'engagement' with the world and the fact of moral freedom, upon a personal and concrete

---

[1] 'A Christian in Philosophy: Maurice Blondel' by the Rev. B. M. G. Reardon, *Theology*, September, 1958, pp. 366 f. But Mr Dru's articles in *The Downside Review*, April, 1962 and July, 1963, although of a more historical kind, must also be mentioned at this point.

approach to human problems which makes the philosopher a participant in them and not a mere spectator. This point of view has become fairly familiar to us here in the work of Gabriel Marcel and of Sartre (and, behind them, of Kierkegaard). But it is hardly at all understood that France has produced a line of thinkers of greater philosophical stature, that the liberation from a stuffy materialism effected in France by Henri Bergson was followed by a movement of thought in which the names of Lavelle and Le Senne are outstanding, and which is now seen to have been in many ways prepared for by Blondel. Nor is his importance to be regarded largely as an affair of history. It is the relevance of his own words to our own time which is being chiefly emphasised. Père Albert Cartier, for example, in his *Existence et Vérité*, claims that Blondel, far from being merely a precursor of Marcel, has a much more solid and satisfying answer to the fundamental philosophical question and so to the atheist existentialism of Sartre and the agnosticism of Merleau-Ponty. But this anticipation of what is positive in existentialism, although perhaps the most striking instance of his originality for most English-speaking readers, is by no means the only one. He goes far beyond the unsystematized insights of the existentialists to offer a 'phenomenology of existence' which prepares for a full-scale religious metaphysics with profound implications for dogmatic theology. And thus his influence upon the French theologians of this century has been profound.[1]

The logic of action

It is not, however, the business of this section of the Introduction to attempt a general assessment of Blondel's claims. These preliminary remarks have seemed necessary, in the present state of astonishing ignorance, merely in the hope that the reader may be encouraged by them to persevere.

All that can be attempted now is to offer such explanations of Blondel's thought as may help to elucidate the texts presented. And, first, the present writer must make a disclaimer and, indeed, offer

[1] See, for example, the importance attributed to him by Canon Roger Aubert in his massive historical work *Acte de Foi* (Louvain, 1945).

an excuse or an apology. He is emphatically not an authority on Blondel's voluminous works, and nothing would have persuaded him to collaborate in an undertaking of this kind had there seemed any likelihood that a more competent person would be found to do so. Moreover, the task would have remained altogether impracticable had not Père Henri Bouillard's *Blondel et le Christianisme* appeared in 1961 to confirm his own hesitant interpretation of the *Letter on Apologetics* and to throw a flood of light on Blondel's work as a whole. It will be seen that the notes appended to the translation of the *Letter* draw very largely on Bouillard's book. And in what is now to be said about *L'Action* (1893), Blondel's first and most famous work, as a necessary preliminary to any understanding of the *Letter* (1896), Bouillard will be our chief guide. The acclaim which his book has received in France[1] would be sufficient of itself to justify a presentation to English readers, derived from him, of those elements in Blondel's thought which are our present concern. (In the last section of this Introduction an attempt has been made to show the reader in what respects Bouillard's conclusions can be regarded by Christian thinkers as importantly controversial and to offer him some grounds for reaching a conclusion on these matters. The section will thus provide a partial indication of the existing state of Blondelian studies which may perhaps be of some use to the reader who decides to explore this uncharted territory.)

In *L'Action*,[2] then, Blondel proposes to show that the problem of human destiny is inevitably set by philosophy. In the end we must choose for or against 'the transcendent'. It is of no use to deny that there is such a problem; the very rejection of 'the transcendent' proves that it is involved. And at this point someone might break in and say that this familiar move is unconvincing. The move, put

[1] With a significant exception, considered in the last section of this Introduction.

[2] Unless otherwise stated, *L'Action* here means the original work of 1893, reproduced by the Presses Universitaires de France in 1950, but never republished in Blondel's lifetime, partly because of the misunderstandings to which it had led, partly because Blondel's position had shifted in certain respects. It is a matter of dispute whether the second *L'Action* (1936) is an improvement on its predecessor or otherwise. In any case it is agreed that Blondel's fundamental inspiration was never abandoned and that his work, from first to last, shows a unity and consistency for which it must be hard to find a parallel.

in this bald form, is certainly familiar, but it is the detailed working-out of it, Blondel's 'dialectic', which is his peculiar achievement. It is impossible even to suggest its force by summarizations.[1] The effect is cumulative. This raises the question whether his method is really a 'scientific' one, as he himself so often claims, or whether it is only a 'technique of persuasion'. And this is a question which, as it stands, cannot be answered because it presupposes just that rigid distinction between intellect and will which Blondel is concerned to deny. The intellect is free: but freedom is intelligent. Philosophy is the progress of the soul. And that is 'action'.

So when Blondel undertakes to show that a 'separated' philosophy, a philosophy closed against 'the transcendent', is illegitimate, he is embarking upon a phenomenology. He points to the character of the human soul in order to show that it is not only a structure but a dynamism. There, he says, are the facts; this is a matter of 'science'. It is an appeal to experience, but not to immediate experience. It is the development of the 'logic of action'. Even those who reject the goal of action are still bound to the law of action. He does not here *assume*, as he has been accused of doing from the first *soutenance de thèse*, that there *is* a goal for action, 'the one thing necessary'. As a Christian, he knows that it is so, but his investigation is that of a 'pure philosopher'. 'Pure philosophy' finds itself inevitably faced by 'the transcendent'. If at that point it remains 'pure philosophy', it has rejected 'the transcendent'.

But we must realize what 'inevitably' means in such a context. Blondel insists that the movement from stage to stage in *L'Action* is brought about by a rational necessity. He writes constantly (as in

[1] But something may be said in illustration of Blondel's method. At every level in the upward movement from the world of matter to the most elaborate human thinking we find a situation which can be explained only by what comes after it. It does not make sense unless it is developed into a higher synthesis. It is not a logical development—*action* must take place. But there is a logic of this development—we can see the direction in which it is engaged and discovers its law. Blondel is not just saying that life is larger than logic. He is saying that there is a logic of life, and that thought is a function of life, springing from it, returning to it and leading it on. The business of philosophy is to show that this development is imposed upon us. What we might call a 'living contradiction' is always breaking out and demanding to be solved.

the *Letter*) about a 'determinism' and about a 'system of affirmations' bound up with one another with an 'inexorable rigour', and (in *L'Action*) that 'we are *constrained* to posit, before our reflective thought, the term which was already present at the beginning of the movement in which an attempt was made to escape it'.[1] Yet it is made perfectly clear also that the 'logic of action' cannot be developed unless it is freely accepted. 'All these sensible, scientific, intellectual, moral and religious conditions of human life . . . although they are implied in us inevitably (*spontanément*), have to be recognized by a free effort; . . . although we may revolt against them, they do not cease to realize themselves in us'.[2] Bouillard,[3] who quotes this passage, also quotes from the second *L'Action*:[4] 'At every stage the temptation arises to halt, to be satisfied with ourselves, to dig ourselves in at the point which we have reached. At every stage we are, not constrained, but sincerely obliged, to pass beyond.' The notion of a purely rational movement of thought in metaphysics, an apodeictic proof the acceptance of which is inevitable and which requires no response on our part, proves to be inapplicable. What *is* strictly inevitable is the 'great option' itself at some point in a man's life, although it may not be recognized as such. Since it is so often not acknowledged, it becomes necessary to 'demonstrate' its necessity by constructing 'the science of action', which, as we shall see more fully, can never supply the place of 'action' itself.

The option

In his concern to show that the 'option', which is always the centre of his thought, does not influence the philosophical argument, Blondel may easily give the impression in the *Letter* that thought and action, 'determinism' and affirmation, belong to spheres which are simply opposed. Philosophy is one thing—the action to which it leads us, the 'option', is something quite different. Only 'action' will bring us to our goal. This is to over-simplify.[5] What Blondel means is that the reason has only to obey its own law in order to be

[1] *L'Action*, p. 490. [2] *L'Action*, p. 464. [3] Bouillard, pp. 238-9.
[4] *L'Action*, 1937, p. 131. [5] *Cf.* Bouillard, p. 240.

faced by the 'option', but that the (good) 'option' itself is the *acceptance* of the discovery that its own law requires it to renounce itself before God, to deliver itself over to him for his purposes. The 'option' is the great 'action', to which at first everything leads and from which everything then follows. But 'live' thought is never divorced from action. Only when action is finally refused does the 'death' of thought occur (and this does not mean that it ceases to register objective existence, but that it now registers it in a negative instead of in a positive mode). The great 'action' is prepared for by the innumerable minor choices of everyday life, any one of which may in fact be the occasion of it. Blondel has often been accused of anti-intellectualism. In fact it is, as Bouillard says, in virtue of the 'reciprocal immanence' of reason and liberty that 'the free passage from one attitude to another carries its own justification along with it . . . if there are necessary truths which are not necessary for our intelligence, they are no less necessary in themselves and in ourselves'.[1] There is no question of a leap in the dark.

It may now begin to emerge that Blondel's importance lies not so much in the conclusions to which he comes as in the attitude which he adopts and the method which he employs—they are in the greatest possible contrast with those of the typical academic philosopher in this country today. The latter will try to find some implication in any suggestion made to him which may discredit it: he will not accept it unless it follows from something which is itself beyond dispute by an inescapable logical nexus; the idea of going out to meet the suggestion of truth, of broadening one's mind to make room for it, is for him merely shocking; a binding up of the moral and spiritual life with the growth of the mind is for him simply meaningless. Philosophy, morality and spirituality will sometimes be found in three separate compartments in a single individual. For Blondel 'Action is that synthesis of willing, knowing and being, that binding force of the human *compositum* which cannot be broken up without destroying what one has disunited; it is the precise point at which the world of thought, the moral

[1] p. 242 quoting *L'Action* II (1937), p. 411. 'In ourselves' because the refusal of them is not without its consequences.

world and the world of science converge; and if they are not united there, all is lost'.[1]

With these general considerations in mind it should prove useful to turn to certain specific elements in *L'Action*. The most important of them, for our present purposes, is the distinction between '*la volonté voulue*' and '*la volonté voulante*'. The basis of the distinction is found in the Introduction to *L'Action*:

> At the root of the most irresponsible negations or the wildest extravagances of the will, we must see whether there is not an initial movement which always persists, whatever one's likings and one's wishes, even when it is denied or abused ...
> An attitude of strict neutrality is essential in this undertaking, not only because it is necessary to take account of all the infinite diversity of human states of soul, but above all because we must find, beneath the unconscious sophisms and unacknowledged backslidings, the original, essential aspiration, so that we may lead all, in complete sincerity, to the term of their free movement (*élan*). So instead of starting from a single point from which a teaching could be derived applicable to a single soul, we must establish ourselves at the furthest extremities of the most widely different lines of entry so as to recognize, at the very centre, the truth which is essential for every mind, the movement which is common to every will.[2]

This common movement of aspiration is '*la volonté voulante*'. What we in fact will, in so far as it fails to be adequate to '*la volonté voulante*', is covered by '*la volonté voulue*'.

This shows clearly enough that Blondel is not conducting a merely psychological inquiry; the conclusion at which he aims is a metaphysical one. And the method is rational, 'scientific'. He wishes to show that, from whatever angle we approach the human situation, we are faced with problems which demand solution. Throughout the course of the dialectic, the discrepancy between what we essentially will and what we suppose ourselves to be willing is always declaring itself. But it is not that the particular objects which we will are not worth willing at all. The trouble is

[1] *L'Action*, p. 28.   [2] *L'Action*, pp. xx-xxi.

that they are insufficient—they are not adequate to '*la volonté voulante*'.[1] We are driven onward from mere sensation to the formation of a body of knowledge. We become aware of ourselves and of the fact of our liberty, which is at the same time an obligation, something imposed upon us. We have to develop our individualities by going out to meet the world around us and our fellow men. We have to look at things from the point of view of a society which broadens out into a fellowship of all men. We form the notion of an absolute morality. And at this point (if not before) we may try to stop. It is this attempt which results in 'superstition'. In Bouillard's words:[2] 'In the end man tries to achieve himself and to be sufficient for himself by attributing a religious value to his natural activity, placing the infinite and the absolute in one of the finite objects which he has so far encountered. But this pretension, which constitutes superstition, is contradictory: one is driven back upon phenomena to make of them infinitely more than they really are. The rigorous system (*l'enchaînement*) in which human action is deployed in its totality thus leads us to the following conclusion: "It is impossible not to recognize the insufficiency of the whole natural order and not to discover a further requirement: it is impossible to find within oneself the means of satisfying this religious requirement. *It is necessary;* and *it is impracticable*" '.[3] '*La volonté voulante*' thus requires that we should perform the great action, the good option, which throws us open to the divine action.

Let us now look at this dialectic in terms of freedom and determinism. This is only another way of saying what has been said already, but it will have the advantage of clarifying some of Blondel's allusions in the *Letter*.[4] The conflict of freedom and determinism, as he envisages it, is again first stated in the Introduction to *L'Action*. 'In practice', he writes, 'no one escapes the problem of practice' (that is, of 'action'). And he continues:

[1] This 'escapes all introspection. It appears only as the result of a regressive analysis, as the condition for the possibility of "*la volonté voulue*", which alone is the object of direct knowledge' (Bouillard, p. 78).

[2] Bouillard, p. 20. [3] *L'Action*, p. 319.

[4] What Blondel calls in the *Letter* 'the method of immanence' is nothing else than the dialectic of *L'Action*.

It is just this necessity which must be justified. How else could it be justified except by showing that it is in conformity with man's deepest aspiration? For I can be conscious of my servitude only by conceiving of and looking forward to a complete enfranchisement. The terms of the problem are thus clearly set. On the one hand, there is everything that dominates and oppresses the will; on the other, there is the will to dominate everything or to be able to ratify everything; for there is no being where there is no constraint. How, then, is the conflict to be resolved?[1]

It proves that precisely in order to gain our autonomy we must accept our constraints—we must submit to the laws, the 'determinism', of action. It is the function of this 'determinism' to bring us face to face with the final conflict in which we encounter the ultimate source of our autonomy. This is the *unum necessarium*, God summoning us.

In a remarkable article[2] on the memoranda exchanged between Teilhard de Chardin and Blondel, Manuel Ossa brings out the force of the dialectic at the point which we have reached:

Liberty is a plenitude of possibles. But in order to know itself as a plenitude, it must realize itself in an act of willing the concrete. Now when the question of a choice or a decision arises, liberty finds the possibility of considering itself as an object among those which present themselves . . . But considering itself as an object—and thus exteriorizing itself in regard to itself, taking itself as its own end—liberty at once despoils itself of what constitutes its wealth, that is, of being . . . the act which organizes all the objects which are exterior to it, assimilating them to itself and adding to them its own infinity.

Thus it is impossible for the will to choose itself directly—yet it is forced to choose itself indirectly in choosing objects *for* itself. It cannot escape itself, and yet it is kept away from itself. Whatever objects it chooses, 'action' seems to be finally frustrated. 'But this

[1] *L'Action*, p. x.

[2] 'Possession de l'Être et Abnégation dans la philosophie de Maurice Blondel', *Revue d'Ascétique et de Mystique*, Oct.-Dec., 1962, pp. 483-509.

apparent frustration of willed action manifests the indestructibility of voluntary action, for I should not be aware of this frustration, if there were not in me a will which is superior to the contradictions of life.'[1] And at this point arises, says Blondel, a 'new affirmation'. It is 'the reality of this necessary presence which makes possible the awareness of this very conflict. There is "one thing necessary". All the movement of the determinism leads us to this end: for it is from this that issues the determinism itself, the whole significance of which is to bring us to it.'[2] This is the 'immanence' of the trans- cendent. '*La volonté voulante*', to repeat, once it has discovered itself, is under the necessity of willing itself. This is the law of its autonomy. But to be under the *necessity* to will oneself *freely* is incomprehensible unless there is 'something beyond' from which our freedom derives and which we have not yet attained. We must surrender our power of willing to the source from which it derives if we are to exercise it as it demands to be exercised. 'Action', to become itself, must make itself passive to the creative act. 'The true will of man is the divine will . . . To appropriate nothing for oneself is the only way of attaining the infinite.'[3] And now we can choose *everything* freely. Everything, including our own action, receives an infinite value.

The 'proof' of God's existence

It is this combination, in the transcendent, of absolute necessity and absolute inaccessibility for our natural powers which provides us, says Blondel, with the true notion of the supernatural: he goes on to speak of 'a baptism of desire which human knowledge is incap- able of producing (*provoquer*) because the very need for it is a gift . . .'[4] This is the point at which Bouillard has made his most important clarification of Blondel's expressions. The supernatural here, he points out, does not mean the supernatural of Christian theology which is, in a special sense, gratuitous (it is this supposition that has caused the most persistent misinterpretation of Blondel's thought), but simply 'the divine action which, in every man, is at

[1] Bouillard, p. 86.   [2] *L'Action*, p. 339.   [3] *L'Action*, p. 387.
[4] *L'Action*, p. 388.

the origin of voluntary movement and which each must, at least implicitly, recognize as such, if this movement is to reach its end'.[1] This would still be the case if the Christian Revelation had not occurred. Thus we are concerned here with an 'undetermined supernatural', and 'the need for the supernatural is nothing else than the thirst for the Absolute, but of the Absolute recognized, by abnegation, in its sovereign liberty'.[2] Bouillard considers that 'baptism of desire' in the passage quoted above is just a way of referring to the 'consent of the reason'; but it is clear that, for Blondel, this consent may be accompanied by 'baptism of desire' in the theological sense. For 'to the man who does what is in him God does not refuse grace', and this theological adage is ever present to Blondel's mind.

The Christian notion of the supernatural is not introduced in *L'Action* until after the 'great option' has occurred. It is difficult to understand how anyone could have failed to see this, for Blondel himself makes the distinction as plainly as possible. The good 'option' once made, it is now for the philosopher to ask himself whether the claims of the *Christian* revelation may not be well founded. The revealed supernatural, says Blondel, the mystery of our union with the Blessed Trinity, is 'a truth which is impenetrable for any philosophical theory, a good which is superior to any aspiration of the will'.[3] Baptism by desire may have taken place already, but the Christian revelation has still to be acknowledged. What the philosopher can do, however, is to see that the hypothesis of such a revelation now makes sense for him. He is prepared for it. He can see that, *if* Christianity is true, then man's needs will have received perfect fulfilment. Thus he discovers 'the practical obligation to accept the supernatural announced by Christian preaching, if this is actually shown to be the supernatural reality'.[4] It is in that sense, and in that sense only, that the Christian notion of the supernatural is 'necessarily engendered'.[5] When, therefore, Blondel says that this notion 'springs from an internal initiative'[6] he means that 'the supernatural order defined by the Christian dogmas answers the undeter-

---

[1] Bouillard, p. 89. 'Gratuitousness' is discussed more fully later.
[2] Bouillard, p. 90. [3] *L'Action*, p. 407, n.1. [4] Bouillard, p. 93.
[5] *L'Action*, p. 406. [6] *L'Action*, p. 397.

mined expectation of the human will, and, by the same token, determines it'.[1]

Bouillard draws attention to a particular formula in *L'Action* 'which has shocked or embarrassed so many readers': 'it is impossible that the supernatural order should be without the actual order to which it is necessary and impossible that it should not exist, since the whole natural order guarantees it by requiring it.'[2]

> We must understand here [he goes on] by 'the natural order' the world in as much as it is the field of human activity . . . by 'the supernatural order' the relation of man and the world to the 'one thing necessary' which entirely transcends the world and human activity. Thus the incriminated formula merely means that the world cannot do without God, and that man cannot achieve himself without throwing himself open to the action of the Creator. In fine, it does not mean anything more than the traditional proofs of God's existence.[3]

This must be continually borne in mind in reading the *Letter*.

Something must be said here about Blondel's attitude to the 'traditional proofs'. It has been thought that, in *L'Action*, the existence of God appears only as a postulate, requiring an option, and that the affirmation of his existence takes place only in the process of the option. And this interpretation might seem to be confirmed by a passage in which we are told that

> in showing that this conception, inevitably engendered in the consciousness, forces us to affirm at least implicitly the living reality of this infinite perfection, there is no question of concluding to the being of God; it is a question of showing that this necessary idea of God leads us to the supreme alternative on which it will depend whether God shall or shall not really be for us.[4]

At first sight, too, the statement that 'really to know God is to bear within oneself his spirit, his will and his love'[5] has an anti-intellectualist flavour. But, as Bouillard very clearly shows, we have only to consider these passages in their context to discover their real

---

[1] Bouillard, p. 95.   [2] *L'Action*, p. 462.   [3] Bouillard, p. 98.
[4] *L'Action*, p. 426.   [5] *L'Action*, p. 441.

meaning. It should be already apparent that in *L'Action* the arising of 'the necessary idea of God' is equivalently 'the implicit and spontaneous affirmation' of his existence (if any further proof were needed, there is Blondel's explicit statement of his intention in a letter of 4th April 1897).[1] What Blondel is saying is that the idea which we have of God's *existence* is never adequate to his *being*. Not only must we *act* on this idea, for unless the good option takes place we shall have no possessive knowledge of God but only a privative one; but also Blondel is insisting that our knowledge of God, even after the option, must be always driving us further. 'As soon as we regard him from without as a mere object of knowledge or a mere occasion for speculative study without freshness of heart and the unrest of love, then all is over, and we have in our hands nothing but a phantom and an idol.'[2] Blondel, then, is unquestionably offering a 'demonstration' of God's existence; but he regards the merely logical arguments as 'partial'.[3]

What does this mean? Blondel continues: 'Such an argument does not lead to being [that is, it does not provoke the option], it does not necessarily bring thought face to face with real necessity. A proof which results from the total movement of life, a proof which is the whole of action, this will have, on the contrary, that constraining force. So to produce the equivalent of this spontaneous force by a dialectical exposition [that is, by the *'science* of action'] one must not leave any loophole for the mind.'[4] In other words, a man may become certain of God's existence by living a human life as it ought to be lived, by 'action'; if he requires to be convinced of it, we must use the indirect method of showing him what life demands. The traditional arguments are not rejected, but they are 'interiorized'. 'The proof of "the one thing necessary",' says Blondel, plainly enough, 'derives all its force and validity from the order of phenomena in its entirety.' Thus the argument from contingency 'instead of seeking for the necessary outside the contingent . . . shows it in the contingent itself, as a reality already

[1] Quoted by Bouillard, p. 174 n.

[2] *L'Action*, p. 352, quoted by Bouillard, p. 175. The present paragraph and the next are little more than a summary of pp. 172-7 of his book.

[3] *L'Action*, p. 341.   [4] Ibid.

present . . . immanent at the very centre of all that is. Instead of proving simply the impossibility of affirming the contingent alone, it proves the impossibility of denying the necessary on which it rests'.[1] The true teleological argument, again, 'does not measure the Cause which it affirms by the scale of its effects; but in recognizing it in them it places it beyond them and finds in the relative beauty of things the very principle of all beauty . . .'[2] I invoke no principle of causality; but I find in the imperfect wisdom of the world and of my thought the presence and the necessary action of a thought and a power which are perfect'.[3] So with the ontological argument: 'We are constrained to affirm it [the "one thing necessary"] in the measure in which we have the idea of it: for this idea itself is a reality'.[4]

Questions of terminology

We have seen that, although the affirmation of God's existence is the very core of L'Action, Blondel can deny that he 'concludes to God's being'. (It should be clear that to put it like this is not to make the thomist distinction between 'essence' and 'existence', which arises in a different context and has different implications.)[5] We must now turn to his use of the word 'being' in so far as it may cause difficulty in the Letter. It is contrasted with 'phenomena', and regularly refers to God's being, *absolute* being, or to God's being and the 'solidification' of created being which results from our knowledge of it *as* created being. To understand this is to understand also another use of language which could otherwise prove equally misleading: Blondel's use of 'subjective' and 'objective'. 'Objective knowledge' is the knowledge of 'being'; 'subjective knowledge' is the knowledge of 'phenomena'. Knowledge of 'being' results from the good option.

As usual it is Bouillard who has fully clarified the meaning of these distinctions in his analysis of the last chapter and the Conclusion

---

[1] *L'Action*, p. 343. [2] *L'Action*, p. 346. [3] *L'Action*, p. 347. [4] *L'Action*, p. 348.
[5] In *L'Être et les êtres* (Alcan, 1935) Blondel makes his position plain. The splendid passage on pp. 162-9 shows that it is still that of the original *L'Action* as indicated above.

of *L'Action*. He explains that, consistently with his whole method, Blondel does not enter upon the 'ontological' question until the complete dialectic of action has been deployed. He then sums up the argument of pp. 481-6:

> Philosophers have been led to look for the absolute of truth and being either in the data of sense, or in the positive sciences, or in a determinism which excludes liberty, or in a liberty which excludes determinism, or in a metaphysic which is closed in upon itself, or in a morality which rejects all further inquiry. Doctrines are thus constituted which are mutually exclusive. To disentangle what is controverted from what is not controversible, we must at first suspend the ontological affirmation, consider the objects of knowledge as they appear, that is, as heterogeneous but bound up with one another[1] (and not exclusive of one another), not looking in one order of phenomena for the truth of another but considering that each must have its own truth and solidity.[2]

Thus, as Blondel makes clear on a number of occasions, 'at the moment when the ontological question is raised, we can affirm the reality of the objects of knowledge all together.' 'By this method', Bouillard continues,[3] he will show 'that spontaneous knowledge included this from the very beginning'. For the whole function of the dialectic is to constrain us to 'the avowal of the truth which is in us . . .'[4] The regressive analysis is immediately concerned 'only with the internal relationships which bind up with one another all the phenomena in our consciousness; but, at the end . . . the practical necessity of raising the ontological problem brings us necessarily to the ontological solution of the practical problem'.[5] The phenomena 'are solidified'.

Just as it is a mistake to suppose that the affirmation of God's existence is, for Blondel, the result of a blind choice, so, then, it is a mistake to suppose that all true knowledge results, in his view, from such a choice.[6] Blondel does not mean to say that we have no knowledge of the truth until the 'ontological problem' has

---

[1] This phrase often occurs in the *Letter* in reference to the dialectic of *L'Action*.
[2] Bouillard, pp. 138-9.   [3] *Ibid*, p. 139   [4] *L'Action*, p. 427.
[5] *L'Action*, p. 425.   [6] For what follows see Bouillard, pp. 148-50.

been raised by the 'practical necessity'. Indeed he says the exact contrary. He tells us that the knowledge which he calls 'subjective', and which includes the knowledge of the necessity of the option, is 'necessary knowledge of the truth'.[1] In fact it is what would be ordinarily called 'objective' knowledge. But Blondel reserves the term 'objective' for that knowledge which is the 'possession' of being, of absolute being or reality. 'The necessary knowledge of the truth is still only a means of acquiring, or of losing, the possession of reality'.[2] That is why he can write that 'it is still only a representation of the object in the subject'.[3] It must be confessed that such language can be extremely misleading; Blondel recognized this, and later adopted 'speculative knowledge' and 'effective knowledge' to refer to knowledge before and after the option. And in the conclusion of *L'Action* he makes the same distinction in terms of the 'science of practice' and 'practical science'. The 'science of practice' (or 'action') is the business of philosophy: 'practical science' is the result of the good option, which is beyond philosophy ('the science of action can never supply for action'). So when we are told in the *Letter* that philosophy can never produce *being*, we must always understand this to mean, as Blondel himself puts it on occasion, that it can never lead us of itself to *beatitude*.

Again, if there should be any suspicion that Blondel was not clear in his own mind about all this, we can turn to his correspondence. He writes to Père Auguste Valensin:

> I had to draw up an indictment of *separated philosophy* . . . I wanted to insist on two capital truths: that to 'attain', to *possess*, the reality of being and especially of Being, it is not enough to know it (in the weak theoretical sense of the word), and that knowledge (in the strong sense, the Johannine sense) implies a profundity of vision which manifests the solidarity of things, the secret of their dependence, the meaning of our present and eternal destiny. That is why I insist so much on two sorts of knowledge—one which precedes, proposes and imposes the option, the other which results from an attitude which we have taken up . . .[4]

[1] *L'Action*, p. 486.   [2] *Ibid.*   [3] *L'Action*, p. 438.
[4] *Bl-Val Corr.*, vol. II, pp. 309-310, quoted by Bouillard, p. 153.

There was a good deal of excuse for Blondel's language in the circumstances of his time.

When he was writing *L'Action*, positivism, phenomenism and [Kantian] criticism imposed on most minds a negation of all metaphysics, or at least a profound distaste for it. He had to start from this position. As with all the positions examined by him, he wanted to take his stand on his interlocutor's ground, to adopt his language, to accept his problematic provisionally so as to show the incoherence of the system and the necessity of adopting a higher viewpoint. This desire to keep in touch with doctrines which were then alive explains the frequent usage ... of terms such as 'science' (for 'philosophy'), 'determinism' (for 'necessary implications'), 'phenomenon' (for 'datum', the object of knowledge as such). This explains the rather odd interplay of opposition between subjective and objective, phenomenon and being, in short, the external form of the ontological problem and its treatment in Blondel's work.[1]

But it is because he was trying 'to say something to someone', as he puts it in the *Letter*, that his work will live.

It must be re-emphasized, in conclusion, that there has been no attempt in this section to offer a conspectus, however sketchy, of Blondel's thought. We have been concerned with it only as it appears in his great original thesis and only in so far as that is a necessary introduction to the *Letter*. An introduction to the thesis itself would need to take account of other obscurities—there is, for example, a recurrent difficulty, towards the end, of deciding in what 'universe of discourse' Blondel is moving. And we have not been directly concerned with a tendency to exaggerate oppositions which Blondel later recognized and corrected in his later work. But it is to be hoped that, in spite of all these warnings, *L'Action* will receive new readers. It is that hope, very largely, which has brought the present volume into existence.

[1] Bouillard, p. 166.

IV. DISPUTED QUESTIONS

The Natural and the Supernatural

It was remarked above that Bouillard's *Blondel et le Christianisme* seemed to have been unanimously acclaimed in France (that is to say, by Christian writers)—with one significant exception. Since such extensive use has been made of the book it is necessary to take account of the exception. In a short article entitled 'The Centenary of Maurice Blondel', *Revue Thomiste*, July-Sept. 1962, Père J.-H. Nicolas, O.P., reviews Bouillard's book and still echoes the complaints which were made in that periodical at the end of the last century about Blondel's failure to preserve the gratuitousness of the supernatural, his subjectivist and anti-intellectual approach to the problem of knowledge and, in general, his misconceptions about the relationship between philosophy and theology.

Père Nicolas begins by paying a graceful tribute to Bouillard's work as an exposition of Blondel's thought, 'the complexity and also the imprecisions of which become clearer perhaps at the end of this remarkable effort of elucidation' (a concluding phrase which shows that the preceding compliments are back-handed ones). He then gives an account of the principal conclusions which Bouillard reaches, laying the proper stress on the most important of all: that ' "the supernatural", the desire and the necessity of which are shown by the *method of immanence*, is "not the supernatural in the *positively determined* form given to it by the Christian Revelation, but the still *undetermined* supernatural, which philosophers, even among the pagans, have descried" '.[1] 'The Christian supernatural', writes Nicolas, continuing this admirable account, 'appears only at the third stage of the genesis of the notion of the supernatural, and, quite precisely, for the philosopher, as the determination of this general and confused notion of the supernatural.'[2]

[1] Nicolas, p. 433, quoting Bouillard, p. 70.   [2] Nicolas, p. 434.

At this point Nicolas turns to the offensive. 'Without wishing to deny', he writes, 'that this [conclusion] corresponds at least to an aspect of Blondel's thought, it is hard to believe that it expresses the whole of it . . .' Bouillard, as we have seen, has himself insisted on the confusion which may easily arise in the mind of the unwary reader about the meaning of 'supernatural' in Blondel's writings. He has also pointed out that there is no need to suspect a confusion in Blondel's own thought, considered as a whole. Blondel may have sometimes failed to realize that he was slipping from one sense of 'supernatural' into another, but the distinction itself was always present to his mind and presided over all his work. Speaking formally as a Christian to Christians, Blondel will point out that if the acceptance of the supernatural is something to which we are obliged on pain of damnation, *we* must be in a position to *choose* it; there must be something in us which enables us to recognize and respond to it; moreover, the 'undetermined supernatural' must arise for every man, for those who are ignorant of Christianity cannot choose anything other than this, and then the good option becomes 'baptism by desire'. He will also point out at times that our destination, *as a matter of fact*, to the Christian supernatural order cannot fail to leave 'traces' of itself in our psychology, but an appeal to direct introspection is not a characteristic of his early works. Speaking simply as a philosopher, he is concerned to show that it is the duty of man, *in any circumstances*, to hand himself over freely to a power which is 'transcendent', the undetermined 'supernatural'. The philosopher as such can only realize that the (hypothetical) Christian dogmas offer man a further advance in the way in which he is already moving. And this development involves a change, not just of degree, but of kind.

Nicolas, however, continues as follows:

Too many [of Blondel's] declarations indicate a discovery of Christian dogmas by the method of immanence alone, and it is impossible to believe that the reflections in the *Letter* on the obligation of accepting the gift of God, on the necessity of a redemptive sacrifice, on the significance of the Incarnation, and also on 'the necessity of dogmas and revealed precepts' derive from a confrontation of the undetermined notion of the supernatural with revealed dogmas: on the contrary, they present themselves as springing from man's reflection on himself.

After what has been already said, the reader may be invited to make up his own mind on the question by examining the incriminated passages.[1] Is it reasonable to find in them a doctrine which is inconsistent with Blondel's attitude as revealed by his work as a whole and expressly repudiated in the *Letter* itself? Blondel's own words are: '*En déterminant la genèse de l'idée de révélation ou en indiquant la nécessité de dogmes ou de préceptes révélés, nous ne ferons jamais autre chose que tracer des cadres vides, dont rien de nôtre ne saurait fixer la réalité ou remplir le dessin abstrait.*'[2] It is clear from the whole context that he is referring to the necessity under which everyone stands to make the option for or against the 'supernatural', to the 'point of insertion', in fact precisely to the 'undetermined supernatural'. The result of the good option is that we are prepared to accept the Christian Revelation, that it is *necessary* for us to accept it, if it proves to be a fact.[3]

But we have not yet come to the real *gravamen* of the charge which Nicolas is making. There is, he goes on to say, the further difficulty, whatever interpretation may be given of the passages in the *Letter*, that, according to Blondel,

the positive, revealed, Christian supernatural appears as the determination of the philosophical notion of the supernatural; in other words, that it is implied in this. If, then, this still undetermined supernatural appears to purely rational, philosophical, reflection as necessary, indispensable, as that without which man cannot achieve his action, then this necessity automatically affects the supernatural in its positive, revealed, form, which is nothing but the explication of the preceding form, and man without revelation appears to himself as unachieved, incomplete . . . if the supernatural is a require-

---

[1] *Lettre*, pp. 87-90 (pp. 201-3 below).   [2] *Lettre*, p. 41 (p. 159-60 below).

[3] To this it might be replied that we should be obliged to accept it in any case if it proved to be a fact. But what Blondel means is that we should not be able to recognize it as a fact without this preparation.

ment of man, God owes it to himself to provide man with it . . .[1]

Thus Nicolas rejects the explanation that there is no requirement that God should reveal himself but rather a requirement that man should accept God's revelation. He adds that the true concept of the supernatural, even in an undetermined form, is a theological, not a philosophical, concept, and that Bouillard's long chapter on the subject 'does not seem to have established the contrary'.

It is hard to believe that Nicolas can have studied that chapter very closely. We read in it: 'The movement to the general and indeterminate idea [of the supernatural] is not of the same type as the movement to the specifically Christian idea; the necessity is not identical in each case, or at least it does not disclose itself in the same way. The first is such that it manifests itself inevitably to every man, at least implicitly. The second is such that its special determination can be apparent only to one who knows Christian dogma and is willing to envisage it, hypothetically, as the eventual revealer of the deep-seated requirements of the will. Certainly both necessities are hypothetical, in the sense that only actual practice [the *action* of acceptance] will effect the realization of what reflection shows us to be necessary. But . . . the second is hypothetical by yet another title—in so far as it will not be discovered apart from the hypothesis of revealed dogma.'[2] And in an earlier passage we are told that the Christian supernatural is not 'virtually enclosed in the former notion. From the undetermined supernatural to the Christian supernatural the movement is not analytic, but synthetic'.[3] Nicolas is not justified, therefore, in suggesting that this movement is a mere making explicit of what is implicit.

Nevertheless, he would presumably say, it remains that man is being defined as ordered to the supernatural, to the Beatific Vision, and this makes it *necessary* for God to offer him grace (he writes of the 'reproach which theologians [that is, the thomists] have always made against Blondel of compromising the gratuitousness of the supernatural').[4] If so, then Nicolas' claim is that man's need for the supernatural, according to Blondel, is one which is essential to his

[1] Nicolas, pp. 434-5.   [2] Bouillard, p. 102.
[3] Bouillard, p. 96.   [4] Nicolas, p. 434.

nature and which therefore constrains God to satisfy it, since it would be unjust for him to implant such a desire without satisfying it. But it is a perfectly respectable and widespread theological opinion, attributed by many to St Thomas, that man *has* a natural desire for the Beatific Vision, although one which is not absolute—it is conditional on God's elevating him to the supernatural order, an 'inefficacious' desire. Whether this makes sense or not it is not our present business to inquire. But it is clear that Blondel cannot be accused of unorthodoxy in saying it, and that he is not committed to saying any more than this. In fact, in his later writings,[1] in which he takes account of the theological concept of 'pure nature' (the state, envisaged as a possibility, in which man would not have been raised to the supernatural order), he explicitly adopts such a theory of an 'inefficacious desire'. If one is not allowed to say that nature requires completion by grace in any sense,[2] if nature is an entirely closed system, then we are faced with the apparent *irrelevance* of the supernatural which was the starting-point for Blondel's thought. It was the need to show his contemporaries that the supernatural is not simply imposed as an alien element but means something for man which remained the motive force for some sixty years. As we have already seen, a result of considering the supernatural as thus *imposed* is what Blondel calls *monophorism*—the attitude of

[1] E.g. *Le Problème de la Philosophie Catholique* (Bloud et Gay, 1932), pp. 25-6. It could be said that Blondel's purely philosophical discussion has been brought to an end by the 'option', and that the need for the Christian supernatural which he introduces at that point is a consequence of the *de facto* ordination of man to the Christian supernatural state. Such a need would not be a property of man's nature, and it would require to be satisfied only in the sense that God, in establishing this supernatural order, would have freely committed himself to satisfying it. In asking the philosopher who had made the good option to recognize the presence of such a need, Blondel would be asking him to recognize a prevenient grace. He would be drawing attention to the conditions of human experience at a certain stage of its development which he thinks of himself as deriving from the Christian supernatural and wishes others to recognize as such.

[2] Fr J. M. Connolly in *The Voices of France* shows very little knowledge of the man whom he calls 'the immanentist Henri [*sic*] Blondel', but he does say: 'Today his work is no longer suspect, save in the most extremely conservative circles . . .' (p. 25).

mind which sees only 'one-way traffic' in the communication to man of supernatural truth, requiring no co-operation by man's intelligence.[1] Thus we find an anti-intellectual authoritarianism in matters of religion bound up with an anti-humanism which keeps the arts, and, in general, cultural development, at arm's length, a mechanical view of tradition, a tendency to regard truth in human affairs as a means to an end and so to adopt certain compromises in public life, a certain disregard for human freedom. It may perhaps become clearer now that the spirit of the Second Vatican Council was the spirit which animated Blondel.

Before we leave this topic of the gratuitousness of the supernatural it may be as well, in the interests of that frankness which Blondel prized so highly, to suggest that there remains, on any showing, a real problem. At first we might be inclined to say that the whole business is a mere fuss about a technical point in theology which seems to have no real meaning. Surely everything is gratuitous, nature as well as grace—we can have no claim upon God, and our business, in his regard, is simply to receive his gifts. It is not, in fact, so simple as that. The Encyclical *Humani Generis* of 1950 laid down that there is a special gratuitousness about grace in that the state of 'pure nature' is one which God *could* have constituted. The difficulty is to see *how* God, with his supreme generosity, could have abstained from giving grace. Encyclicals are not infallible documents, but their teaching must be accepted as a working rule for theologians at least in the existing state of theological development. It may be added that Karl Rahner has proposed, in place of a natural *desire* for the supernatural, a theory of the 'openness' of nature for the reception of a 'disposition' to the supernatural.[2] He points out that we have no means of precisely de-limiting 'pure nature'—what nature would be like if we were not in fact summoned to the Beatific Vision is by no means clear. This is an

---

[1] v. p. 267 above. Blondel considers in *La Semaine Sociale de Bordeaux* the immanentist *efférence*, which is the heresy of modernism, the unilateral *afférence* which might be called the theory of ultramontanism, and the double *afférence*, God's summons to man both exteriorly *and interiorly*, which is a leading theme in the *Letter*.

[2] In the English translation *Theological Investigations*, vol. I, pp. 308 ff.

important consideration which may prove at least to relieve the problem. Rahner acknowledges at the beginning of his article that he had been anticipated here, in principle, by Blondel.[1]

But we must return, for a moment, to Père Nicolas. He devotes a good deal of his article[2] to an exposition and a criticism of Bouillard's chapter on Blondel's dialectic and his conception of Christian philosophy. He does not seem to realize that when Blondel abstains from affirming 'being' in the course of the dialectic he is both guarding against any identification of particular beings with God, the source of being, and also adopting a provisional attitude of neutrality in regard to epistemological questions in general as well as in regard to Christianity. As we have seen,[3] Bouillard makes this perfectly clear. Nicolas thus brings the old charge of 'subjectivism' against Blondel and also objects that he cannot claim to be doing the work of philosophy since he begins by adopting the truth of Christianity as a hypothesis. On the first point, Nicolas insists that it is impossible to suspend the question of 'being' (taking it always in the very special sense which it has in thomism) because all our affirmations must depend upon it. This is precisely what Blondel is saying, in his own way, by showing the consequences of any attempt to evade the 'ontological affirmation'. But how does

---

[1] By whom he is much influenced (unconsciously, it would seem) since he takes a good deal of his philosophy from Maréchal (v.pp. 62-3 above). He had found in an article by L. Malevez, S.J. in Nouvelle Revue Théologique, 1953, p. 79, the following quotation from Blondel's La Semaine Sociale de Bordeaux, Annales de Philosophie Chrétienne, 1939, p. 268: 'It is unquestionably an error to argue as though the natural state of the unbeliever, the agnostic or the apostate were the state of "pure nature", a state which no doubt could have existed, which never has existed, whose real conditions we cannot even precisely define.' (Blondel refers to the former state as the 'transnatural' one; cf. History and Dogma, p. 284, below). Père Malevez here touches on the most important of all books on this subject for our time, Père de Lubac's Surnaturel. Reviewing the book in the same place (Jan. 1942), he had suggested in conclusion that 'the state of pure nature is infallibly [as distinct from necessarily] transcended by God's creative love'.

[2] Nicolas, pp. 435-9. P. Cartier in Existence et Vérité (p. 174 f.) has commented usefully on P. Nicolas' remarks on Blondel in Revue Thomiste, 1948, III.

[3] p. 94 f., above.

Blondel justify his own claims, Nicolas asks, for the option itself takes him beyond philosophy, and, until that has been made, everything remains 'subjective'?[1] The answer is, as we have also seen,[2] that the presentation of the option is itself a philosophical datum. It conveys (or rather demands the recognition of) being, the existence of God and the dependence of 'phenomena' upon him. On the second point, Nicolas writes: 'How can one ask an unbeliever in the name of philosophy, and therefore in the name of rational experience, to begin by entertaining the hypothesis of the truth of Catholicism?'[3] As again we have seen,[4] Blondel does not ask him to do so until *after* the option has been made.

Thus it is not surprising that Nicolas sees in Blondel's work a mass of confusions, resulting from an attempt to settle by philosophical means a theological problem. 'The greatest genius', he concludes magisterially, 'cannot triumph over a contradiction.'[5] This failure to understand what Blondel was really doing also leads him to see in the *Lettres Philosophiques de Maurice Blondel* (which he reviews in the same article) a naturalizing of theology where Blondel is in fact considering the *meaning* which theological dogmas can have for the inquiring mind.[6] But let us grant something to Nicolas. It is true, as he says,[7] that Blondel often caricatured thomism. This is a subject on which we shall touch later.[8]

The notion of Christian philosophy

We must now take up the question of 'Christian philosophy' itself, particularly in view of the controversy on the subject which broke out in France in 1931 and which still continues.[9] So far it has been taken for granted that this expression, referring to a philosophy

---

[1] Nicolas, p. 437.   [2] pp. 85-6, above.   [3] Nicolas, p. 438.

[4] p. 91 above.   [5] Nicolas, p. 439.

[6] 'In thomist intellectualism, the formulas of faith are equally accessible in their *meaning* for every intelligence, believing or unbelieving,' Georges van Riet, *Revue Philosophique de Louvain*, 1963, 'St Thomas et la philosophie de la religion', p. 57.

[7] Nicolas, p. 444.

[8] In the Prefatory Note to the *Letter*.

[9] v., e.g., van Riet's article, *Revue Philosophique de Louvain*, Feb., 1963, already quoted.

which finds in Christianity its 'directive hypothesis',[1] is a perfectly allowable one. That it is possible to make philosophy an apologetic, indeed that true philosophy must lead to the 'undetermined supernatural',[2] is, as we have seen, the argument of *L'Action*. But it is time to observe that 'Christian philosophy' is an awkward expression, for it may suggest that the method of philosophy, as employed by Christians, is different from that employed by others, and that it is not strictly 'autonomous'. Blondel himself soon came to disapprove of the expression. When the controversy broke out, he was quite prepared to agree with Bréhier, although strongly dissenting from his views about the nature of philosophy and about the nature of Christianity, that there is, in that sense, no such thing as 'Christian philosophy',[3] pointing out that he had already said as much in the *Letter*, thirty-five years before.[4] He did, however, go on to suggest in the *Letter* that a Christian philosophy might be constituted,[5] referring evidently to his own conception of philosophy, although he regularly speaks of it there as 'integral philosophy', and in his first reply to Bréhier[6] he withdrew the statement in the *Letter* that Christian philosophy does not exist as being 'too summary'. Again replying to Bréhier and disapproving of the expression 'Christian philosophy', he prefers to speak of 'Catholic philosophy', meaning by this the universal philosophy, which is open to the supernatural, to Catholicism, fructified by it in its own domain, but independent of it in its method and constitution; but he emphasizes that to speak of philosophy in this way is to speak of it '*secundum quid* and not *simpliciter*'.[7]

In this connection a passage from an article by Père Henri de Lubac[8] has been often quoted:

According to M. Blondel's conception of Christian philo-

---

[1] Bouillard, p. 27.

[2] The phrase is used by Blondel in this connection in *Le Problème de la Philosophie Catholique* (1932), p. 160.

[3] *Le Problème de la Philosophie Catholique*, p. 128.   [4] p. 65, below.

[5] Esp. p. 205, below.

[6] *Revue de Métaphysique et de Morale*, 1931, p. 605, quoted by Bouillard, p. 213.

[7] *Le Problème de la Philosophie Catholique*, pp. 162, 169.

[8] *Nouvelle Revue Théologique*, 1936, p. 245.

sophy, it is not *yet* Christian. For it is philosophy proving to itself, in a final stage which is still a work of purely rational reflection, that it does not 'button up'. Thus it is a philosophy which is open to Christianity, which does not proceed from it in any way *de jure*, since, if it wishes so to proceed, it could do this only by taking away from Christianity its supernatural character, at the very moment when it proclaims this by its own last avowal.

This article, Bouillard points out,[1] was warmly praised by Blondel: 'It is there vigorously brought out that philosophy, in its most rational autonomy, covers the whole field of experience and of life as a whole. Many confusions and timidities are eliminated . . .'[2] And this leads us to remember that philosophy is not, for Blondel, *merely* the 'science of action' leading to the option; it comes into full activity only after the option and maintains its function and its rights even when it takes cognizance of doctrines which it receives from a higher source. When Blondel says, in the *Letter*, that Christian philosophy has still to be constituted, he is thinking, perhaps, of Christian philosophy in this sense.[3] Philosophy in so far as it is common ground for believers and unbelievers (and there are obvious reasons for confining its meaning to this, in practice) is 'not yet Christian'. But it is also 'not yet Christian' from another point of view. In so far as Christians are (as they should be) philosophers in their theologizing, *understanding* their faith, they are extending the scope of philosophy. Philosophy is still *becoming Christian*. 'True philosophy is the sanctity of the reason.'[4]

But we must note, with Bouillard,[5] that this exercise of the reason which Blondel calls (quite rightly) philosophical is the regular practice of the classical theologians. It is also, therefore, theological. This is a fact of which Blondel seems unaware in the *Letter*. Misled

---

[1] Bouillard, pp. 263-4.   [2] *L'Action*, I, ed. 1949, p. 311n.

[3] Further examined in the two volumes of *La Philosophie et L'Esprit chrétien*, 1944 and 1946.

[4] *L'Action*, p. 442.

[5] Bouillard, pp. 254-5, where it is pointed out that Blondel in the *Letter*, as a *philosopher*, takes over a theory of speculative theology about the Incarnation (p. 202, below).

by the manuals of his time, he seems to think that the theologian's task is simply to organize the Christian dogmas into a unity; it is for the philosopher to penetrate their meaning.[1] What Blondel is talking about, then, is properly described, not indeed as dogmatic theology, but as both fundamental and speculative theology: 'It is to some extent under his influence that, since 1900, fundamental theology, as we know it today, has been gradually constituted.'[2]

It will help to bring out the importance of Blondel's standpoint if we consider the views of the other disputants in the controversy of the early 'thirties. Maritain considered that there is such a thing as a Christian philosophy because, although philosophy always remains itself, the Christian philosopher is given certain information by his faith which saves him from following up false trails and points him in the right direction.[3] As de Lubac observes,[4] 'Christian philosophy' does not amount to much, on this showing. And he quotes[5] the remarks of Mgr de Solages: 'M. Blondel justifies M. Maritain, for the latter's position would be untenable if the former's were not true . . . only the orientation of nature towards the supernatural can properly explain how the revelation of the supernatural helps the normal working of the reason, how reason enlightened by faith functions better than reason without the benefit of this light.'

Gilson regarded Christian philosophy as a historical phenomenon. Philosophy, as a matter of fact, owes to Christianity certain ideas of the highest importance; that of creation, for instance. De Lubac comments that Blondel's view is 'perhaps still more necessary for that of M. Gilson. For in so far as philosophy has not itself hollowed out "the eventual place of an undetermined supernatural", nothing can take from it the presumption that it is capable of rationalizing everything in the materials which it receives from faith; and so we can ask ourselves whether Christianity does not

---

[1] That is to say, so far as they contain rational elements. Not only do the mysteries of faith remain mysterious and the data presented by the theologians remain inviolable, but the theologian may maintain that the theological virtues lead to an 'intelligence of the faith' of a supra-rational kind.

[2] Bouillard, p. 259.

[3] *De la Philosophie Chrétienne*, 1933.

[4] art. cit., p. 229.   [5] art. cit., p. 240.

destroy itself to the extent to which it provides philosophy with nourishment'.[1] Thus de Lubac is led to say[2] that if, for Blondel, philosophy is not yet Christian, for Gilson it is *no longer* Christian—it is just philosophy which happens to have been generated by Christianity. It simply 'annexes for itself what Christianity supplies'; whereas Christian philosophy for Maritain is not Christian at all: 'if among the elements which it scrutinizes, some happen to be contained in the revealed deposit, that is just a lucky coincidence. These elements, which all belong to the natural order, were, before Revelation, not only knowable, but known—at least virtually—by philosophers'.[3]

So Blondel's is the only one of these views according to which philosophy *formally as such*, of its nature, can recognize the supernatural, formally as such. It is therefore the only one which deserves to be called both Christian and philosophical. 'Neither dependence nor independence nor mere juxtaposition of the rational order and the Christian order; but a sort of heterogeneity in compenetration and symbiosis in incommensurability, that is what Clement of Alexandria tried to pin down under the name of the new philosophy according to Christ...'[4] That, it was suggested, is what Blondel had in mind at the end of the *Letter*. His friend Victor Delbos once said that 'his original thought ... was to dominate the order of external and conventional relations in which Philosophy and Religion had hitherto been placed so as to establish a philosophy which should be religious, not by accident, but by nature, without being so as a result of prejudice'.[5] Naturally Blondel reacted to Gilson's proposals with some violence:

> either, if these adventitious data of the Gospel message are assimilated, as it is suggested to us ... such a Christian philo-

[1] loc. cit.   [2] art. cit., pp. 244-5.

[3] Without forgetting all that we owe to Professors Gilson and Maritain one may be allowed to regret that their rather rigid thomism is sometimes considered identical with Catholic philosophy.

[4] *Le Problème de la Philosophie Catholique*, p. 145.

[5] Quoted by Bouillard, p. 27, who adds: 'To reconcile faith and philosophy the following procedure has often been adopted: first an attempt is made to construct a self-sufficient philosophy quite apart from Christian thought; then the question arises of how to attach Christianity to it.'

sophy dechristianizes Christianity . . . or, if despite everything one wishes to preserve the Christian data as supernatural demands, that is, in their authentically Catholic form,
then philosophy has to submit to an intrusion which is
absolutely unjustifiable from the point of view which has
been adopted.[1]

Finally, in this matter, reference must be made to Mgr Maurice
Nédoncelle's book *Existe-t-il une Philosophie Chrétienne?*,[2] which
has been translated into English.[3] Nédoncelle belongs to the French
metaphysical tradition of which some mention has been made earlier,[4]
and is known as the chief exponent in France of what is called 'per-
sonalist' philosophy. We cannot stop to consider it here, but it is
pertinent to remark that it is, in his view, 'surprising and scandalous
that the metaphysical analysis of the influence exercised by one
mind on another should have been continuously neglected in the
history of philosophy'[5] For this sheds light upon his concept of
Christian philosophy. As we shall see, he accepts Blondel's position
in principle but wishes to go beyond it. One may venture to suggest,
greatly daring, that Blondel would be more ready to accept this
development than Nédoncelle seems to think. But that is to
anticipate.

Nédoncelle holds that 'philosophy examines reality, in any order,
only in the perspective of ideas or organisms of ideas which express
personalities'.[6]

> Certainly [he writes] a human person cannot fulfil his destiny
> without positing and freely constructing a world of his own.
> But this movement cannot be exclusively centrifugal. All
> interpersonal influence, and *a fortiori* the development of a
> divine principle in us, must develop into grateful acknow-
> ledgment. A consciousness is no less autonomous because it
> becomes progressively aware of its causes. The perfection of
> reason is not ingratitude. Reason is fully adult only in so far

---

[1] *Le Problème de la Philosophie Catholique*, pp. 133-4.

[2] In the *Je Sais—Je crois* series (Librairie Arthème Fayard, Paris).

[3] *Is there a Christian Philosophy?*, Burns and Oates, in the Faith and Fact Series,
1960. References are to the translation.

[4] pp. 81-2.   [5] Nédoncelle, pp. 123-4.   [6] Nédoncelle, pp. 150-1.

as it integrates those organisms of ideas which derive from the divine activity, recognizing it as such.

For 'philosophy and metaphysics aim at constituting, in accordance with the requirements of an absolute honesty and an unrestricted reflection, the universal kingdom of true affirmations'.[1] To suggest that, for Blondel, philosophy is 'not yet Christian' in the sense indicated by these admirable passages is perhaps to read Nédoncelle's views into his words. But at least it may be said that, although the originality of Nédoncelle's particular standpoint is not to be denied, these views are a natural development of Blondel's as regards the general concept of a 'Christian philosophy'.

Nédoncelle, indeed, is generous in praise of Blondel. He writes that, of the various conceptions of Christian philosophy in currency, 'the most strictly accurate seems to be . . . that of M. Blondel'.[2] And again: 'Blondelianism proves not to be without its difficulties. But one thing, at any rate, is clear: apart from Blondelianism and the interpretation of it given by Duméry, it would be a vain hope to look for any watertight meaning of the expression "Christian philosophy". . .'[3] What emerges . . . is that the direction of thought indicated by Blondel must be adopted but on condition that it is revised and taken further.[4]

But this reference to M. Duméry raises the question whether Nédoncelle's conception of Blondel's position is the same as that put forward in this Introduction. Nédoncelle quotes from Duméry: 'The supernatural is for the philosopher a necessary hypothesis; only theology can bear upon its reality. Blondel, as a philosopher, does not require that the supernatural should exist; he requires that it should be possible. It is the hypothesis of the supernatural, not its

---

[1] Nédoncelle, p. 144.

[2] Nédoncelle, p. 150. He also writes that Blondel has helped philosophy 'to formulate what it has sought, gropingly and in substance, for two thousand years, and perhaps for its whole history . . . What we chiefly owe to the Blondelian doctrine of insufficiency is our deliverance from the easy-going air and the complacent psittacism which have so often tarnished the renown of Christian philosophy' (pp. 113-14). Of M. Gilson he writes: 'Fundamentally he has little confidence in the autonomous powers of the intellect . . . he believes in the history of philosophy much more than in philosophy' (p. 87).

[3] Nédoncelle, p. 111.   [4] Nédoncelle, pp. 112-13.

reality in actual fact, which conditions the validity of natural ontology.'[1] And this leads him to see in Blondel's account 'a very abrupt demarcation between philosophy and life, as if philosophy were only a logic relative to presuppositions or conclusions, whose reality it cannot judge but only their intelligible connections'.[2]

It will be obvious that the element which Bouillard has shown definitively as the central element in Blondel's argument, the 'undetermined supernatural', has fallen into the background here. Philosophy, for Blondel, does not regard the *undetermined* supernatural' as a mere hypothesis; it *'demonstrates'* the 'undetermined supernatural'. It is not simply that philosophy 'owes to itself to make us give faith a trial', as Nédoncelle puts it,[3] because it recognizes the 'Christian supernatural' as possible. It judges the reality of the 'undetermined supernatural' and itself puts this before us as a fact. Only then are we prepared for the Christian 'supernatural'. And the 'logic of action' presides over all this movement. Submission to reality is the great action of life.[4]

The interpretation of Blondel's thought

We are thus led to the last of the disputed questions which are to be treated here, that of the interpretation of Blondel's work as a whole. Until the appearance of Bouillard's book, Duméry was commonly considered the standard interpreter. An attempt has been made in these pages, so far as space has permitted, to show that Bouillard's interpretation is the correct one, that it is solidly supported by the texts. But no doubt the subject will remain for some time a disputed one, for opinions, once formed, are not changed overnight. It seems desirable, then, at least to bring out more fully

[1] Nédoncelle, pp. 110-11, quoting H. Duméry, *Blondel et la religion* (Presses Universitaires de France, 1959), p. 65.

[2] Nédoncelle, p. 111.

[3] loc. cit. Bouillard's book appeared after Nédoncelle's

[4] The following fine passage from Nédoncelle would surely have been accepted by Blondel: 'When philosophical reflection develops in a Christian soul, it is itself intrinsically Christian; and this includes an ascesis of the mind which dissects, discriminates, advances little by little and is in touch with the corresponding demands which can arise in non-Christian souls' (pp. 124-5).

the difference of view as between Duméry and Bouillard. It will be clear already that Duméry's fundamental error is to overlook the importance of the 'undetermined supernatural', of the option. He sees in Blondel's philosophy essentially 'a critical and reflective analysis'. When Blondel says that man has *need* of the supernatural, Duméry regards him as being unfaithful to his own method of 'immanence', which is confined to the 'formal plan of reflection' and excludes 'the real plan of action'. If the interpreter turns critic in this way, the question must arise whether his interpretation is the right one. When it runs counter to Blondel's plain assertions about the purpose and the character of his method and to the whole tenor of *L'Action*, we must conclude that it is the wrong one.[1] And here it may be noted that Duméry is quite right to say that Blondel is not seeking to find 'a tell-tale sign of the supernatural on the psycho-empirical level', his method being to analyse the 'necessary', but that there is no occasion for complaining, as Duméry does, that when Blondel speaks in the *Letter* of a *felt* need[2] for the supernatural he is again proving false to his own method. Blondel, says Bouillard, 'is not trying to make the unbeliever *register* an awareness of a need, but he hopes, by his dialectic, to *arouse it*, which is a quite different matter, and does not imply, in itself, any *"psychologism"* '.[3]

Duméry, in fact, says Bouillard, is imposing a Plotinian perspective on Blondel's work. In *La Philosophie de l'Action* Duméry tells us that the option is 'only the recognition of an *a priori* normative and an identification with its movement . . . It becomes constitutive of being because, in the manner of Plotinus, it recognizes being as the trace of the One'.[4] Thus the analysis itself is always confined to the sphere of the hypothetical, and it has to be applied to the real if an *ontological* judgment is to be made. This is what happens when the option occurs—and it happens, for good or ill, all the time. It is just one aspect of the process of knowing. (According to Duméry's *Blondel et la Religion*, however, Bouillard points out,[5] the option,

---

[1] Bouillard, pp. 67-70, referring to Duméry, *Blondel et la Religion*, p. 79.
[2] p. 163 below.
[3] Bouillard, p. 79, referring to Duméry, op. cit, pp. 47, 49 and 54, n.1.
[4] Duméry, pp. 113-14, quoted by Bouillard, pp. 144-5.
[5] Bouillard, p. 145, n.5.

understood particularly as the option for or against the *Christian supernatural*, is prepared for by the reflective analysis and follows it.) We have seen[1] that there is a sort of propaedeutic option, according to Blondel, taking place, throughout human experience; 'knowledge is thus always prior to one option and posterior to another'.[2] And we have seen that the great option in face of the 'one thing necessary' may occur at any stage. But this does not justify the conclusion that all cases of option may be reduced to a moment in the general process of knowledge (or to the option for or against the Christian supernatural). If this does not seem to be sufficiently established, one can only ask the reader to make sense of the *Letter*, if he can, on any other basis. A reading of *L'Action* must surely bring him to the same conclusion. Unless he succeeds in disregarding (as Duméry seems to have done) the necessity of 'equating the term willed with the principle of the voluntary aspiration itself',[3] which is at the heart of *L'Action*, he cannot see in the 'determinism of action' (as Duméry does) only 'the intelligible structure of action'.[4]

If we disregard uninformed effusions and the suggestions made, to Blondel's amazement, at the outset of his career, that he was really a kind of Kantian or a pragmatist like James, other interpretations reduce, in principle, to questions of emphasis, according as interpreters concentrate, more or less, upon the various aspects and the various periods of his work. He is sometimes related to the 'existentialists' (Père Cartier's book has been mentioned already),[5] sometimes to the thomists. Readers of M. Claude Tresmontant's *Introduction à la métaphysique de Maurice Blondel*,[6] or M. Jean École's *La métaphysique de l'être dans la philosophie de Maurice Blondel* might

[1] p. 86 above.   [2] Bouillard, p. 146.   [3] *L'Action* p. 406.
[4] Duméry, *La Tentation de faire du bien*, p. 187, quoted by Bouillard, p. 225.
[5] p. 52.
[6] The reader who seeks for an account of Blondel's final achievement in metaphysics—necessarily left aside in this Introduction—should by all means secure Tresmontant's most valuable book. It contains, among other things, a comparison of Blondel's approach to that of Teilhard de Chardin and a discussion of Blondel's epistemological views which very clearly shows him to have been ahead of his time. But it is the account of 'the problem of creation' as treated by Blondel which is of chief importance.

receive the impression that he was being annexed for thomism, although M. École admits[1] that Blondel's attitude to the 'proofs' of God's existence is quite different from that of thomism and is 'unquestionably of Augustinian inspiration'. Nédoncelle remarks,[2] after discussing Roger Mehl's *La Condition du philosophe chrétien*, that 'M. Claude Tresmontant has, if I may so put it, given Blondelianism a twist in a different direction. In his work the affirmation of insufficiency is swallowed up in the joy of renewal'. It is not to be denied that the metaphysical works of Blondel's last period do make explicit much that was only implicit in the earlier works and that they show him to be in agreement with St Thomas on questions of the greatest moment. Thus the earlier works are considered important chiefly as leading to these conclusions. But it may be held that the approach to them is what really matters, and that the earlier works are more immediately relevant for our time. Concentrating upon Blondel's *method*, Étienne Borne, in his very fine *Passion de la Vérité*,[3] has rightly related him to the dialecticians, Pascal in particular, who have emphasized the dramatic and historical character, the insecurity and incompleteness, of human thought. Dr Peter Henrici in *Hegel und Blondel* has suggested that Blondel's dialectic is purely philosophical in contrast with Hegel's, which carries with it a 'theological vision'.[4] Père Jean Trouillard, in a particularly impressive article,[5] has related Blondel to the Platonic tradition in view of his subordination of human ideas to the norm of the One . . . And so one might go on.

[1] op. cit., pp. 196-8, quoted with approval by Tresmontant, p. 329.

[2] op. cit., p. 98.

[3] Librairie Arthème Fayard, 1962. This book contains what is perhaps the most illuminating account of Blondel's dialectic.

[4] Bouillard, p. 269, who very pertinently remarks that 'whereas Hegel practises "the intelligence of the faith" in such a way that the "intelligence", that is, philosophy, goes beyond "faith", Blondel practises it in such a way that "faith", as supernatural adhesion, always goes beyond "philosophy" '. Both bring a dialectic to bear, but with opposite intentions.

[5] 'Pluralité spirituelle et Unité normative selon Blondel', *Archives de Philosophie* Jan.-March, 1961 (Blondel Centenary number, which contains much valuable matter). Bouillard has given the highest praise to this eminent Plotinian scholar's interpretation of Blondel (p. 96, n.2), which is only superficially akin to Duméry's.

These diverse but complementary lines of approach to Blondel may help to suggest that he is a philosopher of stature. It might be suspected that his work is eclectic in a pejorative sense, an amalgam. But such work does not grow in importance as Blondel's is growing. The conclusion must be that he is an original, that is, a first-hand, thinker. Such a thinker may well claim to belong to the *philosophia perennis*, for this, though always the same in substance, must be always changing. A great philosopher must bring to it the contribution of his own time, in which he must therefore be profoundly engaged, building the past into the present, and anticipating the future. This seems true of Blondel. He was anticipated by others in certain respects (by Lachelier, for instance, despite the latter's fideism). But there is ground for saying that his is a genuinely original synthesis. If we consider the Industrial Revolution as the last historical divide, there is ground for saying that he is the first great Catholic philosopher of the present age.

POSTSCRIPT—It was not to be expected that M. Duméry would join in the chorus of praise for Père Bouillard's *Blondel et le Christianisme*. His *Raison et Religion dans la Philosophie de l'action*, which is largely a criticism of Bouillard's book, appeared too late to be discussed in this introduction. It must suffice to refer to Bouillard's reply in *Archives de Philosophie*, Jan.-March 1964. There has also appeared a short but valuable book, *Maurice Blondel*, by Jean Lacroix, consisting of extracts from Blondel's works and an essay on his thought.

PART TWO

PREFATORY NOTE

to THE LETTER ON APOLOGETICS

Most readers of the *Letter* will require some help if they are to understand it. The Introduction has tried to give this help so far as Blondel's main positions are concerned, and the notes appended to the text, in addition to providing incidental information relative to particular passages, recall certain warnings issued in the Introduction (and in the present Note) at points where they are especially relevant. But this Note is also necessary, not only to provide information about the *Letter* as a whole, but also (and in the first place) to explain why it was chosen for translation.

It was not at all easy to decide which of Blondel's writings should be offered first to the English reading public. Ideally, *L'Action* (1893) should have been the answer. But it did not seem practicable (on various counts) to produce so large a book together with all the information and elucidation which it would have required. There was something to be said for producing the last of the works: *Exigences Philosophiques du Christianisme*. And there were other possibilities. But on the whole it seemed best to begin, so far as possible, at the beginning. Of the early works, apart from *L'Action*, the *Letter* and *History and Dogma* were clearly the most important, but they were not likely to be very intelligible (the *Letter*, especially) without a context. The context of the *Letter* is *L'Action*; the context of *History and Dogma* is also *L'Action*, but more particularly a cross-section of history in the early years of the century. The Introduction, which thus came into being, has proved, perhaps, to make a virtue of necessity in providing a rough guide to the significance of *L'Action* and an encouragement to undertake a reading of it.

There are, however, certain disadvantages about the choice of the *Letter* which must be candidly acknowledged. Blondel is a thinker writing for our time; after seventy years we are now at last catching up with him. But his style does date: it is diffuse, repetitive and involved (difficulties of vocabulary have been discussed, in a general way, in the Introduction).[1] There was not much that one could do about that, short of rewriting in an entirely different style, and this seemed undesirable. Then there is the fact that Blondel is fighting on two fronts simultaneously: he wishes to maintain his philosophical rectitude in the eyes of the philosophers of his day, and at the same time he wishes to explain himself to Christians, to his fellow-Catholics in particular. This makes the *Letter* a source of confusions, but, if the point is borne in mind, and with the help of the Introduction and the notes on the text, it should not be difficult to avoid them. There is also the fact that Blondel in *Le Problème de la Philosophie Catholique* (1932) made some severe criticisms of the *Letter* of 1896. Was it worthwhile to translate an essay which its author regarded as unsatisfactory? An affirmative answer to this question must be established.

In the first place, the historical importance of the *Letter* would be a sufficient justification in itself. Its influence has been widespread, and it has been the subject of protracted debate on the Continent; it is high time for us to discuss it here. In the second place, although on any interpretation it has unquestionable deficiencies, it has been acclaimed by Duméry as Blondel's masterpiece.[2] We shall here accept Blondel's own account of these deficiencies rather than Duméry's, but Duméry's verdict is nevertheless important. (It may suggest that a proper understanding of the *Letter* is a first step to an understanding of Blondel's other works.) In the third place, a brief examination of *Le Problème de la Philosophie Catholique* will show us that the substance of the *Letter* was very far from being repudiated by Blondel.

Some criticisms which he made of particular passages are mentioned in the notes on the text. Here we may confine ourselves to his more general verdicts. The second chapter of *Le Problème* . . . is entitled 'Annotated extracts from the *Letter* of 1896: exposition

[1] pp. 94 f., above.   [2] *Blondel et la Religion*, p. 1.

of its essential thesis'.[1] For our present purposes, only a part of it need be considered. Blondel prints only the headings or conclusions of the account (at the beginning of the *Letter*) of the first four apologetical methods which he there criticizes. He has more to say about the other two. Some of the details in all this, he says, 'would seem to date from an epoch which is fortunately a past one; a good many other assertions, of too massive a kind, would require distinctions and further developments; many severe judgments had in view recent deviations from traditional thought and would seem today, now that the true masters are better known, still more unjust than in 1896'.[2] If the passages referred to are relatively (but by no means wholly) irrelevant to present-day conditions, they make up for it by their historical interest. And Blondel modestly allows that several of these examinations are not without lasting usefulness.[3] When he comes to the fifth of them he quotes several paragraphs,[4] emphasizing the importance of distinguishing his properly philosophical approach from the method of apologetics, perfectly proper in its own way if its limits are recognized, 'which had happily inspired many preachers and writers from Savonarola to Bonald, Lacordaire, Gratry, Ollé-Laprune, Fonsegrive and very many quite recent authors'.[5] He goes on to regret that he did not make a distinction between the 'state of pure nature' in the theological sense and what he calls the 'congenital state of rational man'. But this latter state, all-important for the philosopher, 'seemed to me more or less overlooked or misunderstood by what was then called "traditional apologetics" '.[6] Hence the examination and denunciation of a sixth method which Blondel calls 'partially justified by all too many texts and by my wishing to direct attention to the decisive points'.[7]

Blondel's chief point of self-criticism refers to his unwitting

---

[1] Owing to the unpleasant misunderstandings which the *Letter* caused and the general temper of the time Blondel had not republished it. The whole was first made available to the general public in *Les Premiers Écrits de Maurice Blondel* (Presses Universitaires de France) in 1956. Until that time it was available only in *Annales de Philosophie Chrétienne* and in off-prints.

[2] *Le Problème.* . . . p. 22.   [3] *Ibid.*   [4] p. 143, below.
[5] *Le Problème.* . . . p. 24.   [6] *Ibid.*, p. 27   [7] *Ibid.*

unfairness to 'scholasticism' in the discussion of this sixth method. But what he denounced under this name was a reality, and it may at least serve as an awful warning. He gives (without references) a long list of 'assertions which barred the approach to Christianity, even to the consideration of Christianity and any understanding of it, for a mind respectful of philosophical exactitude'. The list is quite horrifying.[1] This was, he adds, the 'integrism' which Benedict XV condemned.[2] He then refers to the dangers to which this state of mind can lead, still referring obviously to the condemnation of the *Action française*, and remarks that 'I may be more easily pardoned for having pointed it out twenty years in advance, even while appearing to call in question not so much the true features [of scholasticism] as the caricature of it which alone my criticisms envisaged.[3]

He then prints, with only a few cuts, section II of the *Letter*, 'for that is where the question of life or death for Catholic philosophy is decided'.[4] A few notes are added, some of them incorporated in the notes to the present translation, or already mentioned in the Introduction. Nothing is withdrawn. Blondel has only to point out that he is still feeling his way in the *Letter* and sometimes introducing 'parasitical preoccupations'[5] instead of concentrating upon the problem of Catholic philosophy; at the end of the note just quoted he adds that 'commonly people have confined themselves too much to accommodating pre-existing systems complete as they stand, like Platonism and Aristotelianism, to the doctrine of the Gospel, considered as something altogether alien, superimposed, no doubt, but not fitted to ferment the philosophical mass below it' (the last words are a clear indication of Blondel's concept of Catholic philos-

[1] To give one example: 'The true and sure method of exorcizing all danger of immanentism is to show that in regard to the reason Catholicism is absurd . . .'

[2] *Ibid.*, pp. 28–9.

[3] *Ibid.*, p. 30. He adds in a footnote: 'the vice common to all the deviations indicated is a sort of passivism which materializes the mind . . . which sometimes invokes the primacy of the intelligence or the life of the spirit itself only for temporal ends' (cf. Introduction, pp. 26–7 above).

[4] *Ibid.*, p. 30.

[5] *Ibid.*, p. 39n.

ophy). The fact that he prints very little of section III should not lead one to suppose that he had ceased to have much use for it. The first of his own notes to section II[1] remarks: 'In a later passage of the *Letter* (a passage which I shall suppress for the sake of brevity) I showed how philosophy has historically and dialectically evolved under the secret influence of Christianity. This is directly relevant to my present purpose'. There is no question, then, of Blondel's repudiating the *Letter*.

It remains to mention a handful of facts about its origin and its consequences. Père Charles Denis became the editor of *Annales de Philosophie Chrétienne* in 1895 and, says Blondel, 'to inaugurate his tenure of office . . . described my project [*L'Action*] as an attempt to free apologetics from its old methods of argument and to lead it on to strictly and purely psychological ground'.[2] The *Letter*, written in reply, was 'improvised month by month during the course of my first year's teaching at the Faculty, when I was in the grip of an emotion and a danger which threatened all my reasons for thinking and living . . .'[3] (he refers to the hostile reception of *L'Action* on the part of so many professional philosophers.). In the passage just quoted he goes on to say that the *Letter* 'contains some ill-chosen expressions . . . to a prejudiced mind, it could easily give the impression, in spite of an intention which is plainly the very opposite, that in criticizing "methods" I am tampering with "dogmas", and that in speaking of "contemporary requirements in apologetics" I am actually ranging myself among the apologists (where it is entirely a question of methodology, and where I am seeking not to weaken but to fortify and vivify the methods which I criticize only in so far as they are found in isolation, so as to lead men's minds to the vital point on which the convergence, the organization and the efficacy of the proofs all depend)'. In fact the *Letter* did give this impression to prejudiced minds, in a big way. Gradually Blondel gained more and more recognition from his philosophical colleagues, but the immediate effect of the *Letter* was depressing in the extreme. He was bewildered by the violence of the attacks made upon him by Catholics: 'Acting on weighty advice, I abstained for fourteen

[1] *Ibid.*, p. 31.   [2] *Ibid.*, p. 13.   [3] Ibid., p. 19.

years from entering personally into these controversies . . .'[1] The *Letter* was delated to the Holy Office; it was rescued thence by Leo XIII, at the instance of Cardinal Perraud.[2] When Blondel is mentioned, the reply is still sometimes evoked from those who should know better: 'Blondel? Wasn't he condemned?'

[1] *Ibid.*, p. 46.   [2] v. Duméry, *Blondel et la Religion*, p. 4.n.

THE LETTER ON APOLOGETICS

I. THE VARIOUS METHODS OF APOLOGETICS AND THEIR IMPORT 129

1. *Of pseudo-philosophy in the service of apologetics*
2. *Of the improper use of the sciences in the field of philosophy and apologetics*
3. *Of the pretension of turning facts into apologetic proofs and of the confusion of points of view in apologetics*
4. *Of the persuasiveness and the philosophical insufficiency of apologetics based on the moral and intellectual fittingness of Christianity*
5. *Of the validity of the presumptions in favour of Christianity based on its identity with the laws of life, and of the philosophical and theological difficulties which arise from such an argument if it is supposed to be rationally conclusive*
6. *Of the services rendered by the old method and its inconsistency from the standpoint of philosophy*

II. THE REALLY PHILOSOPHICAL POINT IN THE RELIGIOUS PROBLEM AND THE RIGHT METHOD OF APPROACHING IT 150

1. *How the philosophical problem should be put if religion is not to be simply a philosophy and philosophy is not to be absorbed in any way by religion*
2. *Of the right method of pinning down the precisely philosophical point of the religious problem*
3. *Of the character and the bearing of the only philosophical conclusions which it is rationally and theologically legitimate to propose with regard to Christianity*

III. THE MUTUAL RENEWAL OF PHILOSOPHICAL AND RELIGIOUS PERSPECTIVES BY A FULLY CONSISTENT DEVELOPMENT OF MODERN THOUGHT 168

1. *How autonomous philosophy has been transposed and defined under the immanent influence of the religious problem*
2. *On the growth of religious awareness through the progress of free philosophy*
3. *The constitution of integral philosophy in integral Christianity*

NOTE: This text is commonly known as *The Letter on Apologetics*. Its correct title is *A Letter on the Requirements of Contemporary Thought and on Philosophical Method in the study of the Religious Problem*. It was first published in *Annales de Philosophie Chrétienne*, January to July, 1896.

It has been laid down recently, in *Annales de Philosophie*,[1] in a discussion about moribund ideas and the development of new ones, that 'scientific apologetics is on the way out', that 'metaphysical apologetics is dead' and that 'nothing is left save moral, psychological and social apologetics which appeals to the innermost needs and the highest aspirations of the soul'. The writer[2] goes on to say that my primary purpose in *L'Action* was 'to put Christian apologetics on a psychological basis'. I agree with him up to a point: science is incompetent, and metaphysics, at least in its traditional form, is inefficacious when we are trying to bring back the men of our time to Christianity. Nevertheless I cannot allow that the proposed method is the only one or even that it has value at all from a purely philosophical point of view or that I have myself undertaken to confine the problem of religion within the field of psychology.

I protest against this allegation which affects the whole approach to religious philosophy, this interpretation which distorts all my thought, and I proceed to explain myself. If this were a purely personal matter I should say nothing. It is painful to be misrepresented, but it is still more painful to protest against another's judgment of oneself and to disagree, on certain points, with dis-

[1] Sept. and Nov., 1895 (pp. 653-6 and pp. 188-90).   [2] Tr. v.p. 123, above.

tinguished persons or beloved masters. But it seems that it would be in the general interest to examine, with all possible rigour and without respect of persons, the legitimate requirements of modern thought about apologetics. So, putting out of mind the persons concerned, I propose to consider those methods of argumentation which seem to me false or defective or insufficient or excessive from the point of view of critical reason even though from other points of view they may have a certain usefulness. If I submit them to a severe examination, this is not for the empty satisfaction of depreciating them or at least of restricting their import, but in order to determine as exactly as possible what conditions must be satisfied, when such delicate problems are in question, by any statement which claims to be strictly philosophical. It is always important not to confuse disciplines which are, in fact, distinct: so I must be forgiven for pointing out to some who suppose that they are philosophizing that they are really doing nothing of the kind, and for shocking, as I doubtless shall, some who are in no doubt about their faith, by my desire not to alienate those who have no other certainty, perhaps, save that of their own incredulity.

It may seem strange to envisage, as it were gratuitously, difficulties which might seem avoidable if one adopted other courses. But the difficulties are real ones. They are obstacles to many of those who have the wit to see them. And they are salutary for us because they compel us, if we face up to them, to raise our thoughts and our hearts to a more lofty conception of Christianity. It must be clearly recognized, then, that we are not seeking easy methods of persuasion; we are trying to see on what terms one can purchase not just a reasonable conviction but one which is strictly and, if I may so put it, technically rational. How is the problem to be presented so that it may be truly philosophical? How can the enquiry be brought to the critical point where the debate can be decided, without falsifying the proper objects either of reason or of faith? How can we restrict the scope and the significance of conclusions which have universal validity and demand philosophical investigation whatever beliefs individual philosophers may hold? Those are the points which must be clarified. One cannot conciliate everybody; for if one tried to make things easy for a wider public, one would run the risk of producing arguments which could not rightly claim to satisfy everybody. So, far from trying to content ourselves with cheap successes, let us seek to satisfy ourselves in the hardest way. Nothing is too much trouble in these matters; and the important thing is not to address believers but to say something which counts in the eyes of unbelievers.

I. THE VARIOUS METHODS OF APOLOGETICS AND THEIR IMPORT

By a rapid review of the various systems of apologetics, beginning with those which have the smallest value and range, we shall be preparing the way for defining the nature of the problem as well as the method which it demands and the sort of solution which it implies. Such systems, to repeat, may have the greatest value from the historical point of view or the moral or the literary or the aesthetic one; all I deny is that they are, in the strong and technical sense of the word, philosophical. This must be made clear.

1. *Of pseudo-philosophy in the service of apologetics*

There is no need, of course, to speak here, since all agree in dismissing them, about the pretensions of certain apologists who suppose themselves to be philosophizing whereas they have only zeal or presumption instead of competence. Yet it is always useful to repeat that there is a wrong way of defending the truth and that, in spite of apparent results, a false method can never give genuine and solid support to religious doctrine.

We must all be more and more persuaded of our obligation to intellectual integrity. There are two sorts of argument: those which satisfy ill-prepared and superficial minds; and those which really satisfy. We must resist those who require from us the wrong sort of arguments; we must resist our own inclinations. Our effort must be to transfer relentlessly from the second to the first of these categories whatever is feeble or insufficient or suspect. We must not discredit ourselves in the eyes of others or allow ourselves to be infatuated by a *pseudo-philosophy*—which is not to be confused with a philosophy which is false: for we can wrong ourselves by resting truths of which we may be, in fact, assured, upon an unsound proof. Here, as elsewhere, the end does not justify the means; and that is precisely the fault which I am pointing out—that of binding up the truth with an erroneous method or an unsatisfactory argument. It is better to be silent than to defend the truth in such a way. When I think of the harm done by foolish friends who disgust truly impartial, legitimately exigent minds by the banality or futility of their reasonings, it seems to me that one cannot be too severe with this pseudo-philosophy.

It will be objected, I know, that many are moved by bad arguments. Is that a reason for using them, even when such people would not be moved so easily by good ones? No—we must be more exigent on their behalf than they are themselves. Apart from the fact that they may discover one day the flaws in the arguments which they once thought sound, we ought never to put forward anything which is not in our own eyes secure against criticism. The duty of intellectual loyalty extends not only to saying nothing which one does not believe to be materially true, not only to establishing truths on the basis of those arguments alone which seem formally valid *to ourselves*, but also in leaving nothing undone to ensure that our claims and our proofs are sound *in themselves*. So it does not matter that certain arguments seem demonstrative to certain untrained minds; we must resolutely refuse to employ them. It is a service which we owe to the truth to deprive it of all bogus supports and to show them for what they are. So much the worse for those who still hanker after them. Those who might have been satisfied by them will be saved from a certain philosophical presumption and may be reached instead by arguments of a very different kind which will not puff them up with empty learning. I hate the infatuation of people who are tough-minded with the tough-minded, who see too clearly to see properly, who are proud of their myopic certainty, who are foolishly indignant at the folly or the intellectual perversity of unbelievers and who, with the bumptiousness of a faith which is bound up with reasons of a too human kind, have neither due respect for souls who are still seeking the light nor a sense of the mysterious profundities of our destiny. It is undesirable that our apologists should be those who are most in need of conversion to the Christian spirit.

2. *Of the improper use of the sciences in the field of philosophy and apologetics*

So far one might hope for general agreement, but what follows will be perhaps less acceptable. In what are called the conflicts between science, metaphysics and religion (I refer not to matters of fact or historical problems but to questions of principle), how many there are who make ingenious efforts to restore harmony between them! How many there are who attach themselves to the findings of the positive sciences as though they were the expression of absolute reality and try to reconcile them with their philosophical opinions or their personal convictions! How many consider that these conceptions about matter, force or physical agents, those which scholasticism has elaborated or (especially) those which the positive sciences are gradually evolving, must be brought into harmony with one another and then form part of an *ontological* explanation and bear witness to the truth of Dogma! I shall perhaps shock a number of excellent people and seem to be absurd in saying that these attempts are pointless. But it must be realized (for, more and more, philosophers who take the data of sensible intuition or the symbols of the positive sciences as materials for their thesis will be disqualified and will not count for those who count) that the time is past when mathematics, physics or biology could be thought to have a direct bearing on philosophy. This is not simply a statement of personal opinion. There is no more continuity between scientific symbols and philosophical ideas than there is between the qualities perceived by the senses and the calculation based on these same data of intuition. If heat as we perceive it in our organs is heterogeneous in regard to the degrees marked by the thermometer or the theories of thermodynamics, there is just as much heterogeneity between physical hypotheses and metaphysical explanations. There is no passage from the one to the other; and the sciences will develop indefinitely without making any contact with what they are mistakenly supposed to signify; for it is no business of theirs to attain or to reveal the final ground of things: their sole task is to constitute an increasingly coherent system of relationships on the basis of their own special conventions, into which a certain element of arbitrariness always enters, and in so far as each of their various hypotheses proves to be in conformity with factual evidence.

Thus to discuss conceptions of mass, of the atom, of affinity and so forth, as if one could derive from the scientific theories which elaborate them some information of immediate relevance for the philosopher, is to waste one's time; worse still, it is to become sterile and to discredit oneself. There is no more agreement or disagreement possible between the sciences and metaphysics than there is between two lines drawn on different planes. When once one has awakened, really awakened, to this truth, which is quite independent of the variety of philosophical opinions, it is impossible to understand how one could have believed the contrary. And then a great deal of time is saved which would have been simply wasted on false problems and a great deal of misdirected effort.

In this sense, then, it is true to say that, so far as philosophy is concerned, 'scientific apologetics is on the way out', indeed that it is dead, that it has never been alive; for, in these matters, what dies is what has never lived. Yet it would be a mistake to suppose that the sciences have no part to play in the solution of the great problems which affect our destiny. If this were the place for it, it would be possible to attempt a whole new philosophy of the sciences so as to show that, although the theories of the positive sciences cannot be taken in any way as the material elements of metaphysical constructions, they are, nevertheless, not arbitrary at bottom or detached from the rest of human life, which forms, as a whole, a single unique problem. A vague awareness of this deep-seated connection explains why so many persist in taking up a false position, although it does not justify their error.

3. Of the pretension of turning facts into apologetic proofs and of the confusion of points of view in apologetics

Turning now with some apprehension to other forms of apologetics, I must indicate at once an essential distinction. Unlike the previous methods' which must be condemned root and branch as both trivial and dangerous, these have a certain value, indeed offer advantages of a high order, and are also easily accessible; in fact, they claim approval, but only on condition that their value is not exaggerated, their character not falsified and their bearing not misconceived. I hope, then, that I shall be forgiven for a frankness which is a mark of my respect for those whose views I am about to examine as much as for the truths which they defend.

On the pretext that 'religion is not only a state of mind, but a fact and a doctrine, and neither dogma nor history belong to the individual consciousness',[1] certain apologists bring their argument to a point from two quite different directions. On the one hand, they disprove the objections of rationalism to the supernatural; and often they confine themselves, on this negative side of the business, to rejecting the pretensions of naturalism. On the other hand, they consider Christianity chiefly as a historical fact to which all the rules for assessing testimony are to be applied. What I wish to say is that the connection which is thus made between these two orders of proof is not an essentially philosophical one, and that, however great the historical value of these proofs may be, it is the conclusion both of reason and of faith that they are not apodeictic as regards the order of revelation; that in consequence it is not within the competence of philosophy to indicate the existence of the supernatural in actual fact and, finally, that if philosophy has *less* competence in the realm of facts than they seem to allow, it claims far *more* in the realm of ideas.

[1] The words of Mgr Baunard, published in the *Annales* for June, 1895, p. 326. Cf. various articles published in the same place by the Abbé de Broglie. I hasten to add that Mgr Baunard considers that 'the rich and profound psychological method' of which I shall speak later should be a preparation for the doctrinal and historical demonstration.

It is well to criticize and to dissipate the negations of rationalism. But is it enough, after that, to examine the history of the great 'Christian fact', if the philosopher's reason is to be ripe for conversion? It is not enough that there should be no impossibility on the one side and certain real facts on the other for the connection between what is possible and these realities to impose itself on my mind, to oblige my reason and to govern my whole life. Why must I take account of these facts when I can legitimately disregard so many other facts which are equally real? How far am I responsible for a voluntary abstention in their regard? These questions remain unanswered, because it is not sufficient to establish separately the *possibility* and the *reality*—it is necessary to show the *necessity* for us of adhering to this reality of the supernatural. Until this connection has been grasped, historical apologetics, although they may have considerable importance for a particular man or for a historian, will have none for a mind which follows the requirements of philosophical method to their legitimate limit.

I go further. Since, by hypothesis, faith is a gratuitous gift, no apologetic, however demonstrative we may suppose it to be, can communicate it or produce it. Philosophy, in agreement with theology in this, will not claim to bring faith to birth in a soul: confined as it is to human methods and natural approaches, it shows (this is its double function) that man cannot disregard the question of faith with impunity, but that he cannot of himself alone put himself in possession of this life which is both necessary for him and inaccessible. Philosophy cannot attach to the supernatural the sort of certainty which it confers on all that it affirms: it cannot therefore pronounce on the question of fact, it can only determine the dispositions which prepare for the understanding of facts and for the practical discovery of truths which emanate from another source.[1]

The proofs are valid only for those who are thoroughly pre-

[1] *Tr.* Père Bouillard comments on this passage as follows: 'when philosophy, according to Blondel, manifests the need for the supernatural, it does not demand that God should reveal himself: it simply reveals the *a priori* by means of which we can grasp and accept the demands of Revelation' (*Blondel et le Christianisme*, Ed. du Seuil, 1961, p. 77—referred to in subsequent notes as 'Bouillard').

pared to accept and to understand them; that is why miracles which enlighten some also blind others. Let us use the strictest language about this: since for philosophy no contingent fact is impossible, since the idea of fixed general laws of nature and that of nature itself is only an idol, since every phenomenon is a special case and a unique solution, there is nothing more in a miracle, if one thinks it out fully, than in the most ordinary events. But equally there is nothing less in the most ordinary events than in a miracle. The purpose of these interventions, which provoke reflection into making conclusions of a more general character by breaking through the deadening effects of routine, is to show that the divine is to be found not only in what seems to surpass the familiar powers of men and of nature but everywhere, even where we are tempted to think that man and nature are sufficient. So miracles are truly miraculous only for those who are already prepared to recognize the divine action in the most usual events. And it follows that philosophy, which would offend against its own nature by denying them, is no less incompetent to affirm them, and that they are a witness written in a language other than that of which it is the judge.

It is therefore asking too much of philosophy to wish to introduce it into questions of detail about the 'Christian fact' and to make it ratify or confirm, in its own way, the autonomous conclusions of historical apologetics. But, on the other hand, it is to ask too little of it if we restrict it to the purely negative function of dismissing the objections of naturalism and procure from it the mere statement of a possibility. If the fact is to be accepted by our minds and even imposed upon our reason, an inner need and a sort of imperious appetite must prepare us for it. How is this expectation to be defined? How is this inner aspiration to be linked up with the truth of the object which will satisfy it? This, unless I am mistaken, is what was called 'bringing existing problems to their proper point',[1] and it was strongly urged that this new and rich approach, which from the analysis of our vital needs promotes the avowal of Christianity's perfect correspondence with them, is that which we should enter upon resolutely in the steps of the master who was referred to in this connection. And it is indeed in this spirit that M. Ollé-Laprune

[1] Cf. *Annales* for Sept., 1895, p. 655.

considers the great 'Christian fact', less as a historian than as a spectator and an actor at the same time, less in its origins than in its whole actual development. Impressed particularly by truths of the moral order and dwelling above all on the personal experience of the inner life, he reveals the profound affinities between Christianity and our human nature, its perfect adaptation to our needs and its internal harmony. He shows it as being desirable and certain because it is attractive and good; as being true and real, not only because it is possible and historically established, but because it is divinely human.

Need I say, even without speaking of the value which it borrows from its user, whom my very gratitude forbids me to praise, how much importance I attach to this sort of proof, this versatile method which, one may say, forces the whole life of the spirit and of the heart to bear its witness? Yet if one examines it closely, does it not contain, once again, in the eyes of the pure philosopher, both too much and too little? Is the link between the natural order and the supernatural defined with the necessary precision? This must be examined.

4. Of the persuasiveness and the philosophical insufficiency of apologetics based on the moral and intellectual fittingness of Christianity

If an analysis of our innermost needs and a thorough investigation of our powers of thinking and of loving leads us to find, in the dogmas proposed for our belief, the harmonious counterpart to them, it must be agreed that this affords a strong presumption in favour of this Christian religion, which thus claims to be a complement to the essential nature of man and its complete satisfaction.

Many of those whom we wish to reach are not capable of having, perhaps not even of understanding, any further requirements. It is possible to show, as did Chateaubriand, that the Catholic spirit is a source of beauty superior to any other, to bring out, despite appearances to the contrary, the fundamental role and the decisive initiative of this spirit in the birth and progress of modern science, to find in the refinements of human affection and generosity, in the joys and even in the sorrows of the human heart, a proof that every upright and developed soul contains an aspiration towards Christianity. It is possible to find in the Gospel the necessary and sufficient principle of moral and social perfection, and to demonstrate the agreement between the Church's teaching and her discipline with the needs of our reason and our will. All these arguments are persuasive and well founded, and I do not wish to depreciate in any way their salutary effects. But in order that they may have these effects, they must be used only where they can find a foothold. And the danger lies in putting them forward as the one properly philosophical argument for the truth of Christianity. A canvas of Raphael's is no defence against the relentless sword of dialectic. So our business now is to discover what our defences are really worth and to arm ourselves, like our adversaries, against ourselves with all the power of reason.

This method of apologetics of which I have been speaking is effective for those who are moved by considerations of a sort which is not strictly philosophical and for those who have tested their faith already in the crucible of rational criticism and preserved it intact and who then delight to see how many admirable consequences can be drawn from the principles on which they have established their thought and their whole life. By the same token it is ineffective or premature for the unbeliever who proposes to take philosophy for his guide and who feels the legitimate need to dig down or to climb up wherever reason will take him. We must not shirk the truth in this matter; we must not claim to take hold of our adversary when in fact we are out of touch with him. We must have the courage to realise this, for it is a fact; we must have the courage to admit it, for the philosophical spirit rightly resists this kind of demonstration. And, in order not to cast justifiable discredit on what we are trying to defend, I feel it incumbent upon me to say, whatever the cost; 'No, that is not essentially philosophical, it cannot be and must not claim to become such'. I go on to give my reasons.

However perfectly expressed and however morally admirable the account may be when such a method is employed, even if one could establish the perfect coincidence of the content of the Christian Revelation with the capacity of the human soul, it remains true that this sort of apologetics considers the supernatural at the outset from the point of view of the natural. It merely exploits the witness of the soul which Tertullian called 'naturally Christian', and it does not radically and necessarily contradict those who accept Christianity as a superior but still human form of morality and doctrine. In short, the very notion of the supernatural remains vague and ambiguous. For consider the strange embarrassments which attend such a position. If one insists on the conformity of dogmas with the requirements of human thought, one runs the risk of seeing in them nothing but a human doctrine of the most excellent kind; if one lays it down at the outset that it surpasses human reason and even disconcerts human nature, then one abandons the chosen ground and the field of rational investigation. Such philosophical apologetics either cease to be apologetics or cease to be philosophical.

It is true that one can explain why Christianity both satisfies and mortifies a man. But then either our natural resistance to the demands of the Gospel is accounted for like that which we oppose to the claims of everyday duty—and in that case we are still on the human level; or else it must be recognized that the supernatural troubles us because it is the supernatural—and then we are faced with the whole question of why this superhuman trouble should be imposed on us as an obligation. In fact, the relationship of this supernatural order with the natural is no more defined on this account than the idea of the supernatural itself. Yet it is this definition which is of supreme importance, since in the end the whole difficulty is to see whether this constraint, which appears to be uncalled for, is not a mere fiction or chimera.

If, then, in the course of a moral analysis or a discourse on religion, one makes a profession of Catholic faith, this declaration remains independent of the dialectical procedure; and then what I would call the formal character of Christian teaching (as opposed to its material content), its demand upon our nature which is both mortifying and necessary at the same time, its inaccessible, impracticable and rebarbative character—in a word, the neuralgic point for the modern mind—has not been touched upon at all.

And it must be added that it cannot be touched upon by this method. For if one tried to begin with the supernatural, treating it as a factual datum, one would be abandoning philosophy. If one tried to produce the supernatural from natural premisses as an apodeictic conclusion, an undertaking which has been condemned under the name of semi-rationalism, one would be abandoning orthodoxy. And if one simply brushed aside these difficulties and tried to produce a really convincing proof by this method, one would abandon both philosophy and orthodoxy. It would indeed be strange to offer philosophers who are hostile to Christianity a doctrine which would be philosophical only if it ceased to be orthodox or would be orthodox only if it ceased to be philosophical —unless it failed to be either at the same time. We may think that people are fundamentally wrong, but we must not play into their hands by the form or method of apologetics which we may think fit to adopt on this or that occasion.

Perhaps it might be objected at this point that there are problems which it is legitimate and even necessary to treat as settled, cases in which it is urgent to accept what is offered us in a provisional way; then, when the account is complete and the solution has been analysed and worked out, the mind can be and should remain satisfied. But it becomes clear that things do not work in such a way in this unique case where the supernatural life is in question when we remember that a man, of himself alone, cannot put himself directly in possession, or remain in possession, of this life which is naturally inaccessible for him; and, if one supposed the problem to be soluble on the human level, finding eventually merely human reasons for justifying the solution, then one would be exposed to the charge of false pretensions. Thus the real reason for adhering to Christian truth, if one used such a method, would be foreign to the method, so that a material element would appear in the conclusions which would not be reconcilable with the formal content. And there, I may remark in passing, is the flaw in Pascal's celebrated argument about the wager.

But I hasten to add that this method, although lacking in demonstrative force for the unbeliever, should be convincing for the believer in a sense which I shall explain. The Council of the Vatican made a distinction, which has been too often overlooked, between those who have received and possess the whole living truth and those who do not possess it or know it only from the outside.

The apostasy of the former is without excuse, but the latter are excusable in their ignorance of Christianity, in their misconceptions of it and in their very opposition to it. That is why it is legitimate to distinguish, as did the Abbé de Broglie, between the use of the reason *before* and the use of reason *after* the act of faith.

And that brings me at last to the singular merit and the solid value of M. Ollé-Laprune's religious writings. Steeped as he is in revealed truth and enriched by its fullness, he has made it part of his own substance, and this has passed from his life into the expression of his thought. The evidence for what he thinks shines out from what he is, and his thought clarifies and justifies his living faith by all the harmony and beauty which it manifests and communicates. Nothing is more decisive or irrefutable than such a witness; nothing is more convincing than the *sufficiency*, if I may so put it, of this living system. There is nothing to add but 'come, see and taste'. When a man has the faith, practises what he believes and embraces in reflection the whole meaning of his belief and his activity, then the circle is closed, there is no room for doubt and the proof is complete.

But to reach this result one must start from the fact of the Christian life—whereas the great need of apologetics today is to start from the fact of a theoretical and practical incredulity. One must suppose the supernatural *as present in one's life*, using a hypothesis which absolutely transcends the philosophical field, if one is to find the expression of it *reflected in one's thought*—whereas one must suppose the supernatural *absent from one's life* in order to show that it is *postulated by thought and action*. And for those who have not the truth, while believing themselves to have it, for those above all who are honestly seeking it, for the beggar and the hungry who stand at the door of the feast, there is something meaningless and even irritating about such an inventory of spiritual treasures, of which they know nothing, or which they consider imaginary, and about the use of unfamiliar language full of complacent sentiments which wake no echo in their own hearts.

But there is something of greater importance to be said by way of ending this discussion. Our reason has not the same lights or the same duties *before* the decisive act of faith and *after* it, but it remains true that the alternatives between which we must choose are bound up with one another. *After* the act of faith, human co-operation remains coextensive with the primary and gratuitous activity of God; thus there is still a natural life to be found even in the supernatural life. *Before* the act of faith, God's secret summons does not leave man's reason and will in a state of legitimate indifference or innocent and definitive neutrality; we must therefore necessarily take account of what might be called the supernatural insufficiency of human nature. And since the refusal of the state to which he is called is not a mere privation for man but a positive falling away, it must be possible to discover, even in a life which is closed against faith, something of what it rejects.

So undoubtedly it is not only desirable in the interests of apologetics for these questions not to be considered simply from the point of view of believers, since (to repeat) it is chiefly important to say something which matters for the unbelieving philosopher, but perhaps it is also more in keeping with the complexity of Christian doctrine, which controls and judges every form of human life, to embrace all minds in one's scope and to theorize about the *absence* of faith in men's souls as well as its *presence*. This becomes all the more necessary when we reflect that by putting ourselves in the place of the unbeliever we are profitably informed about that road which, within faith itself, leads us still more to faith, by showing us on what terms, and at what cost, we acquire it and preserve it.

5. Of the validity of the presumptions in favour of Christianity based on its identity with the laws of life, and of the philosophical and theological difficulties which arise from such an argument if it is supposed to be rationally conclusive

Writing recently about apologetical work in modern conditions or as one reporting other people's ideas, M. le Querdec[1] has pointed out a method which, whatever may have been thought of it, is, in fact, considerably different from the method just discussed and which, above all, whatever he may have supposed himself, is altogether different from that which I myself followed in *L'Action*

[1] see *Annales*, June, 1895, p. 321.

and which I shall define later on. In what does his method really consist? What are its advantages and disadvantages?

In the last section we were considering a method which was concerned above all to show a principle of harmony and light in the faith as that is present to our thought and our life; and it was chiefly in the intellectual order and also in the sphere of morals but finally in that of reflective, retrospective, thought that we observed with joy, as a mark of the truth of Christianity, which reconciles freedom of judgment with the external authority of a dogmatic rule, 'this conformity with the deepest aspirations of human nature'.[1] Now we are to suppose ourselves faced by a soul in search of itself, lacking any rule of thought and, above all, any direction of its life, and we are to see it 'invincibly' led to recognize that 'life cannot be lived without a doctrine of life, since Christianity and in particular Catholicism alone can provide it'. Before Light was being sought through light, *media vita*; now Life is being sought through life, *media luce*.

The advantages of the method thus summarized are manifest. 'All other demonstrations are only aspects and modes of this', since it claims to prove that Christianity *alone* satisfies all the artistic, intellectual, moral and social requirements of mankind. It proceeds by way of elimination, 'driving the opponent from all his positions'; and, since it systematically determines *all* the essential conditions of life, it does more than pile up proofs drawn from the examination of *each* of them, because this complete inventory leaves no loophole for the mind and forms an organized synthesis. Thus it applies the scientific methods of absence and presence; and, embracing the whole complex of life, gathering together its deepest lessons, it does not confine itself to a dialectic of clear thoughts, which is always suspect or incomplete, but makes capital out of all that unconscious labour which goes on at the common sources of both action and reflection. It presupposes, therefore, the effective and instructive testing which is given by action and for which nothing else can supply, all in conformity with the hypothesis of the felt absence or the deliberate refusal of the Christian life.

And yet one must say of this method, as of the previous one,

[1] M. Ollé-Laprune, *La Certitude Morale*, p. 409.

that it does not define, and does not enable a philosopher to define exactly, the relationship of the natural order with the supernatural. Even though it has advantages which the previous method does not offer, it proves to have also certain fresh defects which must equally be pointed out, because it seems to misconceive both certain rights of philosophy and certain necessary susceptibilities of theology.

For can one admit purely and simply what our author calls 'the identity of Catholicism with life', as if Revelation only confirmed and fulfilled nature without bringing with it any new element, any heterogeneous datum, any unhoped for and unsuspected gift?

Can one admit that 'Catholicism is so admirably adapted to the needs of human life that its laws are the very same laws of that life', neither more nor less; as if religious prescriptions merely overlaid, by a sort of geometrical coincidence, the dictates of conscience and the lessons of moral experience?

Can one admit that it is sufficient to juxtapose 'the parallel account of Christian dogma' to 'a thoroughgoing analysis of sensitive, intellectual, moral and social life itself', as if that would not be claiming too much or too little: —too much; for we must not forget that, if Christianity claims to satisfy man's natural needs, it also claims to arouse and fulfil new ones, far beyond anything which we could hope for or suspect, and that the need for the gift, the request for the gift is, like the gift itself, already a grace; —too little; for between these two orders which, I repeat, do not simply coincide, there is a relationship other than a parallelism to be defined, even when we are only preparing to show how each penetrates the other. And so, as before, the relationship of the natural with the supernatural remains undefined, and we oscillate between two extremes without finding the point of adjustment, for, in fine, we can conclude from the fact that Catholicism satisfies all the aspirations of human nature only to its natural human truth; and, if we take it to be supernaturally true, it follows that it is beyond the reach of our premisses.

But there is another more fundamental objection, which stands to the previous ones as cause to effect. M. le Querdec does not take a life which is still closed or alien to the supernatural for what it is any more than the apologists previously discussed, and he does not try to define all the various states and all the possible attitudes of the soul in face of the decisive question, the hidden turning-point of its destiny. Instead of frankly accepting the existence of thought and life which is without faith and grace, and then looking for what is still present in the absence of the supernatural and finding in each individual the criterion of judgment upon each individual, thus keeping to a law of *autonomy*, he tries to show and to add what ought to be there instead of looking only at what is, in fact, there. That is to practise a method of persuasive or prescriptive exhortation, to undertake an analysis of life in order to impose upon it in the end a *heteronomy*, without realising that the extraneous element is not justified philosophically either in its form or in its content.

That is why we hear talk of a mere 'parallelism' between two orders which have quite different origins and, although parallel, are nevertheless made to *converge* in some inexplicable way. And just as one cannot see, in such an account, either what is lacking or what remains to man without the supernatural, so one cannot see what prepares for it, what sustains the acceptance of the gift of grace and what develops its fruitfulness within nature itself.

So instead of constructing a *science*, a science which is applicable to every mind and at all times, a complete science which determines the problem of human destiny, a science which has probative force through the rigour of its dialectic and the universality of its standpoint, our apologists confine 'the *need* of modern apologetics' to the invention of mere makeshifts. They 'bow to the necessities of a new tactical approach'; they give up 'constructing an *apologia sub specie æternitatis*', and leave 'unoccupied' the field of doctrinal apologetics; they grant that 'metaphysics has become useless', and with an inconsistency which indicates the confused nature of these views, after claiming that their method embraces and transcends all the others, they remark that there is another sort of argument, the doctrinal or classical or dogmatic sort which remains in itself the most objective and the most capable of convincing men in general but is not suitable for the 'jaundiced eyes of our contemporaries'.[1]

[1] *Tr.* The phrase was used by George Fonsegrive (v. Blondel, *Le Problème de la Philosophie Catholique*, Bloud et Gay 1932, p. 18), who is criticized here under his *nom de guerre*, Yves le Querdec.

I propose to consider why we should be so sure that the eyes of our contemporaries are jaundiced, whether some of their demands are not just and salutary, whether anything is of value in these matters which does not touch the eternal interests of the conscience, which is a mere matter of tactics or of convenience and which does not penetrate to the basis of our moral being, and finally whether it would be a mistake to think that the old method had or could recover any strictly philosophical efficacity. So here we come to that form of argument which M. le Querdec calls objective or scientific, and which could also be called the doctrinal method of traditional apologetics. What is it? And what is its value?

6. Of the services rendered by the old method and its inconsistency from the standpoint of philosophy

This form of argument, that which is 'always given at the beginning of theology in the treatise on religion' has been rightly summed up for us as follows:[1] 'Reason proves the existence of God. It is possible that he has revealed himself. History shows that he has done so, and it also proves the authenticity of the Scriptures and the authority of the Church. Catholicism is thus established upon a truly scientific rational basis'. More simply still, and without bringing in directly historical evidences which are of another order, one can say that the complete and harmonious account of the truth, with its infinitely rich appropriateness, forms a proof and an excellent one; when it is perfectly understood, it is its own demonstration. In this sense, an anatomy as precise, an inventory as complete, an exposition as well-ordered as that which Thomism offers us of every natural and supernatural *object* of knowledge and of faith is capable of exercising an irresistible force of conviction for anyone who can grasp this powerful synthesis. *Mole sua stat: specie et pulchritudine regnat.* We may add that this supremely harmonious co-ordination of all the elements of the world, human and divine, gives to all who are ready to learn and properly prepared all the benefits of security in its light and of peace in its well-ordered system. When metaphysical and theo-

[1] see *Le Monde*, 20th May, 1895. The report of a conference at Issy on the conditions of modern apologetics.

logical ideas had what one might call their normal and almost automatic sway over men's minds, there being nothing else to fear but heresies, that is to say partial dissensions, it was sufficient to show, beginning with undisputed starting-points, the inner coherence of the truth, multiple in its aspects but single and seamless, like the coat of Christ.

It must be confessed that it is not the same today for most men who think, even for believers. Thomism seems to many an exact but, if I may so put it, a *static* account: as a building-up of elements, but one in which our passage from one to another remains something external to us; as an inventory, but not as an invention capable of justifying advances in thought by the dynamism which it communicates. Once a man has entered this system, he is himself assured; and from the centre of the fortress he can defend himself against all assaults and rebut all objections on points of detail. But first he must effect his own entrance.[1]

And since the thomist starts from principles which, for the most part, are disputed in our time; since he does not offer the means of restoring them by his method; since he presupposes a host of assertions which are just those which are nowadays called in question; since he cannot provide, in his system, for the new requirements of minds which must be approached on their own ground, one must not tend to treat this triumphant exposition as the last word. We are still in the life of struggle and suffering; and to understand this is itself a good and a gain. We must not exhaust ourselves refurbishing old arguments and presenting an *object* for acceptance while the *subject* is not disposed to listen. It is not divine truth which is at fault but human preparation, and it is here that our effort should be concentrated. And it is not just an affair of adaptation or temporary expediency; for this function of subjective preparation is of the first importance; it is essential and permanent, if

---

[1] *Tr.* At this point the reader may need to be reminded that the Thomism of Blondel's time was very different from that of our own, and that he is basing his remarks on 'traditional apologetics' in the *Letter* upon manuals which gave a false impression of scholasticism (see Blondel, op. cit., esp. pp. 27 and 47). It is nevertheless noteworthy that so intelligent and generally well-informed a writer should have been left with such an impression—it was clearly the dominant one.

it is true that man's action co-operates all along the line with that of God.

That is also why we must not be so ready to see nothing but deviations, 'perverted minds' or 'jaundiced outlooks' when we should be considering the great transformations of human perspectives down the ages. Little by little, God's purpose in the governance of humanity emerges from the individual errors, the incomplete views and the particular defects of this mind and that; and what men bring to this process of general development is never negligible or entirely astray from the path where the truth shows forth on our horizon. In our actions and our thoughts there is always something which transcends our intentions and our reflections; and this, although it does not do away with personal responsibility, does make progress possible when true doctrines have become decadent, even through the apparent triumph, for the time being, of false ones: the city of truth is built with the stones piled up against it.

There are two ways of looking at the history of philosophical ideas. Either we remain outside the main stream which sweeps through the world of thought and radically exclude everything which is opposed to the system which we have adopted (for reasons which, judged from our chosen eminence, seem to us sound enough) —and that is to cut ourselves off from the only sort of life which is really fruitful. Or else we try to perceive that stirring of parturition with which humanity is always in labour, we set ourselves to profit by this vast effort, to enlighten it, to bring it to fruition, to kindle the smoking flax, to be less ready to suppose that there is nothing of value for ourselves even in those doctrines which seem most opposed to our own, to go to others so that they may come to us— and that is to find the source of intellectual fruitfulness.

What we do find, from this point of view, if we look at the history of human thought since the time when our doctrinal apologetics, which have not been overhauled fundamentally in the meanwhile, corresponded to the mental climate in which men really live?

At first, that is, when scholasticism was in the ascendant, the natural and the supernatural orders were placed one above the other, but in touch, in an ascending hierarchy. There were three zones, as it were, on different levels: on the lowest, reason was in sole charge, *mundus traditur disputationibus hominum*; on the highest, faith alone revealed to us the mystery of divine life and that of our summons to the feast of God; between the two was a meeting-ground where reason discovered in an incomplete way the more important of natural truths, and these were confirmed and further explained by faith. By thus bearing upon certain common *objects*, these two currents, flowing from different sources, mingled their waters without losing their identities. But there was hardly any thought of examining in a critical spirit what might be called the subjective possibility or the formal compatibility of these two orders.

Soon, however, this dualism began to appear less as a solution than as a statement of the problem, which is, in fact, the great philosophical and religious problem. In a spirit of violent reaction against Aristotelian and Scholastic intellectualism, Protestantism rejected any idea of a rational preparation for faith and began by pulling down the whole edifice of reason and liberty only to build it up again in an independent integrity, no longer regarded as a mere ground floor. Thus there was no longer any middle zone, which might now have become a battleground rather than a meeting-place. The orders were no longer *hierarchically arranged* but merely *juxtaposed* without any possible communication or intelligible relation between them; they were supposed to be united only in the mysterious intimacy of an individual's faith. As a result, when reason, left sole mistress of the knowable world, claimed to find immanent in herself all the truths needed for the life of man, the world of faith found itself totally excluded; juxtaposition led to *opposition* and incompatibility.

Faced by this rationalism which makes immanence the condition of all philosophy, we have to ask whether, in the only order which remains, there does not reappear an imperious need for the other one. I shall be considering shortly the possibility of this and the benefit to ourselves of being thus forced by the new situation to penetrate more deeply into the inexhaustible spirit of Christianity. But it should be obvious already that to lay down without more ado the basic doctrinal affirmations of the thirteenth century is not only to stop up all access to those who think in terms of our own time but also to make a hopeless attempt to recover for one's own mind an equilibrium which has been irremediably lost, which could remain stable only because certain distinctions had not yet been made and certain problems had not yet appeared. To think in our day in precisely the same terms as five centuries ago is inevitably to think in a different spirit.

How far this law of growth and transformation affects even those who ignore it, or suppose that they can evade it, is clear from the fact that an equilibrium which was originally spontaneous becomes, in these conditions, a matter of uneasy compromise. In this dogmatic form of proof, for which reason, history and revealed theology are laid under contribution at the same time, we find a heterogeneity between the data, and it is at once obvious that not only their coherence but their very substance is problematical. And if the synthesis does not work for the minds of our contemporaries with the ease with which it worked heretofore, that is not wholly their fault; for there is, in fact, a doctrinal lacuna to be filled in, which the opponents of Christianity must not be blamed for pointing out to us because, after all, we cannot expect them to regard as sufficient and satisfactory, from the point of view of method, what is, in fact, nothing of the sort.

The artificial and superficial character of this compromise is indicated above all by what was called about the middle of this century 'spiritualism', which became for some 'Christian spiritualism' as though it had not been intended by its author[1] as the one and only religion of the enlightened middle class. This new name is already an old one, and it is perhaps hardly possible or desirable to rejuvenate it. Often what appears new is what ought to grow old, and there are some doctrines which are born old—this seems to be one of them. Compounded at a time when a quite clear and quite sensible philosophy was desiderated by politic persons, as far from the subversive boldness of excessively free thought as from the exigencies of faith in its fullness, this doctrine, which has normally surrounded Christian ideas with a respectful and deadly silence, some

[1] *Tr.* The reference, as Blondel's footnote to this paragraph indicates, is to Victor Cousin.

ᴏ̣ ᴌ̣ᴏ aᴅherents simply admitting them but often in a conventional and watered-down form, this doctrine which deserves the fate of the lukewarm will retain the name of spiritualism in the pages of history. Let it keep the name; traditional philosophy and the fine French language have never recognized it[1].

If, then, doctrinal apologetics, in its old form, leaves intact the problem which seems to us today the very basis of religious philosophy, how is this problem to be put, by what method is it to be approached? What can be said on a subject of such complexity and delicacy which will strike home and remain strictly philosophical?

II. THE REALLY PHILOSOPHICAL POINT IN THE RELIGIOUS PROBLEM AND THE RIGHT METHOD OF APPROACHING IT

If the outworn forms of a supposedly philosophical apologetic no longer make any impression upon the mind of an unbeliever, and if the general movement of modern thought turns more and more against it, this is not, as we have seen, without good reason. We must not complain that the growing weakness of this apologetic is due to an unfair severity on the part of its opponents or that it is a sheer loss or an evil without remedy or even an evil at all—it is not. I should not have undertaken this searching criticism, to which I have felt myself obliged at the risk of disquieting old-fashioned believers or of throwing cold water on their well-intentioned

[1] It is to be found, rarely, in the 17th century as a technical term, and what does it stand for? An abuse of spirituality. Popularized by Eclecticism, it evokes the memory of that School by a legitimate association of ideas, and it shares the discredit into which that School has fallen, so that to use the term is to seem a survivor from 1830, which is no doubt better than to put back the clock to the Middle Ages as we are reproached with doing. Furthermore, it happens that this expression of equivocal origin and doubtful sense seems to have been confiscated by some who hold converse with 'spirits' and are not content to be called 'spiritists', perhaps because 'spiritualists' sounds better. So let us not hanker after the name. Up to Cousin's time those who had better things to talk about than he had dispensed with it. It will be dispensed with after him. It was once believed that it designated Philosophy; it is time to realize that it is only a label. Henceforth it must be confined to the lumber-room.

enthusiasms, if I were not convinced that the crisis of which I speak, though painful for some, will be salutary for all by reason of the fresh insights which it demands and the promise for the future which it holds out.

So it is not sufficient to see that the old positions are no longer tenable. We must profit by the effort of thought which has revealed their weakness and find secure ones instead, borrowing from those who have ruined the weak defences the means of building solid ones. It becomes urgent, then, to determine as exactly as possible: (1) the precise point to which the evolution of philosophical thought has brought the dispute; (2) the method which alone enables one to touch on this decisive point; (3) the character, meaning and bearing of the conclusions to be reached—conclusions in which the most exigent philosopher and the most circumspect theologian will find nothing to blame or to regret.

So, without incriminating anybody, without misconceiving the services which our very adversaries render us, even if involuntarily, but with that intellectual charity which is perhaps the rarest of all, and which by always thinking the best of people often brings it out, let us profit by the beneficent transformation of apologetics which those philosophers who are most alien or hostile to Christianity have made possible and necessary. No good can be done by acting half-heartedly, by making painful and difficult concessions, by coming to forced agreements, as if one stood to lose rather than to gain all along the line. Perhaps, on coming to the end of this inquiry, we may consider that the intensified demands of modern thought are legitimate and profitable, and in conformity both with the philosophical spirit and with the spirit of Catholicism itself.

1. *How the philosophical problem should be put if religion is not to be simply a philosophy and philosophy is not to be absorbed in any way by religion*

In a phrase which must be explained but which indicates at once the seriousness of the conflict, modern thought, with a jealous susceptibility, considers the notion of *immanence* as the very condition of philosophizing; that is to say, if among current ideas there is one which it regards as marking a definite advance, it is the idea, which is at bottom perfectly true,[1] that nothing can enter into a man's mind which does not come out of him and correspond in some way to a need for development and that there is nothing in the nature of historical or traditional teaching or obligation imposed from without which counts for him, no truth and no precept which is acceptable, unless it is in some sort autonomous and autochthonous. On the other hand, nothing is Christian and Catholic unless it is *supernatural*, not only transcendent in the simple metaphysical sense of the word, because there could be truth or beings superior to ourselves which we could nevertheless affirm immanently by the use of our own powers, but strictly supernatural, that is to say, beyond the power of man to discover for himself and yet imposed on his thought and on his will.

Thus, it seems, the chief and indeed the unique aim of philosophy is to assure the full liberty of the mind, to guarantee the autonomous life of thought, and to determine in complete independence the conditions which establish its sway. Can there be, then, any possible connection between philosophy and Christianity, since the one seems to exclude the other? The first step, if their very coexistence is to be conceivable, is to show that they can meet and collide; it will be less difficult to show, after that, that this collision is not possible unless there is agreement at the heart of the conflict. The initial effort, without which no other has any philosophical value, is to indicate the point of encounter—that and nothing else.

If we would lead men to face the question of the Christian life, the question of *everything or nothing*, is it our business simply to stir up in them sentimental aspirations, as found in those rather odd people who are content to keep a mystical consciousness and a scientific one in different compartments, or simply to rouse from the depths of the mind a yearning for the ideal, even if that is a Christian ideal of a vague sort—which is the religion of a number of our contemporaries? No, what is good and useful as a preparation or a means becomes ineffective and dangerous, to say no more about it,

---

[1] *Tr.* It is to be observed that Blondel does not commit himself without reserve to the 'notion of immanence' as here described.

if it is taken to be a satisfactory end. For what we find in ourselves is precisely *not* what we have to receive;[1] and we shall never face the real difficulty by this method, we shall turn our backs on it, for it is not the object or the gift themselves but the form and the circumstances of the gift which form the obstacle. Even if (to suppose the impossible) we were to recover by some effort of human genius the whole letter and content of revealed teaching, we should have nothing, absolutely nothing, of the Christian spirit, because it does not come from us. To have this not as given and received but as found issuing from ourselves is not to have it at all. It is this that scandalizes the reason, and that is what we must fix our gaze on if we are to probe the wound of the philosophical conscience among those of our contemporaries who live a life of thought.

Let us look at it more closely; the wound is deeper still and the scandal greater; and we shall never approach the problem fruitfully unless we see it in its entirety. For to this fundamental intellectual and moral subjection, which requires of a Christian a sort of death in order that he may live, is added a whole series of other trials. 'Let us be clear', we are told, 'that in man's fallen state, the supernatural end being still imposed upon him, whereas he has none of

[1] *Tr.* Blondel thus rejects 'the notion of immanence' in the form in which he referred to it above (see previous note). Commenting on this paragraph (op. cit., p. 33. n.1.), Blondel observes that 'it was perhaps ill-advised to seem to make common cause with the adversaries of the Christian spirit by acknowledging, even provisionally, a tragic conflict between the natural movement of the reason or the will and the gift of grace, since Christianity elevates and completes far more than it humbles and represses. My excuse is my desire not to alienate the unbeliever and the opponent by seeming to give colour to their prejudices. In any case one must not overlook the necessity of an ascesis in the Christian preparation, which aims at giving life to the whole man by subjecting him to a phase of mortification' (note dated 1908). On the same page in a second footnote Blondel comments on the next paragraph of the *Letter*: 'Moreover it is not only our fallen state which explains the necessity for surmounting a spiritual crisis: even in man's original state a trial was imposed before he could be confirmed in the happiness of the supernatural state. Thus there is a fundamental condition which has to be accepted and fulfilled in any circumstances, and it becomes clear that this is a question not of arbitrary contingencies or decrees subsequently enacted but of an element which is essential to the destiny of a creature summoned to participation with the divine' (note dated 1930).

the means necessary to attain it, he is in a truly miserable condition'.[1] Now what is here pointed out in passing, as a *fact* or a truth to be believed among other truths and after other truths, is just what prevents many from believing at all, because here there is a question of *principle*, which controls everything. Here is the gate by which we must enter if we are to be Christians; and to cross the threshold we must admit that we are powerless to save ourselves, but powerful to ruin ourselves for ever, that we are incapable of purifying ourselves, but capable of sullying ourselves irremediably, and that the gift which is gratuitous and free in its source becomes for the subject of it inevitable and obligatory—so that there is no symmetry, it seems, between the alternatives, since what we cannot do of ourselves becomes imputable to us personally if we have not done it, and since a gracious gift turns into a rigorous debt. *Qui autem non habet, et quod videtur habere auferetur ab eo.*

This cruel dilemma is more or less obscurely felt by men and keeps alive in their hearts a sort of hostile unrest or nagging suspicion as if there were at the heart of Catholicism a repellent harshness against which one should rebel in the name of some new ideal of justice and loving-kindness. The fact that these difficulties do not rise to the surface in many cases does not prevent them from troubling consciences; above all, it does not justify us in doubting the sincerity, sometimes haughty but often agonizing and generous, of those on whom they weigh. For most the obstacle is all the more insurmountable in that they cannot clearly see it: and so it is a service of the first importance to show it to them plainly and not to cast stones at those who are held up by it. For if they are 'sick' it is the great and inevitable sickness of man before God from which they suffer, the supreme human sickness.

In fact, it is only on condition of envisaging this sickness in its full extent that one can succeed in asking the right question—which is the essential aim, the capital point. If Christianity were a belief and a way of life added to our nature and our reason as something optional, if we could develop in our integrity without this addition and we could refuse deliberately and with impunity the crushing weight of the supernatural gift, there would be no intelligible con-

[1] M. Ollé-Laprune, *Le Prix de la vie*, p. 356.

nection between these two levels, one of which, from the rational point of view, might just as well not exist. Not to climb upwards would not be to fall down; and to renounce the higher vocation would be simply to remain on the lower level where men could grow spontaneously—so that no philosophical problem about a Revelation could conceivably arise. But as soon as this Revelation seeks us out, so to speak, on our own ground and pursues us into our inner fastnesses, as soon as it regards a neutral or negative attitude as a positive backsliding and a sort of culpable hostility, as soon as the poverty of our limited being can contract a debt which must be paid for in eternity, then the encounter takes place, the difficulty stares us in the face and the problem is set. For if it is true that the demands of Revelation are well-founded, then we are no longer simply on our own ground; and there must be some trace of this insufficiency, this impotence, this demand in man simply as man,[1] and an echo of it even in the most autonomous philosophy.

Is it now clear on what ground the debate must be engaged and that the real problem differs *toto genere et tota natura* from the efforts which are made to dress up dogma in a way which should make it luminous and attractive for our reason, that it is not a question of dealing with this or that particular point or of presenting a system of doctrine historically defined, that the philosopher is not concerned here with questions about facts or individuals, that it is not the problem of believing in certain truths but the problem of faith in its formal and integral aspect, in a word, that it is a question of seizing whole and entire the indivisible kernel of the difficulties which, unless they are solved, will leave us without any possible Christianity? Above all, is it now clear that, unless one goes to the furthest limits of the most precise and most searching demands of

[1] *Tr.* This demand, as Père Bouillard has found it necessary to point out (p. 74, n. 2—against H. Duméry), is not a demand in man *for* the supernatural but the demand made upon man *by* the supernatural. When Blondel speaks of 'man simply as man', Bouillard continues, he is not considering the theological hypothesis of a 'state of pure nature', but man as he is today (p. 74, n. 3—Blondel has pointed this out himself, op. cit., p. 38, n.): 'the *Letter* is addressed *directly* to believers . . . to explain to them the legitimate requirements of philosophers, and then to show *indirectly*, to philosophers . . . the rational character of Blondel's undertaking' (p. 75, n. 3).

full Catholicism, there is not even any means of rationally conceiving the meeting or the coexistence of a religion which is not simply a human construction and a philosophy which does not abdicate and become absorbed into the ineffable? One can indeed defy anyone who does not envisage these searching demands in all their profundity to propose the essential problem of religious philosophy without destroying either the very notion of religion or that of philosophy.

2. *Of the right method of pinning down the precisely philosophical point of the religious problem*

The bold and successful move which it now seems indispensable for us to make in our own defence is to have recourse to the 'method of immanence' and to apply it to the full, with an inflexible rigour, to the examination of human destiny: nothing else will define the difficulty and nothing else will resolve it; and then the solution, like the problem itself, becomes possible only by forcing us to be equally faithful to philosophy and to orthodoxy, or rather by forcing philosophy, like orthodoxy, to remain faithful to itself.

In what does it primarily consist? Does it consist in declaring straightway that man can find, of himself and in himself, all the truths necessary for his life and that his whole salvation comes from himself alone? That would be to prejudge the question and to begin with an answer to it. Does it consist in adopting the critical standpoint (which in fact is not critical enough) and in excluding any transcendent reality and making human subjectivism into an absolute? That would be an infidelity to the method which one pretends to be adopting by making use of an ambiguity in the words 'immanent' and 'transcendent' of which we must take careful note: for our idea of transcendent truths or beings, whether real or imaginary, is always immanent in so far as it is our own; and before we can pronounce upon the significance of what we are thinking it is important to decide what in fact we are thinking; that is, we must go over the whole series of our inevitable ideas and their necessary implications apart from the mutilations or partial restrictions which the superficial intervention of our reflective decisions seems to bring about when we are preoccupied with moral and ontological problems. The method of immanence, then, can consist in nothing else than in trying to equate, in our own consciousness, what we appear to think and to will and to do with what we do and will and think in actual fact—so that behind factitious negations and ends which are not genuinely willed may be discovered our innermost affirmations and the implacable needs which they imply.[1]

If the meaning of modern philosophy escapes so many who have not lived the life of their own age but in the past, if so many current doctrines seem to them vague or enigmatic, this is doubtless because they have quite failed to grasp the principle of this method, which has become and will be more and more the soul of philosophy. They sometimes complain that philosophy has become an affair of technical subtleties, confined to initiates; what must be allowed (but it is no ground for complaint) is that philosophy is becoming more and more a field of knowledge specifically distinct from others— and therefore a technical one. And its special business is to criticize all the phenomena which make up our inner life, each one in the light of the others, to adjust them, to study the connections between them, to show all their implications, to discover what principles are presupposed by thought and by action, to define on what conditions we may ascribe reality to the objects or the means of salvation which are inevitably conceived by us, to study (for example) our idea of God, not just as God, but in so far as it is our necessary and effective thought of God, or again to analyse the conception which we are led to form of revealed beliefs and practices, not just as religious and redemptive Revelation, but in so far as we can see them as answering to our needs—in short, without attempting to add to this conception what it cannot give us.

Thus the immanent affirmation of the transcendent, even of the supernatural, does not prejudge in any way the transcendent reality of the immanent affirmations—a radical distinction which no one, perhaps, has preserved with complete consistency, and which enables us to construct in a scientific manner, without distracting preoccupations or fruitless or premature discussions, the entire phenomenology

[1] *Tr.* This paragraph and those which follow are intelligible only in the light of Blondel's *L'Action* (1893)—see Introduction, pp. 83 f.

of thought and of action. It is the only distinction which is capable of securing the mutual independence of the two orders and it is, moreover, in conformity with the very letter of the dogma which maintains the pure liberality of the author of grace together with the obligation laid upon us men. Formally identical with objective faith, subjective faith is entirely at the mercy of rational criticism, while objective faith remains untouched.[1]

It remains to show—perhaps to the surprise of certain philosophers and equally of certain theologians—that the only possible religious philosophy, which is truly religious and truly a philosophy, results from these principles.

For when we study the close-knit system of our thoughts, it becomes apparent that the very notion of immanence is realized in our consciousness only by the effective presence of the notion of the transcendent.[2] The idea of an absolute intellectual and moral auto-

[1] *Tr.* Even in the light of *L'Action* this paragraph is, on the face of it, baffling. Père Bouillard (pp. 112-13) explains it by referring to Blondel's letter of August 19th, 1896, to Père Semeria in which 'subjective faith' stands for 'the system [*l'enchaînement*] of phenomena . . . which, in default of a known and defined *credo*, offers to every soul of good will and in a form which cannot be precisely determined that "baptism of desire" which is always possible and necessary for salvation.' Blondel goes on to say in this letter: 'My sole aim is to describe the subjective dispositions and the practical attitude of a sincere mind, of a soul which is consistent [*conséquente*] with itself. And if we happen to have knowledge already of what I have called "objective faith", that is, of revealed truth defined by the Church's authority, philosophy has no right to make use of this knowledge and to introduce it into the series of its own autonomous affirmations: it can only register the fact that these data . . . correspond with an incomparable precision to its own demands [*appel*] and its own needs' (*L.P.*, p. 93). Thus, as Père Bouillard remarks, (p. 113, n.) 'subjective faith', which receives the offer of the supernatural only in an undetermined way—not as determined by the Christian Revelation, is not identical in *content* with 'objective faith'. He thus sums up the matter (p. 108): 'The Christian notion of the supernatural order is relevant to philosophy only in so far as it appears as the ultimate determination of the undetermined idea which arises in every man, even in the absence of Christian teaching'.

[2] *Tr.* Blondel (op. cit., p. 35, n.), commenting on this passage, points out that he is emphasizing the need for transcendence in all our thought—'without it', he says, 'we should not be aware of anything, we should not have the least notion even of the relative' (this must not be taken to mean that we know things only 'in

nomy is conceivable only on condition of our conceiving also, and necessarily, of a possible heteronomy. And if the method of immanence is confined to determining the dynamism of our experience, without pronouncing in the first place on its subjective or objective significance, it is simply a matter of analysing this inevitable idea of a dependence of human reason and human will with all the consequences which it implies. Then there would be no longer any ground for saying that the problem of the supernatural, resulting as it does from the hidden workings of thought which I have just indicated, is inconceivable or inadmissible or unphilosophical; on the contrary, it is the very condition of philosophy as it is now presented in its intransigent independence. And this movement of free thought and exclusive rationalism, becoming fully conscious of itself and reaching, so to speak, the very end of its course, was precisely what was required so that there should arise as a philosophical hypothesis the religious thesis on which this whole movement logically depends, so that one may see clearly what its very existence implies. It is when it is fully developed that it becomes most clearly incomplete. Thus we are in line with the defenders of the rights of reason and in a state of philosophical grace. And, at the same time, we are on safe ground in regard to theology.

But here we have to watch our step. If we are to remain consistent with ourselves in this task of integration, we must always remember that we must not go beyond the demands of our own consciousness, that the supernatural will not remain in conformity with the idea which we conceive of it unless we acknowledge it to be beyond our human grasp, and that in determining the genesis of the idea of revelation, or in showing the necessity of dogmas or of

---

God'). He goes on to distinguish this general necessity for transcendence from a 'second stage' in which we establish that 'our real idea of a transcendence implies the acknowledgment and the effective presence of that which is not reducible to anything which we can produce or extract *ex nobis*, even when we discover a certain effect, a certain clarity, *in nobis*. And this shows the legitimacy of a further question: can the absolutely inaccessible, naturally inscrutable and fundamentally ungraspable transcendent reveal itself and give itself to us supernaturally, and on what conditions?'

revealed precepts, we never do anything more than indicate blank spaces which cannot be filled in or established in their reality by any resource of ours. Even when we show that this system of rational requirements rests upon the most concrete living experience, and even when we determine the conditions which seem to us necessary if what we think and will is to *exist*, it is not our philosophy, integral though it may be, which will produce, as in a seedbed prepared for it, being itself, the living truth, the gift which brings salvation. And it is just by the acknowledgment of this impossibility that philosophy is reconciled with theology.

For both faith and reason teach that the supernatural must be humanly inaccessible. What faith imposes upon us as a reality, reason conceives as necessary but impracticable for us. The one declares to be gratuitously given what the other can only postulate inevitably, so that they coincide not by overlapping but because one is empty and the other full.[1] Even when their affirmations seem to cover something of the same ground *sub specie materiae seu objecti*, they remain radically heterogeneous *vi formae*. And perhaps one must consider that even the rational truths which are ratified or consecrated by Revelation have, under their theological aspect, a bearing quite other than that which they have under their philosophical aspect,[2] because doubtless one cannot realize absolutely the total ordering even of natural things without at least an implicit reference to him who is called by St Paul *primogenitus omnis creaturae, in quo constant omnia*, and of whom it is said that without him all that has been made by him would return to nothingness.

To sum up, theology cannot allow philosophy to reach the reality of the supernatural order, or to deny its truth or to admit its intrinsic possibility (which would be again both too much and too little), or to declare itself indifferent and alien to it, or to juxtapose itself to it, judging itself sufficient and satisfied in its enclosed

---

[1] *Tr.* Blondel (op. cit., pp. 48-9) points out that such metaphors are unsatisfactory both as suggesting that we can prepare for the supernatural in a too positive way and by seeming to overlook the necessary co-operation of our natural powers with the work of grace.

[2] *Tr.* Blondel gives the impression of thinking that this was an unusual suggestion. In fact it is a theological commonplace.

inviolability. There is only one relationship required—that which is determined by the method of immanence, which considers the supernatural not as a historic reality, not as simply possible like an arbitrary hypothesis, not as optional like a gift which is proposed but not imposed, not as appropriate to our nature and belonging to it as its supreme development, not as so ineffable as to lack all foothold in our thought and our life, but (with the precision of the scientific spirit, which is concerned neither with the merely possible nor with the real and should give us nothing more nor less than the necessary) as indispensable and at the same time as inaccessible for man.

Yet to speak of *necessity* may seem to make a dangerous connection between the two orders and to bring the freedom of the divine gift within the system of human action in a way which is illegitimate.[1] It is not really so, and in forestalling this fear we shall be led to explore more deeply our own solution.

3. Of the character and the bearing of the only philosophical conclusions which it is rationally and theologically legitimate to propose with regard to Christianity

1. To say that the method of immanence, like all methods of a scientific character, shows us nothing more nor less than the 'necessary' is not to use the word in an ontological sense as if it were a question of absolute existence or of truths whose contraries would imply contradiction; it is merely to observe that our thoughts are inevitably organized in a close-knit system, and it is this determinism, underlying as it does even the use of our freedom, which makes it possible to constitute philosophy as a science. Thus to say that the supernatural appears as 'necessary' to the philosopher and as inaccessible at the same time is not really to misconceive the liberality of the

---

[1] *Tr.* Blondel (op. cit., p. 37, n. 2, dated 1910), after remarking that he has been so often misunderstood as claiming a demand for Revelation in man, adds the following comment: 'But once charity has determined to summon men to the supernatural, there is a concrete logic which requires a real coherence and, in the words of Deechamps, "God owes it to himself not to leave his work of loving-kindness in a half-finished state" '.

giver, or to compromise the freedom of the receiver, or to do away with the gratuitous character of the gift, or to deny the possibility, for man, of remaining ignorant of the means of grace while yet sharing in a hidden way the efficacy of that which he does not know, or to deny that a neutral state is conceivable in which a man has not been called upon to use his reason or to receive as a pure grace the communication of the mediating power;[1] still less is it to bring the reality of the supernatural order within the determinism of nature. *What*, then, is necessary?

What is necessary is that, in some form which cannot be defined to cover particular cases, the thoughts and actions of each one of us together make up a drama which cannot reach its conclusion unless the decisive question arises, sooner or later, in the consciousness. Each one of us, simply by using that light which enlightens every man coming into this world, and by the use of his own resources, finds himself called upon to pronounce upon the problem of his destiny. For, in order to make the simplest considered affirmation about the reality of the objects which make up our thoughts, in order to produce deliberately the most elementary of those acts which enter into the determinism of our wills, we must reach implicitly the point at which the option becomes possible (at which, in default of any other enlightenment, it becomes necessary and decisive) between the solicitations of the hidden God and those of an egoism which is always evident enough.

So without there being *real* continuity between the sphere of reason and that of faith, without in any way bringing within the determinism of human action the order of supernature, which is always beyond the capacity, the merits and the demands of our nature or any conceivable nature, it is legitimate to show that the development of the will constrains us to the avowal of our insufficiency, leads us to recognize the need of a further gift, gives us the aptitude not to produce or to define but to recognize and to receive it, offers us, in a word, by a sort of prevenient grace, that baptism of desire which, presupposing God's secret touch, is always accessible and necessary apart from any explicit revelation, and which, even

---

[1] *Tr.* Again (cf. note, p. 104) there is no ground for supposing that Blondel is envisaging 'the state of a pure nature' as a theological hypothesis.

when revelation is known, is, as it were, the human sacrament immanent in the divine operation.

And if, indeed, for those who can be instructed only by nature, there are substitutes for the supernatural act, this is again a consequence of that secret requirement which brings everyone necessarily face to face with the data of the problem and with the means of resolving it: certainly man does not find in himself alone the whole solution; and it does not follow from the fact that he does not always need to recognize it distinctly that he does not always need the efficacy of a real mediation. But, finally, if the law of action *sine addito* seems to break down, it is because our action contains of its nature a point of insertion. We can be responsible for a refusal only if we are intimately disposed and constrained by our very sincerity to will and to accept that which it is always possible but not legitimate to thrust aside—and which we can never suppress. There is an ineffable and unsuspected overplus in the gift which we receive, and 'yes' provides infinitely more than the mere contrary of 'no'; but it remains true that 'no' damages this point of insertion and the natural requirements of the soul.[1] For if our nature is not at home with the supernatural, the supernatural is at home with our nature; so it is inevitable that the titles of naturalization which it gives us should never disappear without trace; to turn away from one's destiny is not to free oneself from its control. That is the meaning of the *necessity* which connects these two heterogeneous orders without infringing their independence. And so we must reject the complaint that we are making any confusion or committing any trespass here, and point out that by any other method our critics would strain or break those very delicate relationships which philosophers and theologians are equally concerned to respect if they are not to run the risk of implying either a real continuity or a formal incompatibility between philosophy and theology.

2. Here, then, as in all cases where our method requires scientific necessity, the reality or rather the realization of what is proposed as necessary is subordinate to another factor which is alien to science: only practical action, the effective action of our lives, will settle for

[1] *Tr.* What is 'naturally required' is that the soul should 'open itself' to the reception of a gift, the character of which remains at this stage undetermined.

each one of us, in secret, the question of the relations between the soul and God. Thus from the very meaning which this hypothetical necessity proves to have it follows that the legitimate scope of philosophical conclusions stops short at the threshold of that real operation in which alone the human act and the divine act, nature and grace, can unite. Philosophy therefore remains and cannot but remain on this side of that mysterious marriage; and it remains for us to gain a full understanding of this restriction with all that it implies.

For from presupposing the Christian life or infused faith, what we have to do, if I may borrow theological terms which will convey my thought on this point, is to address not only those who may belong to the body of the Church, not even only the unknown multitude of those who belong to her soul,[1] but everyone indifferently. Nothing counts as philosophical which does not precede, embrace and transcend these distinctions. For we have not to impose any prescriptive formula on consciences or any imperative rule, but rather to make a complete study of their possible attitudes so as to unearth the 'immanent' springs of conduct and the 'necessary' consequences. Only the simple recognition of what they actually are and how they actually behave will make our teaching fruitful for them.

Not only must we work out a universal and abstract theory of the real absence or the hypothetical presence of the supernatural in men's souls, but we must also sedulously avoid any concrete and particular application of our formulae and conclusions, however exact they may be in themselves. For we never know exactly what is required in particular circumstances or for a particular conscience, or what the sufficient substitutes may be in each case. The precept 'you shall not judge' is without exception in these matters. Perfect justice coincides here with perfect charity.

And that is not all. Since philosophy, even when it constructs a complete science of the practical, cannot touch that incommunicable knowledge which only the practical itself provides, since, even when studying the supernatural, it cannot pronounce on its actual

---

[1] *Tr.* This distinction between the soul and the body of the Church has been very properly replaced in our time by the distinction between those who are visibly united and those who are invisibly united with the Church.

presence or its historicity or its operations here and now, it becomes possible to discuss questions which concern religion of the most positive kind without making this religion itself a matter of dispute, without pronouncing on what it offers or trespassing on its preserves. And the serenity of such a discussion can remain even when a free inquiry leads to diverse conclusions; for those who claim to belong to the Church's body must not cut themselves off from her soul by cutting off from it those who perhaps belong to her soul but not to her body.

It follows again that, even in the heart of a Christian society, and even when one has before one's eyes the whole organism of Christian dogmas and Christian precepts, one must continue to respect with all scrupulousness the limits of philosophical investigation. Undoubtedly this great spectacle is incomparably instructive for determining the insufficiencies of our nature and for indicating the fulfilment of our rational requirements and aspirations, but it is all the more necessary to resist the temptation of confusing disciplines and competences, and of *rediscovering* rather than actually *discovering*. For, in the sense in which the expression is ordinarily understood, 'Christian philosophy' does not exist any more than Christian physics: philosophy, that is to say, is applicable to Christianity in so far as Christianity exercises, in the last analysis, control and judgment even over men who are ignorant of it or reject it.

Is there, strictly speaking, a philosophical apologetics? Yes and no—No, if this means that philosophy lends its services and, so to speak, commits itself in advance, or that its conclusions can be homogeneous or continuous with those of theology or subordinate to them, or if it is expected to take account of claims which exceed its competence or to sacrifice, even on a single point, its method and its scientific autonomy. Yes, if it means that, while entirely distinct from other forms of apologetics by reason of the question which it asks and the bearing of its answers, it and only it is capable of clearing away the fundamental objections, of determining the nature of the supernatural and of throwing clear light on the requirements and insufficiencies of our nature.[1]

[1] *Tr.* Blondel, in reproducing this passage (op. cit., p. 39), omits the misleading phrase 'determining the nature of the supernatural' and substitutes 'thus making

Now that a context has been prepared for them which protects them from their peculiar inconsistencies, we could find room once more for several of those apologetical methods which we had to criticize. But, after all, if there is one which deserves to be called philosophical to the exclusion of all the rest, it is that which follows reason to its furthest limits and admits no heterogeneity which it does not itself see to be the guarantee, the consequence or the extension of its own autonomy.

There are two ways of philosophizing, we may say, although there should be only one by rights: one which does not really go back to the ultimate questions, although it purports to do so, and develops dialectically by using principles which have not been dialectically established (as, for example, deduction when used as an ancillary and incidental process in the inductive sciences); and this way of philosophizing might be called 'philosophoid'; another which forms an integral system of notions which are all equally subject to critical examination, without intrusive elements and with its own proper bases and its relative sufficiency. Now philosophy, that which is really 'philosophical', can never overlap other forms of apologetics any more than it can allow them to enter its own territory. Does this mean that its conclusions are uncertain or vague or imperfect, and that reason cannot make any conclusive or apodeictic statement in these matters? Far from it: it means, on the contrary, that philosophical reason must formulate rigorous, scientifically determined conclusions, and therefore it must be maintained with scrupulous exactness that the real and effective synthesis of nature with the supernatural comes about only through effective action, and by grace; hence a concordat between philosophy and dogma, on the one hand, and historical or moral or 'philosophoid' forms of apologetics, on the other, involves a heterogeneous element which is not amenable to rational criticism.

Does this suggest a return to what has been called 'separated philosophy' in a disguised form? The whole argument up to this

precise *a contrario* the nature of the supernatural' (pointed out by Père Bouillard, p. 207, n.). In an attached footnote he refers to the incomplete conception of Christian philosophy suggested by the *Letter* (see Introduction, p. 106).

point should refute that idea because, instead of putting aside the religious problem, our whole effort has been to show that it cannot be eliminated, and that philosophy is not free, is not complete, is not itself, unless it envisages it in its most acute and pressing form. But there is a claim to be made on behalf of philosophy which must be respected. Theologians do not permit philosophers to trespass upon their domain: they are right, for they should not and cannot do so; but it follows, and this must be recognized, that philosophers, if they really know their business, should not and cannot allow theologians to enter their own field; the distinction cuts both ways, and the domain of each science remains inviolable. Just as the knowledge of the positive sciences can produce nothing which is formally incompatible with metaphysical doctrines (these belonging to another order), so properly philosophical assertions, as we have seen, cannot legitimately impinge on points which only Revelation can determine. It is good to warn anyone who is not enough of a theologian or enough of a philosopher not only to understand the true solidarity but also to accept the necessary independence of the two realms that he is running a great risk if, possessing as he does by his faith what is immutable and absolute, he claims to bring into the field of philosophical discussion and to impose on human reason expressions, formulae and doctrines which are mutable and perfectible in their human significance. One must never bring down from heaven, on the plea of analogy, solutions which can only be deceptive and tyrannical when their meaning and their implications have been transposed into another register; nothing is more irritating than to use words with an overtone of metaphysical meaning, talking down to people as if from the clouds of heaven, or to say 'speaking as a Catholic' when, with a piously egotistical zeal, and without charity for the only enemies whom we should recognize as such, a man takes upon himself the infallibility of the whole mystical Body and extends it for his own purposes to everything on earth. No, philosophy cannot be a mere instrument or a means; together with it and for the sake of it, theology accepts that conclusion, and it will not charge it with unjust burdens.

Only on this condition can it be effective; it is fruitful and plays its full part as a precursor only if it is free and impartial. It stands for man's part, and nothing but man's part, in the drama of life; but this part is essential. As St John shrank from baptizing Christ, but it was required of him so that human action and divine action should coexist, so reason and nature remain immanent in grace. Let no one, then, suppress them. Just as pleasure is all the better when it has not been sought, just as charity is all the more lovely when it contains no element of pious calculation (even the unselfish intention of being a good advertisement for piety), so philosophy will serve all the better the cause for which some would make it unduly responsible by not turning itself into an apologia. And if it is true that it cannot develop its complete autonomy without facing the religious problem, neither can it touch it fruitfully save at the price of an intransigent and jealous discretion which is both the avowal of its incompetence and the safeguard of its dignity. *Non libera nisi adjutrix, non adjutrix nisi libera philosophia.* We must claim this liberty for philosophy in all its fullness.

Nevertheless I shall not be failing in the disinterestedness which is required by scientific research if I show, in the latter part of this essay, how an apparent conflict between autonomous thought and the preoccupations of apologetics has, in fact, provided advantages for both sides.

III. THE MUTUAL RENEWAL OF PHILOSOPHICAL AND RELIGIOUS PERSPECTIVES BY A FULLY CONSISTENT DEVEL-OPMENT OF MODERN THOUGHT

We must now face the fact that the question of method which we have had to raise here as a particular problem is at bottom a quite general and essential question of philosophical doctrine. For it seems that only a thoroughgoing renewal of both method and doctrine can take full advantage of the great movement of human thought which has been taking place during the last five centuries. So I should like to offer a summary of the teaching which those centuries have bequeathed to us so as to show that it is neither desirable nor possible to ignore it, but also, and above all, so as to determine the conditions which must be satisfied by any undertaking, if it is to be both philosophical and apologetical at the same time and is not to condemn itself to sterility at the outset.

So far I have considered the problem of religious philosophy only as a difficulty limited to a special sphere; it must now be shown that this problem, far from being a subordinate and restricted one, determined by conditions which are independent of it, is itself the presiding and determining one: from this more commanding point of view all the criticisms and all the requirements which we have to set forth already will be enhanced or intensified. For if we are to profit by the beneficent renewal of perspectives opened to us by a fully consistent development of modern thought, we must renounce certain ancient philosophical errors once for all and not confine ourselves to putting new patches on old garments. It is true that one cannot touch these outworn envelopes without seeming to lay violent hands on those essential truths which, for the time being, they happen to contain and without making oneself an object of suspicion for so many people who confuse their scholastic prejudices with the cause of which they make themselves the privileged champions. But, however painful such suspicions may be, we must not be deterred by them; we must even fear, in advancing our criticisms, lest we fall into that flattering discretion which Aristotle calls εὐτραπελεία, and we must enter boldly upon the frankest possible account of our position with the liberty of a philosopher even in these delicate matters and to the fullest possible extent.

So to those who try to put back the clock or who ignorantly protest against modern thought or keep always just behind it, dragged on, as it were, at the chariot wheels of their opponents, or who try to restore ancient Reason or ancient Philosophy on their previous foundations, or who consider enigmatic or needlessly complicated the new methods of philosophizing which they do not try to understand and so declare to be unintelligible, hoping to achieve their ends by simpler methods—to all these I cannot refrain from saying with all possible emphasis: 'No, your task is an impracticable one; your project is an illusory one; your intervention merely hinders progress.'

Perhaps this vigorous language will seem less offensive to them if they conceive as possible, beyond the misunderstandings and the existing conflicts which so rightly distress them, the mutual renovation and reciprocal promotion of philosophic thought and the Christian spirit. If they would only rise above all movements of merely obstinate reaction or attachment to the past (especially their own past), all temporary expedients, provisional concessions, dialectical artifices, interested arguments, bogus palliatives, prudent reserves and tacit postulates! They must give up objecting that anyone who contests their principles fails to understand them or that theological certitudes can and ought to dispense from philosophical dissatisfactions. Things have now reached a point at which one has no longer the right, if one wants to be both a philosopher and a Christian at the same time, to start off covertly on the basis of one's faith and then pretend to reach it for the first time, and one can no longer keep one's beliefs discreetly at a distance from one's own thinking. And it is no longer a question of one's personal attitude, of settling one's own conscience, or of a state of mind confined to certain persons or certain times, or of a particular psychological or moral crisis of any kind, or even of a general but limited problem of metaphysics. We are faced with a permanent and profound transformation within the constitution of philosophy as a whole, and my desire is to show why this must produce both a religious development for philosophical thought in its entirety and a human development for the religious consciousness and for the very understanding of Christianity.

It is not that I propose to enter into any corner of the theological reserve or to compromise in any way, after jealously defending it, the autonomy of strictly human thought. In speaking of the advance of the religious consciousness, I mean that certain truths become clearer, not *in themselves* but *in us*; indeed it is because they are immobile in themselves that humanity, like a marksman continually advancing to a fixed target, cannot envisage them except in a continual movement. I want to show (1) that philosophy has been transformed little by little and determined precisely in itself by the misunderstood and rejected activity of the Christian idea; (2) that the requirements of religion will be better satisfied, in the end, than they have ever been by the development of doctrines which seemed at first directly opposed to them; and (3) that after a secular misunderstanding, caused by the notions of a false Christian philosophy and a false rationalism of an exclusive and inconsequent kind, there must arise the only sort of philosophy which is compatible with Catholicism or rather, to speak in absolute terms and in a precise and scientific sense, philosophy itself—and that this is not to go outside the field of strictly rational study or to break the necessary continuity of the dialectical process: for philosophy exists only where the problems are homogeneous, free from intervention from outside or foreign elements, and where the development of these problems is complete, without lacunae and without reservations.[1]

1. How autonomous philosophy has been transposed and defined under the immanent influence of the religious problem

My words will seem scandalous, and to justify them I must say this: 'On the one hand, philosophy has never been exactly delimited so far and, therefore, never scientifically constituted: the difference between what it has been and what it is in process of becoming will appear, perhaps in the near future, as great as or greater than (*mutatis mutandis*) that between physics before and after the 16th century, or that between chemistry before and after the 18th century. On the other hand, and with all the more reason, there has never been yet, strictly speaking, a Christian philosophy; what goes under that name does not deserve it at all, either from the philosophical or the Christian point of view; if there can be one which fully deserves it, then it is still to be constituted. And the two problems are bound up with one another or even are one problem.' The unfamiliarity of these theses should not evoke protest before one has faced the reasons which support them: one must consider that a few centuries are a short time in the history of ideas and in the growth of the Christian spirit among man, and that such an evolution must be looked at from

[1] *Tr.* Blondel (op. cit., p. 40, n. 1) characterizes the historical section which follows as 'too cavalier and pretty artificial', and issues a general warning in regard to it as being likely to mislead the reader at certain (unspecified) points. It should be read, therefore, rather as illustrating Blondel's own philosophical position than as a piece of pure history.

a height sufficient for the discernment of those great general movements which are obscured by the details of individual efforts and in the turmoil of conflicting doctrines.

I therefore propose to indicate very rapidly:

first: how the very conception of reason and philosophy which has been accepted by scholasticism as a heritage from the past is responsible for all the attacks against the Christian idea since this conception became current;

second: how the mere presence of Christianity forced this rationalism, at first improperly submissive to it, then illegitimately hostile to it, to work itself out and to transform itself according to its own law of development;

third: how the evolution of this hostile philosophy, apparently spontaneous and increasingly autonomous, leads it, the more it progresses, to define itself or, if one may so put it, to undergo a conversion in just that way which Christianity would desire for it, since, in fact, Christianity has presided invisibly over its inception.

First: When we examine the principles or postulates on which scholastic philosophy is based and the type of problem which it discusses we see that it is first and foremost an adaptation of the thought of the ancient world and a sort of inheritance from the free spirit of Greek speculation, no doubt recast and gaining in wisdom and completeness, but not essentially renewed in the light of a new teaching which has a quite different origin. Now in virtue of its method and of its whole orientation this ancient philosophy tended to engross the whole order of thought and of reality so as to pronounce absolute verdicts about the truth on every sort of subject, so as to put theory above practice or to substitute the former for the latter, and so as to find in itself, as having both the first and the last word about everything, a sort of divine sufficiency.[1] Its implied postulate is the divinity

[1] *Tr.* This passage and those which follow appear at first sight to show an anti-intellectualist tendency. What Blondel really means (as is clear from *L'Action*; cf Bouillard, pp. 151-2) is that philosophy cannot of itself give man the divine life, beatitude. But in recognizing its insufficiency it reveals the *presence* of the Absolute. This theoretical knowledge of the Absolute is valid in itself, but it must be *accepted practically* if we are to *possess* 'being'. 'Being', that is to say, stands here for the Absolute. The intellect is presented with 'being', but cannot attain to it

of Reason—not only in the sense that God is Λόγος, but in the sense that our speculative knowledge contains the supreme virtue and of itself consummates in us the divine work, Ὁ νοῦς δοκεῖ ἄρχειν καὶ ἡγεῖσθα καὶ ἔννοιαν ἔχειν περὶ καλῶν καὶ θείων, εἴτε θεῖος ὢν καὶ αὐτός, εἴτε τῶν ἐν ἡμῖν τὸ θειότατον.[1]

So, far from finding this alliance of the peripatetic philosophy with scholastic theology a quite natural and straightforward affair, we should ask how it is that history succeeded for so long in reconciling what logic would have declared irreconcilable—and in fact that is just what it came to do in the end. How did this mixed marriage work? No doubt, in view of the double manifestation by reason and by revelation of the same divine Λόγος, both the distinction and the harmony of human wisdom and of faith seemed equally natural; but above all this was due to the disclosure of a new domain, beyond anything that ancient thought could conceive or control, which transcended man simply as such and seemed to extend his horizon indefinitely without limiting or diminishing his ancient pretensions. Thus reason submitted itself to the triumphant discipline of the faith without any feeling of constraint, because it had been so far enlarged that the division of its empire passed unnoticed; reason did not have to retreat, it could even grow and advance, without refusing to give up, politely as it were, a first place which it had never occupied or coveted or even imagined. Nevertheless, behind this manifest exaltation of human reason a principle of limitation was secretly established, altogether opposed to the spirit of ancient thought which had a simple faith in its own unique sovereignty and self-sufficiency.

Aristotle, of course, speaks of a life which is more than human and which we are sometimes allowed to reach, becoming gods. Ὁ δε τοιοῦτος ἂν εἴη βίος κρείττων ἢ κατ' ἀνθρωπον, ἀλλ' ἐφ' ὅσον ἐνδέχεται ἀθανατίζειν χρή. But for him it is the activity of rational

---

through its own resources. 'Being' is a gift. When Blondel insists on the 'subjective' character of philosophical knowledge he means, therefore, that philosophy of itself is incomplete. What he repudiates is the philosophy which considers itself self-sufficing.

[1] Aristotle, *Nic.-Eth.*, X, 7.

contemplation which effects this divine life in man, an activity which has its beginning and its end in ourselves; and it is metaphysics which is the full knowledge of being, which encloses being, which gives us being and, if one may so put it, gives us salvation—so that, instead of finding in this a point of insertion for the supernatural, we should recognize that it implies in advance the exclusion of the supernatural and that this sublime and aspiring doctrine makes pure philosophy a candidate for the highest place of all, however high this proves to be.

Thus, as reason, nurtured in the protecting warmth of the Schools and still operating in its ancient forms, became more and more conscious of its own powers, an antagonism could not fail to show itself: and that is why the *Middle Ages* are well named; they enjoyed a state of provisional, but always unstable, equilibrium. Let us not speak, then, of a complete break between those times and ours: the philosophic spirit which engendered scholasticism is the same spirit which took up arms against it; the spirit which destroyed it is the same spirit which, working itself out, will assist the progress of the Christian philosophy. It is this continuity which we must grasp, behind all the movements in its chequered history, if we are to distinguish both the splendid fruitfulness which must attend the efforts of 'Neo-Scholasticism' and the incurable sterility which also attaches to it (for the sense of the expression is an equivocal one). If only this scholasticism, which needed to be revived since it had really succumbed, would stop trying to reanimate the ancient enemy which it used to harbour and which too often it insists on regarding as a friend—which, in fact, is its murderer not only because it has already killed it once but because it will always prevent it from coming to life again so long as scholasticism shelters it or welcomes it back, being dead itself and a principle of death!

In fine, then, scholasticism took over a content which could not be assimilated by the reason of antiquity and a form which could not contain this content, so that in the end a parting of the ways or a head-on collision was inevitable. There was great danger in this alliance. And it is to be remarked that this dangerous and treacherous combination was denounced not in the name of reason as against dogma but in the name of dogma as against reason. For what happened at the Reformation? Holding on to the idea that reason is not and cannot be for the Middle Ages what it was for antiquity, Luther forbade it to touch the principle of Christianity, which it could not control without degrading it or submit to without degrading itself. How comes it, then, that Protestantism, beginning with the *De servo arbitrio*, has seemed to repudiate its origins so quickly by the development of *private judgment*? It is not only because, in fact, this doctrine of a subjection of the reason was in fact a rebellion; it is also because, in rising up against the intellectualism of Aristotle and the scholastics, Luther authenticated that form of rationalism in which the reason reasoning laid claim to an absolute empire, as if it were everything or nothing. There is the subtle connection of ideas which succeeded in consecrating this rationalism when its implications came to be more clearly realized, through the very fear which it seemed to be inspiring.

After that there was really no way back to the equilibrium of the two disparate elements and no means of finding a new equilibrium in philosophy alone by divorcing faith and reason. And it is precisely because scholasticism had opened to human reason the immense horizons of the faith that reason, now left to itself, could not forget the world which it had once glimpsed or give up hope of finding its equivalent: there is, in man, a supreme position waiting to be occupied; whose shall it be? No, things are not and cannot be what they were. And by reason of the very fact that emancipated philosophy tends, as before, to maintain that thought is the divine element in man and that it is self-sufficient, thought is no longer what it was. Unwittingly it sets before itself an ideal which in reality is not proper to itself alone. Thus it prepares for itself, on the way to its promised land, a chequered history of experiments and trials which are unfailingly fruitful because they are all in their different ways disappointments—until human thought, now enlightened in regard to its own nature and to its limitations, becomes capable of determining all that it is and all that it can do by the consciousness of what it is not and of what it cannot do. Thus, even while claiming its full independence and transforming itself according to the law of its autonomy, it is in reality worked upon by the Christian idea with which it is in conflict: in triumphing, it returns upon its tracks, but it is very different from what it was when it set out upon its course—it is vanquished in its apparent victory, victorious in its apparent overthrow.

Second: Let us measure the great discrepancy between the starting-point and the eventual position in the vast movement of thought which has filled the last three centuries. On the one hand, in the 16th century, philosophy is more than ever determined not to restrict itself in any way or to doubt its competence: diffused and indeterminate, it is all in all; it has a simple faith in its own powers, in its validity and in its absolute pretensions; it claims to attain to reality and to apprehend truth—so that between itself and being, between knowledge and life itself, there is an identity which is simply taken for granted. On the other hand, philosophy at present tends more and more to specify, to criticize and to limit itself. That is, it no longer regards knowledge as the complete substitute for actual existence; this means that thought, on its own admission, even if it were supposed to be adequate to reality or identical with being, does not suffice, as such, to make *us* adequate, 'equal', either to ourselves or to things, and that, if every speculative system can be outdated by advances in speculation, the only doctrine which can contain at its heart a definitive truth is that which does not seek for self-sufficiency, and finally that theoretical solutions cannot be satisfactory unless they seek for something beyond themselves, showing the necessity and determining the conditions of a life and a thought which are fully obedient to their own internal law.

But there are many connecting links between these two forms of philosophy, forms which are so different from one another that unless one considered these connections it would be impossible to understand the significance of such a transformation. How slow and complicated is our collaboration in a common task! What efforts of insight have to be piled up to effect the change of perspective! And we realize, as we contemplate this vast process, that it would be absurd to attempt a breaking-down of this fine and firm network, woven by so many great minds whose thoughts cannot be simply dismissed unless we fail to understand them or at least cannot be condemned wholesale lest we misconceive the wonderful workings of divine providence. Let us consider this for a moment if only to observe how narrow and fragmentary even the most penetrating views are shown to be, or rather if only to appreciate the advantages, gradually built up, of this general transformation which, after having brought low, one through another, the supernaturalist philosophy, the philosophy of transcendence and the philosophy of immanence, effects through these conflicts and these catastrophes the only durable peace and the only legitimate alliance.

[1]When once philosophy had broken with theology at the beginning of the modern era, it began to speculate independently *but* without any idea of ousting faith from its position, not yet distinctly recognizing that it could not disregard theology without replacing it and substituting for the supernatural a doctrine of transcendence. So it emigrates into the natural order where it feels at home, *but* without realizing that it would limit its scope instead of limiting its object and its competence, and without seeing that it could not restrict its curiosity and its aspirations, which would be to give up the chief reason for philosophizing at all. It applies itself to the knowledge of things, and, by the critique of sense-knowledge, it lays the foundations of the scientific knowledge in which it hopes to find its feet, *but*, without suspecting that it will have to turn its critical reflection upon itself. So it rediscovers the power of knowledge and its legitimate extension in a realm which had been supposed for so long to be reserved for magical operations and to divine power alone, *but* without seeing that this science of nature does not suffice, even from the natural point of view, to resolve the problem of life or that such an inquiry is destined to form a range of knowledge specifically distinct from the philosophical—that of the positive sciences. Worked upon by the need from which it arose, it then takes its stand in the world of metaphysics and hopes to find 'the true method of reaching the knowledge of all things which the mind can know'; *but* because it is still orientated to the field in which man can remain simply man and where knowledge tends to become merely positive knowledge, it shrinks from touching upon man as a believer, while already claiming that empire over man in all his

---

[1] *Tr.* This next long and intricate paragraph, a conspectus, from Blondel's point of view, of three centuries and more of philosophy, is not a necessary part of his argument.

thoughts and volitions and actions which it exercised over all the world of nature. In the end it reveals its pretensions (inscribed upon its horoscope from the beginning) to a total and absolute hegemony, aspiring now to secularize religion itself, to provide from its own resources the complete equivalent of faith and to lead man to beatitude by its own power, *but* without recognizing that such a method of immanence, once its own conclusions are granted absolute value and its object attains an apotheosis, can only be, like all forms of monism, a concealed anthropomorphism or a subjectivism: for, as Schelling observes, Spinoza unwittingly conceived of Substance, the Object and the Not-Self under the form of the Self when he identified it with the absolute principle. Then it discovers, in any metaphysic of transcendence or of immanence and in the traditional ambition of rationalism to make itself adequate to being and to life, a contradiction analogous to that which rationalism had revealed, working the other way, in scholasticism; and in its turn this intellectualism has its Luther in Kant, *but*, if it now sees that knowledge is not sufficient for life and that there is something which thought cannot supply, it interprets this discovery still in terms of its previous doctrines; instead of simply recognizing that different points of view are involved, it asserts an ontological opposition; instead of just describing the whole phenomenon of thought and action in man's consciousness (which would have been consonant with the critical spirit), it still claims to provide the equivalent or even the reality of all the *noumenon*; and, although it allows that the two aspects of this dualism are irreducible, it continues to imply that this dualism itself is the ἕν καὶ πᾶν and that the whole solution is contained within it. Thus it returns to monism, though in a new dress, and supposes that 'the true criticism demands simply that philosophy should develop from the side of the subject instead of from the side of the object' so as to undertake, as in Schelling, the total reconstruction of Christianity; *but*, if it thus discovers that there is unity and complete continuity in the philosophical problem, it still continues to believe that this subjective and immanent solution has an objective and absolute value, and that it is sufficient to itself and to ourselves. It comes to realize that 'the method of immanence' excludes a 'doctrine of immanence'; that is, one cannot make a transcendent truth of the negation of the transcendent or of the supernatural, and one cannot exclude ontology except from an ontological point of view; it proposes, then, to content itself with explaining the manifold interdependent and heterogeneous aspects of thought by one another, and to reintegrate all forms of life into the unity of a single determinism; a metaphysical system has thus become a mere scientific method, a pure phenomenalism: *but*, just when it is guarding itself against the ever-recurring temptation to provide of itself alone the substantive secret, the ultimate salvation, it continues to say that the whole problem is both stated and resolved by itself, and that, in its scientific and phenomenalist conception of things, there is, as Taine claimed, 'an art, a morality, a theory of politics and a new religion'; so it still refuses to entertain the idea of its own insufficiency, or the idea of a solution which would be sufficient, or to determine the conditions which such a solution, in view of our human requirements, must necessarily fulfil. Despite its implicit avowal, it still seems bent on eliminating all that is not just itself, and on establishing this right of exclusion or this principle of contradiction on the absolute basis of its own full possession of truth and of being. It recognizes as the conclusion of this secular task of elaboration the 'truism', 'the most natural corollaries of which have not yet been resolutely drawn', that 'we can only be given states of consciousness, and the mind cannot pass beyond these internal phenomena by any of its procedures so as to reach realities, if such there be, of another order'; *but* it does not cease for all that to regard these states of consciousness or these internal phenomena as realities, immanent realities no doubt, but complete realities which are sufficient in their own way—so that it does not always notice (and this is the all-important point) that in our most 'immanent' thought and action there is something heterogeneous or transcendent in regard to the knowledge which we have of it, which is logically the very condition for the scientific point of view which philosophy claims to adopt; for it is not philosophy's business to penetrate this, to affirm it or to deny it: it has only to study the idea of it with all that it implies.

So what remains for this philosophy which, through so many efforts and gropings, aspires to give itself a constitution? In order to reach its goal, to come to birth after this long labour, it must free itself from its last shackles and accept all the consequences implied by this affirmation which is so simple but yet evolved with so much toil: 'To oppose the transcendent to the supernatural as contradictory solutions is always to presuppose that speculative conclusions are beings, realities equivalent to life actually lived and thought actually exercised, which, substituting themselves for these latter, explain them or take their place, as if the knowledge of reality were itself the only true reality. The fundamental principle on which philosophy depends as a specifically defined science is that even the complete knowledge of thought and of life does not supply or suffice for the activity of thinking or of living; that, on the one hand, what is immanent in us, action and living thought, is yet transcendent in regard to the reflective or philosophical view which one takes of it, and that, on the other hand, this philosophical knowledge is a phenomenon which is ulterior or transcendent in regard to that which it represents'. So instead of using one of these terms in opposition to the other and insisting that one must stand for appearance and the other monopolize reality, we must simply consider them as interdependent. Instead of considering one as capable of being the substratum of the other, while remaining itself a complete and substantial entity independent of everything else, we must determine on what conditions we can conceive of them as each equally realized, being what they are, both as constituting our knowledge and as constituted by it.

Philosophy, in fine, giving up the pretension of containing and controlling *totum et omne de omni et toto* and the contrary but correlative pretension which makes it only a construction of thought or an epiphenomenon on the surface of life, must now precisely define its own competence and scope, including its own dynamism in the whole system of determination which it studies. Just as the knowledge of the senses and of positive knowledge involve a critique (as we have come to understand better and better) which restricts their significance without lessening their relative value, so we shall see more and more clearly that philosophical knowledge (which is of a quite different order) is no more empowered than they are to provide of itself alone the whole of the effective solution, even though it can determine the necessary and sufficient conditions for that solution.

For no science can be precisely defined unless we recognize the presence and, as it were, the pressure, of a limit beyond which other perspectives lie open, determining both what it is and what it is not. And the difficulty for philosophy is just to discover this determination without detracting from its universal competence and without abandoning the point of view demanded by its method of immanence: for it must find in itself that which goes beyond it, an immanent transcendence. We must consider our own *action*—and by this word we must understand the concrete activity of living thought which expresses to ourselves both ourselves and everything else, although we shall never become 'adequate' to the least of our ideas, and also the initiative by which our instincts, our desires and our intentions are expressed in everything else, although our constantly renewed efforts to attain to ourselves never make us 'adequate' to ourselves.[1] If then we consider our own *action* in this way, we find that this immanent activity is always transcendent in regard to every equilibrium provisionally established by it and to all knowledge extracted from it, and we do philosophy the service of providing it with that matter and that form which alone, by adapting themselves to one another, constitute it in its own essence. For, on the one hand, its precise object and its ever-present idea is to determine the content, the internal relations and the requirements of action, although it can never claim to provide them itself, however rigorously and necessarily it defines them. And, on the other hand, simply because it is not self-sufficient, it helps to stimulate the movement from which it arose, opening before itself an indefinite field for expansion but without abandoning its attitude of reserve in face of the mystery of action, or its precise conclusions in regard to life's demands. And at this point one can regard the conflicting doctrines of the past, which regarded themselves as self-sufficient closed systems, only as different species of the same kind of metaphysical alchemy, all of

---

[1] *Tr.* This sentence, as Père Bouillard remarks (p. 35), shows that Blondel's aim is not to down-grade thought, but on the contrary 'not to confine thought to representation, but to reintegrate within it the very act of thought and the whole of life'.

them equally incompatible with philosophical science and with Christian philosophy. The ancient conception of the hegemony or, more exactly, of the αὐτάρκεια philosophical reason is thus destroyed by the progress of reason itself.

Third: At the end of this evolution, which revolutionizes philosophical perspectives through the hidden pressure of the religious problem set at the beginning of modern times, we find that the following conclusions emerge from the turmoil of doctrines and, as it were, at the intersection of the demands, apparently opposed but really convergent, of rational speculation and the Catholic consciousness:

1. The function of philosophy is to determine the content of thought and the postulates of action, without itself providing us with that being of which it studies the notion, without containing that life of which it analyses the requirements, without sufficing for that of which it defines the sufficient conditions, without realizing, making real, that of which it must say that it necessarily conceives of it as real. It must show on what conditions it subordinates to itself the reality of all that it affirms: but, although it is itself a living force which develops effectively as an integrating element in the scheme of things and contributes its own dynamism, it must come to a stop before what is required of it and by it, always remembering that it cannot satisfy its own requirements. And it must make of this essential reserve a central principle of doctrine and of explanation; the principle may have already revealed itself accidentally, but this altogether simple truth, this 'truism', remains inoperative and obscure if its immense scope is not envisaged. Here is the new development; this is what presupposes a prodigious integration of thought and all the accumulated effort of philosophical reflection and Christian awareness.

2. Philosophy, although it must abstain from any effective solution, must not abstain from any solution in regard to postulates or exigencies. That is, the study of the most detailed phenomena of the religious life is within its competence just as much as that, for example, of sense-perception; for, since it restricts the formal significance of its conclusions to the limits of its method of immanence, it is at home with Christian phenomena as much as with any others

182

but without claiming to supply the effective solution in the one case any more than in the others. It must also be a complete account, analysing the determinism which unites the various interrelated problems which must be treated by it. Indeed, it is precisely by considering this system in its integrity that it will always escape the danger of attributing to itself a sufficiency which never belongs to it. For, even if it were ideally parallel to or identified with the reality of the act in operation and of the being under consideration, it must always remind itself that in us concrete thought and life actually lived are transcendent in regard to our immanent knowledge even of the transcendent and even of the supernatural.

3. Confined as it is to adjusting all the aspects of this integral determinism to one another, philosophy is nevertheless not reduced to being a purely explanatory critique, without power of judgment; and in order to judge it needs no external criterion. In the transcendence of immanent thought and action it finds an internal principle of absolute judgment; and in the binding-up of phenomena into a whole of interdependent parts it discovers a mechanism which gives to all its conclusions a necessary character. That is to say, there is in our wills, considered in all their generality and their depth, a logic whose actual exigencies (implied in what we actually think and established by what we actually do) have only to be discerned for us to be able to uncover the all-embracing laws of thought and of action and to rediscover, beneath the fragmentary appearances of a life in process of development, that which it ought to be, thanks to a clearer understanding of what it cannot fail to be.[1] In this way not only does philosophy determine in detail the effects which bind together all human attitudes of mind and which work themselves out in the end according to a law of compensation, but it also demonstrates that each human destiny, under the most diverse appearances, constitutes a unique problem, and it shows the necessity which controls the general solution. Were it not for this character of internal necessity which expresses the ultimatum to which we are subject in our actions and at the same time defines our true responsibility, the rigours of the sanction would not be justified.

[1] *Tr.* It is particularly necessary at this point to recall *L'Action* (see Introduction, p. 88).

So we may challenge any other philosophy except that of which we speak to affirm that there is something necessary in our moral and religious life, or to admit the rewards and punishments of this life and the next, without violating the whole idea of equity and goodness.

I must not be reproached for underlining the importance of the doctrines which have filled the history of ideas since the Renaissance; it cannot be exaggerated. Nobody can hope to disregard them; nothing can destroy their vigour and fecundity. Nor is it any use to take only a half-hearted interest in the movement of modern thought; it is bound to reach its goal in any case. I have perhaps said enough about the advantages which may accrue from it for philosophy to prevent certain misconceptions; they ought to be singularly precious to us in themselves if it is true that they consist in specifying philosophical science, maintaining its sovereignty in its own domain and reconciling it with what it could not tolerate heretofore without compromise: they are still more to be prized if we realize that they are due to the hidden power and, as it were, the constraint of the Christian idea. So, after indicating what the progress of free thought essentially owes to Christianity, I can now show with greater ease what our Christian conceptions owe to the progress of this free philosophy.

2. *On the growth of religious awareness through the progress of free philosophy*

Far from drawing up an indictment against the tendencies of modern philosophy, we must rather reproach it for not having worked them out completely; we have only to ask that it should be wholly faithful to its principles so that it may find in its fully developed conclusions a wonderful conformity with the Christian spirit and, better still, may throw us open more wholeheartedly to this spirit, of which one must say that, if it has been the cause of progress, it is nevertheless unceasingly in progress itself among men. *Crescamus in eo per omnia semper.* It is well to have some picture of this beneficent advance.

Basing myself, then, on the precise notion of philosophy as it emerges from this secular task of elaboration, I propose to show how it satisfies, illuminates and encourages pretensions which had appeared previously to be incompatible. In it, and only in it, all the lines which had been divergent or confused come together as in a geometrical figure, and opposing theses are reconciled, not by concessions or liquidations, but by showing that each of the adversaries was more in the right than he realized—so a harmonious complex will be formed and a solid body of doctrine, solid precisely because one may survey all its manifold aspects and continue to discover in their very contrasts the most profound congruities.

Since it is impossible to give a complete account of these unsuspected harmonies, it must suffice to enumerate a few of the advances made by philosophical and by Christian awareness, presenting them in each case as a pair in their interdependent aspects.

1. Faithful to its method of immanence, philosophy *restricts* its scope to the inner determinism of thought and action without trespassing upon, or supplying for, the real order. It constitutes, then, a specifically defined and strictly limited form of knowledge and of life. Thus it prepares us for a growing realization that analytic and explicative formulae do not exhaust their object and that there is something in life (and this the essential thing) of which science and abstract reason are not the possessors. Since philosophy cannot claim to substitute itself for the real even in its own domain, the field lies open for a dogma which governs life and thought in virtue of a quite different title, and speaks the language of the absolute. In this sense theological doctrines, even in regard to the natural order, have a scope and a significance quite different from the philosophical theses which they might appear simply to overlap. We must break down entirely the misleading solidarity which a certain sort of scholasticism has favoured and which it persists in trying to restore in spite of its fatal consequences and in spite of the Vatican Council's declaration: '*Duplex cognitionis ordo, non solum principio, sed objecto.*' What deceives so many minds, otherwise in possession of the truth, is the ambiguity of the meaning and function of the reason: as if, by speaking of 'the use of reason, rational knowledge, reasonable adhesion' one meant necessarily 'philosophy, philosophical science'. But, just as the reason is used in the field of sense-knowledge and is indispensable for the elaboration of positive science without thereby operating in the philosophical sphere, so too it works on dogmas and revealed data, which are a sort of experience of the divine and a supernatural empiricism, *argumentum non apparentium*, in order to constitute a sacred science. There, and there only, it is *ancilla theologiae*, just as it is also *ancilla naturae et scientiae*. For theology properly presupposes this rational organization of elements which are not themselves the product of reason; and, in this sense, it applies what we may call a philosophical form to elements which are foreign to philosophy; and therefore its results, while remaining always distinct from rational truths reached by rational processes, have a fixity, a scope and a value of a quite different kind, even when they appear to coalesce with those of philosophy strictly so-called. Philosophy itself, then, free from all alloy, consists not in the heteronomous application of reason to some material or to some object, but in the autonomous application of reason to itself. It is impossible to insist too much on this necessary distinction in that it is especially difficult for minds brought up on the idea that thought, without being the object, can be adequate to the object; they must try to understand that the conclusions of philosophy cannot be in any way combined with the teachings of theology, and that one cannot juxtapose (*materialiter*) to the legitimate *objectivism* of the faith any intellectual *realism*. For, once more, unless we distinguish the rational element in theology from the rationality of philosophy (as also that of science, which again belongs to quite a different order), we run the risk of throwing everything into confusion, of misunderstanding completely the directions of the Church and the claims of theologians, and also of misconceiving in a disastrous way the most legitimate pretensions of philosophers. How many there are, among the masters of the sacred science, who are still in the same position in regard to philosophy as people were in the 17th century in regard to science, when it was supposed that the rational physics of Galileo was in contradiction with the rational theology of orthodoxy!

At the same time, and precisely because it determines and restricts its scope, philosophy *enlarges* its competence. So long as it thought itself capable of engrossing the reality of what it knew, it could not touch dogma without assaulting or degrading it or even study the mere notion of a supernatural or the practices of revealed religion with impunity; and so for centuries we have assisted, in France and in the Catholic countries, at the strange spectacle of 'the whole duty of man' divorced from honest scholarship, from genuine art and from living thought. If, in the countries of Protestant culture, for example, the religious problem and the question of Christianity have more directly or, as it were, more officially interested science and philosophy, is it because Catholicism is incompatible with the philosophic spirit? Not at all. We must conclude, on the contrary, that, on the one hand, theological rationalism has been too often taken for the whole of philosophy, through a failure to realize that there is room for a philosophical discipline below it (which excludes the intellectual rationalism to which people rallied so perilously in defence of the theological kind), and, on the other hand, that if Catholicism was irreconcilable with certain provisional and moribund forms of philosophy, reserving itself to correspond with a further development of thought, this was because it was the invisible agent of a more profound labour of the human reason, preventing the establishment of a premature equilibrium, and constraining philosophy to continue the search for its own true self until such time as it should be constituted as a genuine science. In fact, when the function of certain religious doctrines offered as philosophical comes to an end, that of Catholicism, from which philosophy seemed to have nothing to accept, at last becomes evident. We may now see not only that philosophy becomes capable of treating all questions, even the most detailed, about the Christian consciousness without being false to its own nature or to theirs, but also that it cannot fail to examine them in the same spirit as all the other questions whose intimate connections form one same determinism. And this is what, on the one hand, answers to the imperious need of the human reason which protests against what has been called 'separated philosophy' and lays claim to the religious problem (just as it does to every other, and indeed more urgently), and, on the other hand, is in harmony with theology, which forbids entrance to its sanctuary but also forbids a disregard of it—for, if the supernatural, which is humanly inaccessible, is present there, there is also the *unicum necessarium*,[1] so that, whatever we think or whatever we do, in spite of all life's illusions and frustrations, we cannot treat it *de jure*, or indeed *de facto*, as irrelevant.

Thus we reach a distinction, more radical than we could have realized or even imagined, between the philosophical and the theological points of view, and a condemnation of a misleading and dangerous combination of these; by the same token we establish a connection, closer than ever before, between the philosophical and the religious problems, or rather their continuity, their unity and their necessity, and an absolute condemnation of a false separatism— and so we have a first pair of theses, apparently opposed to one another and previously irreconcilable, but in reality bound up with one another like the logically inseparable surfaces of a solid body.

2. If it is true that philosophical knowledge and theological knowledge differ radically *principio et objecto*, how careful we must be not to abuse the certainty and the fixity of the latter by employing it against the mutability and the legitimate liberty of the former, despite the very natural tendency to extend and apply the science of faith to science in general. How difficult it is, for one who loves the truth and desires to see its unity here and now, not to fall into the temptation of using what he believes for the benefit of what he knows, as if, all forms of knowledge being homogeneous, one could simply string them together in a row! What excesses need to be corrected, and what improvement is to be desiderated in the behaviour of certain theologians, who make revealed truth stand or fall with the prejudices of their particular school, and their sound theological rationalism with their rational pseudo-theology, turning into heresies, with an unwitting perfidy which is all the more dangerous for working below the surface, divergences which are at least deserving of toleration.[2] So, far from making dogmas of our

---

[1] *Tr.* This is an elliptical way of putting the central contention that, whereas the supernatural is, in itself, beyond human control, the one thing necessary for us is to throw ourselves open to the demands made upon us by it.

[2] It is this method (which must really be called odious, when one considers the serious consequences which so many have suffered from it and the delicate suscep- tibilities which it has offended), this art of making sacrosanct the partialities of a sectarian spirit and of compromising, indirectly, the simplicity of the spirit of

rational doctrines and convictions, binding up what we have to discuss with what we have to believe, and tending to divinize all the human supports of our belief, it is a duty to distinguish points of faith with the utmost care from all explanations, or inductive processes or analogical arguments, and from the working of reason upon reason itself. This is not, to repeat, a denial that faith itself serves as a starting-point for reasoning, but, if we are not to compromise theology by laying to its door fallible opinions and unjust condemnations for which a sectarian or partisan spirit is solely responsible, we must try to distinguish what is of faith or bound up with faith on the plane of faith from what is of reason and antecedent to or merely consonant with faith on the plane of reason. If, even in regard to Christian verities themselves, it is necessary to distinguish what is clearly and expressly defined from what is not, still more must one distinguish what belongs to human science from what is of divine inspiration. And this task of discrimination is now more urgent than ever it was. Theology, then, must be itself, its whole self and nothing but itself. Theologians and those who have the duty and the grace of disseminating the sacred science must remain fully theologians, and realize that they have nothing to gain by covering up or complicating their proper function, by humanizing their teaching, by basing themselves on philosophical arguments, by telling us primarily or exclusively what perhaps we know better than they do when we expect from them what they alone can give us, by placing themselves on their opponent's ground to deal with subsidiary or sometimes otiose difficulties, and by campaigning about questions of opinion and advocating causes which can be

---

faith—it is no doubt this of which Descartes speaks, in accents of indignant grief which I cannot blame, in his discussion with Burmann recently made known to us by the discovery, at Göttingen, of a manuscript of first-class importance: *Ante omnia haec Scholastica exterminanda est, praecipue cum hinc adsueverint Theologi adversae parti omnia affingere et calumniari, ut calumniandi artem plane sibi familiarem reddiderint, et vix aliter quam calumniari, etiam inadvertentes, possint.* It is certainly a calumny to bring charges of heterodoxy against legitimate philosophical divergences. I have stigmatized false philosophy; one must be still more severe, in so far as greater interests are involved, with false theology, with what purports to be theology and is not.

abandoned without loss and which ought indeed to be deliberately abandoned, For it is not really their business to take up the offensive or the defensive, but simply to let the sun's light shine upon the godly and the ungodly, developing before our eyes the rational system of the faith, that is, showing that the coherence of dogma, considered as such, forms an organic synthesis and that the sacred science really is a science. At a time of confusion and, above all, of religious ignorance, the first duty of an apologist is to reveal, in all its definitive unity and in all its rich simplicity, the logical synthesis of Catholic dogma. Everything else belongs to a different order, must be put on a lower level, and must be handled by other methods and another competence.

At the same time, precisely because theology does not absorb philosophy, and because (conversely), on pain of a false separatism, philosophy must lay claim to the religious problem in its entirety and thus forms a link between the exposition of dogma and all subordinate forms of apologetics, the believer, the apologist and the theologian, in whom all that is human must subsist with all the exigencies and aspirations of human nature, must labour, with an increasingly intelligent respect for the susceptibilities of the human mind, to speak of science only as a man of science, of the problems of history only as a historian, of the perplexities of modern thought only as a philosopher, and of life itself only as one of the living. He must not suppress or disregard the natural foundation of the supernatural. Just as it is necessary not to confuse functions and competences, so it is vital to break down the watertight compartments which would cut off the Christian, the man and the citizen who is also the man of God, from the world's progress.

Thus with the theologians brought back to their proper place in the interest both of their own authority and of the legitimate freedoms of human thought, Christian activity, by the same token, is more intimately involved with the world of thought and action, and the apostle summoned to work once more as a man among men precisely because, if he is himself more than man, he never ceases to be a man. And these are the two needs which many of our contemporaries feel so keenly. It is no insignificant service to them to show that these seemingly incompatible aspirations can be satisfied at the same time, that they cannot be fully satisfied in any other way, and that these tendencies or desires, which many of those who experience them can only vaguely express, are justified by the precise definition of a method and a doctrine which both reconciles them and prevents their confusion.

3. Since it is not the business of philosophy to provide us with the absolute of truth, with the truth which is substantial and salutary, whereas its duty is to investigate the conditions in which this truth can be made known to us, it follows that it is not its business to elaborate the principles of faith as if these were, in the ultimate analysis, nothing but the discoveries of the reason or more or less symbolic and mythical intuitions. It is not its business to improve upon them, under the pretext of giving them a profounder or exacter sense; it must not prefix its own spirit to the letter which expresses the fullness of a spirit other than its own if it is not to fail in the reserve which it owes to itself and sin against its own nature. Thus it will be in line with this definition of the Vatican Council: 'Neque enim fidei doctrina velut philosophicum inventum proposita est humanis ingeniis perficienda; sed is sensus perpetuo retinendus quem semel declaravit Ecclesia, nec unquam ab eo sensu altioris intelligentiae specie et nomine recedendum.'

The employment of reason in the preserve of dogma and under the discipline of the faith thus consists in ceaselessly penetrating the infinite depths of a fixed truth which it seeks not to renew but to understand. No doubt there remains for it an ample liberty of investigation; and an unlimited field lies open for speculative reflection, since the significance of dogma is inexhaustible. It is none the less true that reason, starting from what is certain and changeless, and uniting itself firmly with the faith, constitutes theology, provides definitive explanations, offers interpretations and organizes a system of demonstrations which, without being ever an absolutely closed one, constitutes a solid gain. And in this sense one must say of scholasticism, which is rigorous in its method and perfect from certain points of view in its constitution, that it proposes a rational objectivism in which we have no fault to find, since it represents the most authentic organization of the truths which the Church has in her keeping; it must be added that nothing could be more opportune for the healing of men's minds than the setting forth of such a doctrine of apologetic teaching, presented in all its purity and with all the candour which belongs to its supra-philosophical character, and (finally), as Leo XIII has said, that faith can hardly receive from reason more numerous or more powerful weapons than those which it owes to St Thomas—so that, after a radical criticism of scholastic pseudo-philosophizing, one cannot lay too much emphasis on its theological rationalism[1] (indeed, it was in order to praise scholasticism with a clear conscience that it was necessary first to criticize it relentlessly). But as we recognize how reason, in its intimate synthesis with revealed objects, receives a peculiar perfection from these data of a higher order and from this, so to say, divine experience, we recognize too that it still has its own proper use in a quite different order; for this theological employment of reason might be called the philosophy of faith and the rationalism of the supernatural—it is not the reason of philosophy; it is not philosophy itself, which, I repeat, has still to be constituted.

So, while there is perfect justification for the claim of theological rationalism to evolve a doctrinal corpus of truths formed by the synthesis of human thought and divine revelation, it remains that philosophy in its own domain keeps that freedom of invention, that right of initiative, that duty to renew its theories by an effective advance in its definitions—in fine, all those characters to which, as we have been rightly told, the doctrines of faith must not be assimilated by a false analogy (which in fact implies that these characters are different from those of theology and that they have their own proper foundation). It does not follow that there is nothing in philosophy but what is mutable and perishable: the fact that it always needs to revivify itself by developments and fresh starts does not mean that its labours are not useful, progressive and, in a sense, definitive; all that follows is that it has not to seek anywhere but in itself for the principle and the guarantee of its competence to reach its own conclusions. Hence, even as regards the solution which it can and should give of the religious problem from its own point

---

[1] Tr. This is not an adequate account of Thomist theology. Indeed Blondel's conception of the theologian's task is in general a rather limited one. The reader may be referred to Père Bouillard's discussion (esp. p. 247).

of view, it must always be open to it to determine its method and its object more precisely by successive approximations, if only to understand more fully its own limits and insufficiencies.

In this way there will be a better understanding and a more complete justification not only of the stability of those points which are strictly of faith but also of all that theological rationalism which makes up the doctrinal body of Christian teaching and the soul of the Catholic tradition in the Church; at the same time there will be a more lively and more accurate recognition of actual conditions, of collective progress and of individual efforts in the order in which philosophical reason is competent. These are the two aspects which must always be envisaged simultaneously, if one is not to leave faith without reason or to close reason against faith: *fides quaerens intellectum: intellectus quaerens fidem*—it is this double truth which results from an absolutely precise distinction between the theological and the philosophical functions of human thought.

4. As soon as philosophy defines, and restricts itself to defining, the conditions which it judges necessary for solving the problem of human destiny, without actually solving it and without containing in itself our life or our salvation, it follows at once that speculative ideas remain variable and disputable whereas the living and salutary truth is not. The exigencies of reason, even if imperfectly realized, can thus serve in their various ways as abstract vehicles for the concrete reality of the solution, and, for souls of good will, certain intrinsically insufficient or false forms of belief and of action can be the equivalent, in default of fuller knowledge and higher grace, of the reality of which they are ignorant, making them in an invisible way, and in their heart of hearts, sharers in what they are not aware of possessing in their thoughts or actions.

But at the same time, if the imperfect or the insufficient can suffice, the sufficient must exist and have its function. This broadening of the notion of the Church's soul is far from compromising the idea which one ought to have of the Church's body[1] as organized with the greatest precision and of the rigour of its definitions or obligatory practices, for it is not possible to understand this hidden extension of supernatural life where men are ignorant of it if one

[1] *Tr.* cf. note on p. 164, above.

does not maintain the necessity of living openly by it where it is recognized. And so one must also note the difference between those who have always been ignorant of the Christian life, I do not say theoretically but practically, and those who know it by the active possession of it and by infused grace: ' *Si quis dixerit parem esse conditionem fidelium atque eorum qui ad fidem unice veram nondum pervenerunt, ita ut catholici justam causam habere possint fidem, quam sub Ecclesiae magisterio jam susceperunt, assensu suspenso in dubium vocandi, donec demonstrationem scientificam credibilitatis et veritatis fidei suae absolverint, anathema sit.*'

Thus there is an infinite variety in the various abstract vehicles which may subserve the unique and concrete working of the spirit which blows where and as it wills, and at the same time there is the absolute rigour and permanent necessity of the defined letter and of the revealed practice, as the authentic condition of possible salvation—the necessity of effective Mediation and Redemption.

5. Since philosophy does not touch the real mystery of action and does not penetrate the secret relations of the human soul with itself, it follows that we cannot base ourselves on external forms of life and thought in order to condemn an individual even when his ideas and his deeds are in themselves most deserving of condemnation. Since we do not know, in the particular case, the obstacles which have been encountered, the light which has been given or the efforts which have been made or the help which has been received, it is never our business to scrutinize the interior forum or to allow human compulsion or the secular arm to interpret the claims of divine morality, or even to determine exactly the obligations of an entire and absolute sincerity for particular persons. Faith is possible and salvation is accessible for everyone, but we have not to decide under what form *in concreto*. It is the merit and the beauty of the philosophical method of immanence that it establishes, in each one of us, that which judges each one of us. *Ipse quisque sibi lex.* Without allowing us to impose a ready-made external criterion, but without preventing us from submitting life and thought to the rigorous necessity of an internal judgment, it leads us to understand and obey with an entire generosity of mind and heart, and even as regards those truths on which our destiny depends, the formal

precept: 'You shall not judge', and at the same time to escape the reproach so often merited by a false zeal: 'You know not of what spirit you are'. But, while we are led to respect the mystery of consciences inviolably, *de facto* and *de jure*, and to realize that the most generous inspirations of charity are one with the demands of intellectual justice, we find that there is the double rigour of a double necessity in this extreme condescendence. For not only is it impossible for the religious question *not* to be raised, and necessary that philosophy should examine the elements of it as completely as possible, but it is also impossible that it should not give a necessary character to its conclusions: what conscience imperiously demands, if it is to remain sincere and loyal to itself, cannot be merely optional. The formal necessity of the problem and the formal necessity of the solution are thus defined on the side of the subject. But that is not all. Not only is the determinism of the religious exigencies of thought imposed upon thought indispensably according as thought determines them from within, but further, once these formal exigencies have been positively determined and practically known from without, they become necessary with a material or literal necessity. Thus it would not be legitimate to seek to give dogmas a new meaning or precepts a looser sense, nor to water down the disciplinary code, nor to interpret the authentic signs and positive requirements of the supernatural order according to the caprices of personal devotion, as mere inspirations of the individual conscience symbolically projected upon the facts. '*Si quis dixerit revelationem divinam externis signis credibilem fieri non posse, ideoque sola interna cujusque experientia aut inspiratione privata homines ad fidem moveri debere, anathema sit.*'

Thus two attitudes of mind, normally antagonistic, are reconciled, and two equally ardent and generous desires are satisfied: on the one hand, the need to extend the invisible kingdom of grace and mercy to the furthest limit, to understand and to love forms of thought and life other than our own; on the other hand, the need and the duty of a rigour in the dogmatic and practical spheres which is quite intransigent. And in order to justify this complete liberality and at the same time to condemn all the accommodations of liberalism, this was the point which it was so urgent to reach, so difficult to approach, since on neither side could any concession be properly made.

6. Since, then, philosophy has the function of withdrawing the innermost heart of morality from human judgment and the always insufficient clarity of human thought, it follows that doctrinal theses, even those which, in so far as theological, have an absolute value and formulate concrete truths, always remain, in their application to particular men, no more than abstract and general rules, however precise and vigorous they are in themselves. They need to be brought alive in practice, but one cannot humanly decide with certainty about the degree of merit or of culpability either in the adhesion which one gives to them, or the fidelity with which one observes them, or in one's neglect or violation of them. No one knows absolutely whether he deserves love or reprobation. So even authorized and more than merely human condemnations, which specify the application of these rules in particular cases so as to denounce and to stigmatize a scandal, still leave us the duty of loving those who are condemned, the only enemies whom we should really recognize as such—and of enfolding them in that charity which rests on a respectful and a just reserve.

But at the same time, while our compassion for all must remain unbounded, without relaxing the strictness of the rule or weakening authority, our rigour in regard to ourselves must be all the greater. For, philosophy being what we have shown it to be, the difficulty which it encounters in the problem of apologetics is such as to affect both believers and unbelievers, and for the same reason: it is not a question of a theoretical adhesion to a dogma which is external to us, but of the practical insertion into our hearts and our conduct of a lifegiving truth—a truth which is the better known the better it is practised and which, when better known, is more demanding as it becomes more generous. So it is first of all ourselves whom we should interrogate when we inquire into the nature of conversion and of the obstacles to conversion. If we are not to give colour to Montesquieu's quip 'devotion is the belief that one is better than others', we ourselves must first bear all the weight of the demands and severities of conscience. There is no doubt about the preference of our contemporaries for those who, in Pascal's phrase, seek with groanings in the sincerity of their hearts rather than those who dogmatize and condemn, triumphing in the assurance of their superiority. We must let our deepest experience reveal to us in the practical order the whole series of our intellectual, moral and religious obligations; we must not use the artifices of dialectic against other people, as if we were not ourselves the first to be judged. And when to justify these obligations we use an indirect but cogent method which manifests their burdensome necessity, when we declare that the natural order is not sufficient for our nature, which nevertheless rebels against the supernatural, and that action, as it is performed in us and by us, requires more than it is possible for us to do by ourselves, when we consider all possible ways of escape so as to establish that we cannot rid ourselves of what weighs upon us most heavily, then let us not give the impression that we are saying all this for the pleasure of imposing burdens on others which we do not bear ourselves, that we do not pay the price ourselves first of all, that this account of the soul in flight from itself and in search of itself is only a pretence, that we have not struggled against our reason and our heart to avoid what we are reproached with calling the inevitable, that we have not had to strive not to hate what is hateful, that we have been able to embrace the faith without finding the crown of thorns, and that (finally) we do not fully realize that the truly philosophical apologetic is the permanent and personal work, a work made visible before men's eyes, of inner conversion. In short, just as it has been necessary to condemn the false separatism which isolated the religious problem from philosophical problems, so we must condemn the false separatism which isolates the work of speculative thought from ascetical efforts and from the painful teaching which is given to us by life itself.

Thus we find that the spirit of charity must persist and intensify even when the necessary condemnations are made with all their rigour, since we must always remember that doctrinal definitions and even the most precise prescriptions are only theoretical abstractions in regard to the innermost and altogether concrete dispositions of individuals, to whom they cannot therefore be applied *in tota et concreta persona* by constraint or by corporal sanction: we have a higher idea of the value of the human person, of his right to respect, of the worth and the mystery of his actions, and, further, an ever-increasing vigilance and exigency in regard to ourselves, since it is illegitimate and impossible to limit the true task of rational specula-tion and of religious philosophy to the merely speculative; we have a more lively sense of our responsibility, of our infirmities and of our solidarity—and do not these theses, properly understood and resting upon definite principles, constitute a clear advance in Christian awareness?

7. Again, since philosophy cannot demonstrate or produce the supernatural, for it cannot even provide or contain the reality of natural action, it follows that it must proceed, like the sciences properly so-called, indirectly, eliminating incomplete solutions one by one, determining what can give them the appearance of sufficing and trying to find how, in certain conditions, these rough drafts of unco-ordinated solutions, containing as they do the germ of further development, may become the instruments of the solution itself. Instead of including within itself revealed data or merely juxtaposing them in an unintelligent descriptive list of heterogen-eous elements, philosophy, using a complex and cogent method, with which it can include all forms of thought and life within a single determinism, has as its task to show us both what we inevit-ably have and what we necessarily lack so that we may integrate into our willed activity all that is postulated by our spontaneous activity. Without taking anything for granted, without introducing anything from outside, always taking persons and ideas for what they really are, it claims nothing more nor less than to bring to light the inner mechanism which moves them and to determine the bearing of it, measuring the final stage by the initial impulse. Since it has not to give us the reality of the solution, it has only to show us that we cannot disregard it legitimately and with impunity, and so it aims at taking into account as exactly as possible the mysterious system of compensation and interplay which controls the elements of this life of ours and makes it what it is. Philosophy does not allow us to veil these depths from our own eyes any more than it allows us to reach the solution of our problem by our own unaided resources.

But it also follows that philosophical conclusions, in virtue of this attitude of reserve, are necessary ones, even in regard to the religious question, and constitute an apodeictic demonstration. So long as one attributed to them a realist or ontological meaning, if I may so put it, it was necessary to forgo deriving from them too conclusive an apologetical proof, so as to leave the field free for whatever grace might prove to do; one had to say that 'to believe by way of reason is not so to believe that the mind cannot entertain a doubt or scruple'; one had to avoid trying to explain how it is that we are necessarily held responsible for what is nevertheless not necessarily demonstrated; one had to eschew a directly philosophical inquiry into the nature of the supernatural and to refrain from justifying the utility of revelation at the bar of reason, merely indicating that without it the essential truths would be too little known, too slowly discovered and too much involved in error. It is thus a matter of the highest moment that one should now be able to say that philosophical conclusions, in so far as they express the innermost demands of the conscience and the postulate of action in its entirety have, because they are limited, an apodeictic value over their whole range, and that, if they leave untouched the mystery of the real and the mystery of the supernatural, it is not because they lack precise and compelling proof but because, beyond all speculative demonstration, there still remains the reality, the essential element of personal effort and the acceptance of grace.

This delimiting and unifying of rational apologetics, which gives it at the same time all the continuity and all the scientific rigour which it had never before enjoyed, is perhaps the most important and most striking of the conclusions to which we have been so far led. For if it is indispensable to bear in mind the gift of God in saving faith, it is equally indispensable, if our thought and our life are to judge us eternally with a sovereign severity, that we should be able to judge them ourselves, here and now and in all their exigencies, with a sufficient clarity.

8. Since philosophy considers the supernatural only in so far as the idea of it is immanent in us, and since it considers natural reality as transcending the knowledge which we have of it, it prepares us to understand better and better that we cannot disregard

nature nor confine ourselves to it; that the human order has its
share in everything but finds its sufficiency in nothing; that our
natural being, although incapable of achieving itself and despite the
devastating claims made upon it by the supernatural which it has
failed to recognize, is nevertheless indestructible; and that, in its
radical insufficiency, man's action remains coextensive with that
of God, according to the theological doctrine so rigorously summed
up by St Bernard: '*Non partim gratia, partim liberum arbitrium, sed
totum singula opere individuo peragunt; ut mixtim, non singillatim;
simul, non vicissim per singulos profectus operentur. Totum quidem hoc,
et totum illa; sed ut totum in illo, sic totum ex illa.*'[1]

So philosophy shows us that man can never legitimately or in
reality confine himself to the human level, that, even when he
appears to do so, this appearance conceals, if he is sincere, a real
participation in what he fails to recognize, and that, in a word, no
natural solution is a solution at all; but it also makes us realize that
the rejection or systematic disregard of what is found to be implied
by human action is not simply the privation of a higher and super-
erogatory state, but a positive failure, and that the human order is
not only sufficiently solid and subsistent to be the foundation for all
divine projects but also remains indestructibly itself even beneath
the weight of eternal responsibilities. Thus, it seems, fresh light is
shed upon a question which is a source of scandal and distress to our
contemporaries, the question of damnation. And thus again the
much misunderstood doctrine of 'vicarious satisfaction' is clarified:
in view of the providential plan and the unity of the divine purpose,
which is free in principle but bound up together in all its parts, man's
supernatural vocation implies that sin is deicide; that man should
be what he is, and from the moment when he became a sinner, it
was therefore a matter of strict necessity that Christ should suffer
and die;[2] and it was further necessary, in order that sin should be
pardoned and effaced in man, that this necessary death should be at

---

[1] *Tractatus de gratia et libero arbitrio*, chap. xiv, § 47.

[2] *Tr.* This excursion into 'philosophical theology' is far too brief to be satisfactory. For an exposition of Blondel's thought on the Redemption see, in
particular, *Exigences Philosophiques du Christianisme* (which appeared posthumously
in 1950), pp. 122 f.

the same time willingly and lovingly accepted; it was necessary, again, for this necessary and freely redemptive oblation to be efficacious in each of us, that each of us should consent to it and should co-operate in the saving expiation, which, though sufficient and superabundant in itself, is incomplete in us unless we do our part.

Thus we discover man's natural incapacity not only to reach his supernatural end but also to enclose himself in his own natural order and to find an end of a kind in that; but we discover, too, the astonishing power which this same man has, despite his dependence, since he can not only lose his soul without abolishing himself but also rise up against God and lead him to death—or follow him in life; and this shows, more than anything else could do, the consistency and the dignity of man in his greatest weakness, the divine cost of his life, the extent of his human duty, and the solidity of fundamental human nature, since God, who can be content with the fulfilment of these natural human obligations, cannot dispense man from them.

9. Man, thrown back upon himself and cut off from the higher life, whose source is not in himself, is condemned simply because he has not changed: and this shows, from the point of view of the concepts which philosophy can only study in their relationships with one another, the absolute distinction between the natural and the supernatural: the opposite results of the alternative are not symmetrical, and 'yes' provides a superabundance infinitely greater than the positive declension which is brought about by 'no'. So, beyond the divine drama which is at work in the consciences of all men, there is now, for souls who believe and are alive, a new mystery of grace which Revelation alone can disclose to us and only to some extent.

While the distinction between the two orders remains complete and unplumbable, we gain a deeper insight into their connection and their harmony. Since man has his share in everything and his sufficiency in nothing, none of his thoughts or acts, despite their indestructibility, can validate itself, or, if one may so put it, be adequate to itself unaided. If in the study of sensible reality and even of the lowest forms of existence, we find, in so far as we try to disengage some objective element, that our thought loses itself in an endless flight and continually goes beyond itself without ever being able to pin down this sensible or scientific or metaphysical phenomenology, it is perhaps because we can never touch being at any point without encountering at least implicitly the source and bond of all being, the universal Realizer. Neither sensation, nor science, nor philosophy terminate absolutely in themselves οὐ τελευτῶσιν. Yet they cannot leave in mid-air or suppress these appearances which give them life, χαίρειν ἐὰν τὰ φαινόμενα ἀδύνατον. It would be a fine thing for philosophy to prepare or encourage one of the dogmatic definitions with which the future will perhaps enrich the ever-increasing treasury of the faith. There are two theological opinions, either of which we are at present free to choose: according to one, the Incarnation of the Word has as its motive simply original sin in view of the Redemption upon the Cross; according to the other, the original plan of creation embraces the mystery of the Man-God in such sort that the fall of man determined only the sorrowful and humiliating conditions which Christ accepted together with the superabundance of grace and dignity which is the fruit of this superabundance of love. It is possible that the Church will decide between these one day, and in favour of the second. For if it is true that the least of sensible phenomena and the most elementary of corporeal existences cannot be conceived as real unless we see an element implied in it which cannot be accounted for by the merely creative decree of the First Cause; if it is true that we cannot bring our action to completion or remedy our faults or even have a real and living idea of God himself without appealing to this mediator; if it is true, as St Theresa teaches, that it is an illusion to think that we can detach ourselves better from material things and have a purer knowledge of God if we leave aside the humanity of Christ, whereas in fact this sacred humanity, 'which ought not to be put in that class',[1] remains the only Way as well as the Supreme Truth, so that without it nothing in heaven or earth is intimately

---

[1] *Tr.* That is, not a humanity like any other humanity. The rather baffling notion of Christ's mediation as the final *explanation* of objective knowledge was entertained by Blondel throughout his career. It must not be taken to deny that our knowledge of reality is objective in itself (cf. Bouillard, pp. 159-63).

known, then it seems that philosophy, by demanding an element distinct both from nature and also from the Author of nature himself in order to conceive the effective realization of the whole order of things, would clarify and justify, from its own point of view, what is perhaps an implicit dogma, Emmanuel as the final cause of the creative plan.[1] So, after having first put aside, in order to define the notion of the supernatural, all questions of fact or of particular individuals, we should be led in the end by this unique route, and in a manner which is at once discreet and imperious, to suggest in its most precise form the need for the concrete reality of the Word, to prepare at this point alone, which alone the philosopher can touch, for the insertion of historical apologetics, and to justify the necessity of studying, acknowledging and bringing alive for one's own mind the fact of all facts, the divine fact of Christianity. And then this sublime postulate of philosophical reason would be in harmony, without any confusion of roles, with the most human of the sciences, the science of history, as well as with the loftiest teaching of theology.

[1] Not, of course, that God is to be made passive, by reaction, to the activity of things or made subject to the necessity of perceiving or submitting to them in order really to produce them. But if we enter upon the labyrinth of sensible existence, if we consider that knowledge and being on this level form the first solid link in the whole chain of our representations and realize that the consistency and fixity of all the rest depends on it, and if finally we try to conceive the conditions on which all the realization of phenomena depends, including those which we call secondary or subjective qualities, those, in short, which manifestly presuppose, in order to exist, rational perception in a corporeal organism, then it will certainly seem that this reality must be inevitably conceived as bound up with the organic and rational activity of a mediator capable of attaching this form, inconsistent in itself, to the existence of the absolute being, who alone, in seeing, brings what he sees into existence, but who sees it *aliter per divinitatem, aliter per carnem,* whether one must find this mediating flesh in man united to the Word who enlightens every mind, and whose part would thus be to act as the universal bond of being throughout all history, or whether one must, in fact, have recourse to Christ's Incarnation itself.

3. The constitution of integral philosophy in integral Christianity

From what has been said it is perhaps legitimate to conclude that the conflict between rationalism and Catholicism can be resolved to the material advantage both of philosophy and of the Christian conscience. So we should like to say to unbelievers and believers alike: 'There is only one religion which carries with it and demands Philosophy'. And it would be necessary to add: 'There is only one philosophy which leads to and calls for Religion'. But the relationships between religion and philosophy have been so misunderstood that friends have been taken for enemies and enemies for friends. And I have desired above all to put on their guard against these misunderstandings so many men of good will who unwittingly frustrate their own intentions.

In the secular duel which party succumbs and at whose expense is reconciliation achieved? What remains dead upon the battlefield, as the one deplorable cause of the misunderstandings and as a sort of pledge of a final agreement, is (among all the elements which scholasticism has put together) neither the Christian idea nor the philosophical idea but the middle term by which they had been united—the ancient conception of the divinity of reason, the realism, both ontological and intellectual, of a thought which controls everything and is everything, the doctrine of the self-sufficiency of metaphysics, the belief in the intrinsic consistency of objects apart from any mediating activity and simply as they are apprehended by the mind; in short, a false philosophy which sought to persuade us *a priori* that the rational order contains all the rest in an eminent degree. It appeared victorious, but hardly seems so now except to some who should have rejoiced in its defeat. For its victims still insist in trying to restore it because they wrongly think it the loyal servant of a theological rationalism which, itself legitimate, fundamentally condemns it. Let us at least learn the lesson that by bringing everything back to thought we are inevitably led to suggest that thought, in ourselves, is sufficient for everything.

What is it, then, that triumphs? It is Philosophy itself, thanks to the gentle and secret influence of the Christian spirit which it seemed to combat and which seems to resist it, the Philosophy which springs from the evolution of human thought not as a passing phase but as an acquisition justified in itself. For it is supremely instructive to see how, left to itself, exclusive rationalism or the bastard form of philosophy comes to limit itself in the way which is most in conformity with the fundamental requirements of Christianity. In fact, to be opposed to the recent transformations is to work against those who are working for us and to deny to them what they are offering to give us in large measure. It has needed the whole of a slow and laborious evolution of thought to reveal the true perspective, to bring to birth the only method which allows the constitution of an integral philosophy in integral Christianity, to lay the only foundations on which a new 'School' can be built—let us not lose, then, in the future, the advantages offered to both sides by the position which has now been reached. To insist on restoring what is dead in the old School, killed by a dead rationalism, is to fall inevitably under the assaults of the double critique which has destroyed the Christian pseudo-philosophy by the metaphysics of transcendence and the rationalist pseudo-philosophy by the doctrine of immanence, and is now itself outdated.

No doubt, whatever one does to justify this total transposition of philosophical questions, even if one shows its necessity and its advantages by a detailed account of it, it will not be possible to make contact at once with the majority even of reflective minds, precisely because of the value and the novelty of the points of view laid open: too many conventions and interests are at stake. Many perhaps, finding that a good deal of trouble has to be taken in order to reach conclusions which seem not very different from those familiar to them, will prefer, through mere habit or human respect or fear of effort, to make charges against what I have written or cast suspicion on it instead of considering it, without troubling to argue and without saying whether they take their stand on a defined dogma or a supposed philosophical orthodoxy. And here I must remark that if I have confined myself to questions of method it is because the way in which one reaches conclusions helps not only to make them valid, but also to define them, to renew them, and to enrich them. Above all, so long as Catholicism does not take this road, it will remain outside the pale in the world of philosophical thought and will not be able to encounter thinking men or to be encountered by them. And here is a fresh source of mutual recriminations. For those who are perhaps already disposed to approve the method or capable of grasping the necessity of it will reject the conclusions, and those whom the conclusions might attract will reject the method. However, if there are always in Christianity latent virtualities which each age discovers in proportion to its needs, one may hope that from the great movement of thought in our time there will emerge, little by little, the philosophical form which is in keeping with its religious requirements. Protestantism, swept on by the current of its logic, has not been able to stand up against its own principles: its prompt and facile agreement with an ephemeral pseudo-philosophy has been so far only a superficial crisis. After so many transient experiments and hasty improvisations the time has come perhaps for the truly Catholic idea to show its power and to promote a philosophy which is the more appropriate to it the more autonomous it is, a philosophy which only gives proof of its solidity by being more difficult to constitute and more impersonal. We must not complain of having to make a greater effort if it leads to a greater result: on the contrary, we must rejoice to see that easy-going hopes are disappointed, that egoistical pessimism is condemned, that an attachment to our own way of thinking has become impossible, that the demands of an impatient or interested zeal have been rejected and disallowed by events. France, which has been accused of lacking the philosophical spirit by reason of its Catholic formation, is perhaps the more capable of sustaining trials and troubles because it is the more capable of finding truth and goodness. It is time to realize these disregarded potentialities. Looking, then, to the future, let us descry in these present conflicts the ultimate triumph of the Christ who was humble and hidden in his life and is still humble and hidden in his progress through human history, even leaving to his temporary opponents the apparent initiative for those great inspirations of justice and of reason which have their secret origin in himself.

Perhaps this philosophy which boldly claims that it cannot leave aside the problem of the supernatural, which is more closely bound up at all points than heretofore and which at the same time goes further in the critique of the very notion of religion, which lays bare the neuralgic points and faces perilous paths by going beyond doctrines of the most advanced kind which have been most justly condemned[1]—perhaps this philosophy will seem temerarious to some. But the danger does not lie there. Two hundred and fifty years ago Pascal was forced to touch on burning topics with a frankness which seemed to him to violate certain reticences of the Christian soul, and he uttered this cry of indignation in his private notes: 'The wretches who have obliged me to speak about the heart of religion!'[2] For of course, with his Jansenist and fideist tendencies, he feared to lay a sacrilegious hand upon that mystical foundation of all authority which he found in custom and even in mere outward show;[3] but perhaps, with the perspicacity of genius, he realized that reason was not yet armed to face, in the full light of day and in the spirit of criticism, the terrible combat which Bossuet too saw to be in store for Christianity. That combat is now ours, and we have still to sustain it without disguise and without reserve. In its boldest effort to close the door to faith reason has gathered strength to open it. After all its endeavours we have nothing to compromise by frank speaking. The only danger now lies in abandoning the strict rules of a discussion which must go on relentlessly to the end. To obey these rules, in a matter in which silence or lack of interest are supremely injurious, is the greatest claim to intellectual respect and the only bond—but one most close and strong—between souls who are apparently sundered by an abyss of positive beliefs but who should

[1] *Tr.* What Blondel presumably means is that these doctrines confused the supernatural with the natural by failing to tackle the problem on the profoundest level.

[2] Pascal, *Pensées, fragments et lettres*, Ed. Faugère, I, 282.

[3] *Tr.* '*Même dans le grimace*'—Blondel seems to be referring to Pascal's advice to take holy water even if one feels a distaste for it. This passage must not be taken as implying a general depreciation of Pascal, with whom Blondel has much in common (see E. Borne, *Passion de la Vérité*, and Introduction, p. 47). Commenting on the last paragraph of the *Letter*, he remarks (*Le Problème . . .* p. 41) that his expectations for modern philosophy have been to some extent disappointed, but that his peroration (although 'sentimental rather than illuminating') 'at least indicates the true direction of my endeavour and of my hopes, which have not failed entirely of fulfilment'.

be fraternally united in their anxious search. For this search, which precedes and can even substitute for possession, must always accompany it, follow it and vivify it; it is the human response to grace and the intellectual condition of charity. And the more frank and unyielding it is as between discordant minds, the more salutary it is through the esteem which it engenders at the price of a radical sincerity. Let us say, then, contradicting Pascal's remark in a spirit of peace and of truth, that we are 'happy to be able to speak, to be obliged to speak, to see so many constrained and eager to speak, about the very heart of religion'.

PART THREE

PREFATORY NOTE

to HISTORY AND DOGMA

The *Letter on Apologetics* had been written in self-defence and was a reply to specific criticisms and misunderstandings. In the following year, 1897, Blondel began assembling material for a full-scale work, *L'Esprit chrétien*, in which he intended to re-state his position in the crisis and criticize his opponents, of the right and the left. But the work hung fire, he could not find a satisfactory form for what he had to say, and in the meanwhile the situation was changing rapidly. The crisis had taken a leap forward: the Modernist Controversy was in full swing. The biblical question had been growing in importance. The encyclical *Providentissimus Deus* (1893) had given official welcome to scriptural studies; Mgr d'Hulst had promoted them, and in Loisy had found a scholar of the highest quality. In 1902 Albert Houtin's book *La Question biblique chez les catholiques de France au xix siècle* publicized the situation, and in the following year Loisy published *L'Évangile et l'Église* which amounted to putting a pistol to the heads of the authorities. Père M-J. Lagrange's *La Méthode historique* appeared later in the year. Blondel was already deeply involved. *L'Esprit chrétien* was to have contained a chapter on the exegetical question. He had corresponded at length on the subject with Loisy (Feb.-March 1903) and with von Hügel (Jan.-April 1903).[1]

Blondel had been very much impressed by Houtin's book, which had made him realize more fully than hitherto the seriousness of the position. The Abbé Wehrlé shared his view. 'In the crisis through

---

[1] The letters are published in *Au Cœur de la Crise Moderniste*. Several passages in *History and Dogma* are taken from these letters.

which we are passing we need sharp-shooters, men who will risk everything and, I would add, make an authority, which *will never retreat* before mystical and candid souls, reflect. For it, too, fear will be the beginning of wisdom . . . Make them realize that *apologetics for others* is of no value for anyone, whether for those inside or for those outside. *Apologetics for us* is one which justifies our beliefs *to us ourselves*, in the full sincerity of a conscience at last returning to honesty.'[1]

L'Évangile et l'Église made Blondel decide to intervene publicly. Its success, even with his friend Wehrlé, made him see the danger of the alternatives of Modernism and Veterism. He was not only fully informed about Loisy's historicism; he was no less well prepared by his controversy with the Abbé Hyppolite Gayraud to measure the inadequacies of Veterism. Gayraud, Deputy for the Finistère, formerly a Dominican, was a typical scholastic controversialist, neither willing nor able to see his opponent's meaning and solely concerned to win a verbal victory. 'You will have seen,' Mourret wrote to Blondel in November 1903, 'that the Abbé Gayraud has still not understood an explanation given to him twenty times already.' Rivière in his history of modernism[2] says that: 'The traditional positions were firmly held by H. Gayraud.' Blondel's alarm at the ease with which Loisy's *historicism* was swallowed, and at the blind confidence of those who did not accept it in the shallow *extrinsicism* of Gayraud, is hardly to be wondered at, and dictated the form which this second letter—addressed to his friend Fonsegrive —was to take.[3]

History and Dogma is, as Blondel says in the opening paragraphs, his answer to the crisis which, but for the 'brutal facts',[4] the author-

---

[1] *Au Cœur*, p. 153.   [2] Riviere, *Le Modernism*, p. 126.

[3] Blondel more than once disclaims any intention, in the section on historicism, of criticizing a particular writer, obviously Loisy. He was not so concerned about the first section on extrinsicism. He had no wish to get Loisy into trouble with the authorities. This needs to be said in view of the fact that M. Poulat, in his history of Modernism, makes out that Blondel was being pharisaical. This is not the only occasion on which M. Poulat's prejudice against Blondel eludes his control and makes him forget the exacting standards of impartiality at which he aims.

[4] *History and Dogma*, p. 230, below.

ities of Catholicism would have liked to ignore. And although he confined himself to one particular point, he thought that his answer to historicism and extrinsicism—the notion of Tradition put forward in the third section—would indicate his attitude in other matters. The essay is Blondel's answer to the crisis as focused by the biblical question.

'Had he been born sixty years later,' Henri Bremond wrote, 'Newman would not have written the *University Sermons*, nor the *Grammar of Assent*, he would have written *L'Action*.' This was not of course meant to be taken too literally; all Bremond meant was that there was a certain cousinship of mind between Newman and Blondel, and that circumstances had changed very considerably. He might have added in the same vein that Newman would not have written the *Essay on Development* but *History and Dogma*, Blondel's 'Essay on Tradition'.

Like M. Jourdain, who had to be taught that he spoke in prose, Catholics had to be taught that they lived by Tradition, and what Tradition was.

No doubt as long as Christian beliefs seemed to coincide immediately with Christian facts, there was no need to look elsewhere than in history for the basis of dogma. But for informed minds, the development of critical research and the progressive analysis of religious psychology make that immediacy impossible. If then, one thinks, as I do for my part, that Catholicism is definitely tied not only to essentially human states of consciousness but to divinely incarnated realities, it is absolutely indispensable to accept a thesis analogous to the one which I tried to defend from the point of view of a philosophy of action, by showing how 'Christian knowledge' organises itself within the Church's tradition. . . . It is the legitimate progress of historical and religious sciences which urgently demands an analogous progress in philosophical and theological methods. To believe that the initiatives and discoveries of criticism can be joined without danger to the old scientific mentality and with speculative methods dating from a period when the problems of today were not suspected—that is the illusion, the extreme danger which I cannot stress too much.[1]

The need for a developed notion of Tradition had grown with the critique of traditional beliefs and quite simply of the value of Tradition which Bayle and Richard Simon had begun. But nothing had been done to answer that criticism (with the exception of Vico's attempt, which no one, and least of all his co-religionists, attended to) and when, after the shock of the Revolution, the idea of Tradition began to seem of the highest importance, those who used it used it as a shield against change and revolution. Tradition was viewed in a political light and, regardless of what it was applied to, came to mean the conservation of a heritage, of an object, and in Christianity of a clearly defined object, the 'deposit of faith'. The handing down of this 'deposit' was looked upon as an impersonal process; the whole emphasis fell on *what* was handed down, and no thought was given to *how* it was handed down. The common view of Tradition was mechanical, and it would hardly be a caricature to say that it was so objective as not to imply any believers to hand down the deposit. This impersonal way of conceiving Tradition led inevitably to what Blondel calls *fixisme*, the notion that nothing whatsoever should change and therefore in practice to *un rétrogradisme meurtrier*, a fatally retrograde attitude towards intellectual questions. The doctrine of development was not—though it might imply—a complete doctrine of Tradition, and it was conceived and allowed as the one answer to the appeal to 'the Bible only'. Blondel's essay implies a radical change of scene.

This can perhaps be indicated by saying that Blondel's notion of Tradition was conceived not in a political light or context, but in a cultural or aesthetic one. He was not trying to defend continuity; he was not concerned in the first place with *what* was handed down, but with *how* it was handed down. In *Reflections on History* Jacob Burckhardt observes that 'one of the marks of higher cultures is their capacity for renaissances'. In the Christian sphere that capacity is Tradition, an apanage of the Church, of the community, of the

[1] *De la Valeur historique du Dogme, Les Premiers Ecrits de Maurice Blondel*, Vol. III, pp. 235-6.

collective, not of the individual—it is, as it were, the Church's culture. Tradition, Blondel says, is not another word for evolution, which is the result of external pressures, nor is it 'a mystical empiricism', nor 'a dialectical movement', but *a living synthesis*. His notion of Tradition is, of course, conceived 'from the point of view of a philosophy of action', and this needs to be stressed since otherwise his use of such expressions as 'collective thought' or 'unconscious thought' may sound dubious if considered exclusively from the point of view of discursive thought. Not only what Blondel says in *L'Action*, but perhaps still more what he says in *La Pensée* would have to be invoked if everything he says and implies were to be developed and examined. Some of the difficulties which his articles raised at the time were put to him by Joseph Segond, who succeeded him as Professor of Philosophy at Aix. Blondel's answer may help to prepare the way for the third and most important part of the essay:

First of all, I do not consider Tradition to be a separate element which can be reduced entirely to its intellectual justifications; I regard it as the living synthesis of all the speculative and ascetic, historical and theological forces: 'It embraces' I said, 'the data of history, the efforts of reason and the experiences of faithful action'. In consequence of which, secondly, it must be recognized that the 'efforts of the reason' are never commensurate with the synthesis which we have only to show to be legitimate without claiming to be a judge of its assertions; in a word, we must not suppose that each one of us can constitute his Tradition by himself, or justify to himself all the acts of the Church; for even after having recognized the legitimacy and rationality of the general and permanent authority of the Catholic Tradition, it is normal that one should not be able to discern the particular and actual applications of that authority immediately and with individual certainty. Therefore, thirdly, one must avoid bringing back the fact of Tradition and the facts which it affirms to our ideas; it is our ideas which must submit and be brought back to the facts: for the facts affirmed by the Authority of the Church presuppose the work of the collective reason, and are not therefore answerable to the individual reason alone.[1]

As Père René Marlé says in his *Postface* to *Au cœur de la crise moderniste*,[2] the problem of Tradition 'is at the same time that of the relations of Scripture to the Church, that of an eternal truth given "once and for all" the manifestation of which develops in time. It is the problem of a "deposit" which subsists in certain respects objectively in a letter and an institution divinely fixed in "the fullness of time" and which nevertheless only finds its truth in a subjective appropriation, indissolubly personal and communal'. It involves a theology of history, of the Church's 'contemporaneity with Christ' (Kierkegaard), for 'development is continuous creation, starting from a germ which transubstantiates its nourishment'.[3]

In spite of the originality and importance of the articles they were neither published without difficulty nor received without suspicion. Before finally agreeing to Fonsegrive's request, Blondel bound himself to abide by the opinion of his friend Mourret on the advisability or otherwise of publication. When Mourret received the first of the three articles (on Extrinsicism) he was seriously alarmed that what could be taken as a caricature of thomist extrinsicism would get Blondel into difficulties and so jeopardize all his future work (as was to happen to Laberthonnière a few years later). Mourret was of the opinion that Blondel's views were perfectly orthodox, but he knew the dangers, the vindictive mentality of the *Action française* and the implacable attitude of the neo-thomists. Blondel's position, he thought, was altogether too delicate to allow of such a risk. Blondel himself was dismayed by the reaction which his article had produced and wrote at once to Wehrlé, who, being in Paris and knowing Mourret, could discuss the matter with him. He had, Blondel explained, only one thought, to do everything in his power to prevent the disaster he feared, *religio depopulata*; and he had written his article moved by 'an inner light'. His wife and his family, too, had urged him not to expose himself to danger, but he felt with his whole being that what he had to say should be made public. Wehrlé was finally won over and after further consultations with Mourret it was agreed that Blondel should publish his articles —a last minute decision communicated by telegram so as to give

---

[1] *Au Cœur*, p. 201.   [2] *Au Cœur*, p. 351.   [3] *Au Cœur*, p. 129.

Blondel time to inform Fonsegrive that after all the articles were to appear (in *La Quinzaine,* 1904).

History and Dogma was by no means welcome either to the right or to the left. Duchesne, Mourret wrote, 'does not appear to have found great interest in your articles and obstinately continues in his malicious contempt for philosophy.' Vigouroux, the 'orthodox' biblical critic, did not bother to read it; Battifol was, like Duchesne, though more disingenuously, irritated by a criticism of Loisy which trespassed beyond the field of history; von Hügel appears to have forgotten how much he had agreed with Blondel and rushed to the defence of Loisy in an article translated by Bremond: *Du Christ éternel et de nos christologies succéssives.* But though the points which he made were well argued he does not seem either then or later to have grasped the importance of what Blondel meant by Tradition. The criticisms which appeared in Battifol's *Bulletin de Toulouse* by M. Venard were the result of misunderstandings and these Blondel answered in *La Valeur historique du Dogme.* Only Blondel's friends, Goyau, Wehrlé, Bremond, were satisfied. But at least Cardinal Mathieu had expressed his approval. Mourret felt that Blondel had had a lucky escape: 'You were well inspired to call your synthetic principle by its *traditional* name, *Tradition.* If you had called it "the collective expression of the Church" or "the action of the infallible spirit on the Christian community", or some analogous expression, you would have been thoroughly compromised'.[1]

---

[1] *Au Cœur,* p. 188.

HISTORY AND DOGMA

I. THE PROBLEM   *page* 222

II. INCOMPLETE AND INCOMPATIBLE SOLUTIONS   224
    1. *Extrinsicism*
    2. *Historicism*

III. THE VITAL ROLE AND THE PHILOSOPHICAL BASIS OF
    TRADITION   264

My dear Sir,

You have asked what my attitude is to the difficulties raised by the biblical problem in its present state, and how, in so far as it falls within my sphere of competence, I envisage the methodological and doctrinal questions by which many minds at the present time are disturbed. I will answer you as clearly as possible; and if you consider the following pages would help some of your readers to make the required distinctions, strengthening their faith without infringing on the legitimate requirements of thought, I should be happy to see them published: these are critical times, when everyone is beset by a common anxiety, and it is the duty of even the most reticent of believers to proffer his humble testimony to those he can usefully address.

With every day that passes, the conflict between tendencies which set catholic against catholic in every order—social, political, philosophical—is revealed as sharper and more general. One could almost say that there are now two quite incompatible 'catholic mentalities', particularly in France. And that is manifestly abnormal, since there cannot be two Catholicisms. I shall not pause here to define these two attitudes or their complex unity, nor to demonstrate the solidarity of the diverse tendencies within their antagonistic systems; that will be the object of an extended work which I am preparing on *L'Esprit chrétien*.[1] I shall confine myself to one

---

[1] Tr. Never completed in this first form, but the title was used in 1944 and the book retained certain of its original characteristics. The two attitudes were, however, defined, and some of the material of *L'Esprit chrétien* was used in *La Semaine Sociale de Bordeaux*, published in *Annales de Philosophie chrétienne*.

particular point, closely connected, however, with the rest, on which you and one or two others have questioned me, to the problem of the relation of dogma and history, and of the critical method and the necessary authority of doctrinal formulae. Perhaps the solution which I propose to that painful and dangerous conflict will indicate the direction in which the solution to the other conflicts should be sought.

I. THE PROBLEM

It is important to determine the real point at issue at the very outset. But the difficulty in the way of doing so is greater than appears. For both sides claim to say things which are valid for an independent mind, and to avoid begging the question, and disclaim starting from faith on the pretext of arriving at it. Both sides claim to recognise in practice and to justify in theory the divine character of Christianity and the legitimacy of the Catholic Church's claims. Both profess to believe in the inspiration of Scripture and the truth of positive revelation. Both affirm that if facts are to support faith they must possess an independent consistency, and that faith in its turn illuminates and guarantees the facts; in a word, that the Bible upholds the Church just as the Church upholds the Bible. Both claim to speak in the name of historical accuracy and the given facts of tradition, in the interest of faith and of a truly Catholic sense. And yet both sides reproach one another with endangering religion, both the spirit and the letter of religion. Which side, then, is mistaken, and how is it that, starting from premises which appear to be formally identical, they end with contrary conclusions?

It is useless, in this instance, to invoke the facts and texts without further ado in the hope of elucidating and reducing the conflict.[1] Everyone invokes them, and everyone makes them testify in his favour, only to end in further disagreement without arriving at its

---

[1] It goes without saying that I exclude the sovereign role of authority from discussion as being above everything. But its decisions, although above rational justification, need nevertheless to be understood with the ears of the spirit in order to be accepted as they should be, *rationabiliter*.

real source and in consequence without engaging in a discussion which might be both clarifying and pacifying. Nor would it suffice to determine, by way of a preliminary discussion, the legitimate claims of the historical method and the rules for the interpretation of official documents; for they are interpreted in opposite senses, since the rules of exegesis and the necessary prolegomena of biblical criticism are themselves dominated by the problem both old and new which we have to solve. As a result of not having dealt explicitly with the problem and all the new facts, neither side understands the other even when using the same words, nor do they, in fact, meet, even when seeming to come to grips over the essential matter under discussion. What, then, is this primordial question, the source, it would appear, of misunderstandings and divergence of views?

If Christian facts (history) and Christian beliefs (dogma) coincided in the light of immediate experience or complete evidence; if one only had to *believe* what others have *seen* and affirmed, the difficulty would not arise. But it is generally agreed that there is, as it were, a double movement between fact and faith, a sort of coming and going passing over two obscure intervals: for while it is true that historical facts are the foundations of the Catholic faith, they do not of themselves engender it, nor do they suffice to justify it entirely; and, reciprocally, the Catholic faith and the authority of the Church which it implies guarantee the facts and draw from them a doctrinal interpretation which convinces the believer as would a historical reality itself, but on other grounds than those which the historian is able to verify. In order that that circle should not be a vicious one, it would seem that, apart from simple fact and dogmatic ideas, and without having immediate and exclusive recourse to divine grace, there must be an explanatory principle and a source of movement which accounts for the double coming and going—the movement from the historical data to a faith which goes beyond what these provide for an ordinary witness—and the movement from faith to really objective affirmations and to realities which constitute Sacred History inserted into the heart of ordinary, everyday history, and incarnating the ideas in the facts. Where, then, shall we look for the light and the strength to enable us to take that double step, in a word to achieve the synthesis of history and dogma while respecting their independence and solidarity, which are both equally necessary?

Now if it is true that this is a fundamental question for Catholic exegesis, it is also true that it has hardly ever been treated for its own sake, under its twofold aspect and distinguishing the two senses, the initial and the final ones, of history—the two senses which we must try to unite and harmonise instead of substituting or sacrificing the one to the other. In fact, no doubt, the difficulty is solved where the believer is concerned; and that is why Catholic apologists and historians do not begin by examining it. But an effective solution to a problem, an implicit solution which allows one to discuss further questions explicitly, is one thing; and quite another the scientific method which is not content to juxtapose supposedly scholarly theses and broad affirmations without critical discussion. The weakness of basing research or speculative constructions on principles which have been insufficiently analysed will appear as soon as we begin our examination. For it will then be seen that contrary to their own declarations, but impelled by the logic of hidden postulates, some tend to behave as though history had to depend absolutely on dogma, others as though dogma had to proceed exclusively from history and be subordinate to it. And yet the whole point is precisely to discover what is the authority proper to each, in particular from what source dogma derives what is original and authoritative in it; how, in a word, history and dogma still continue and will continue to verify and vivify one another. For the way in which theology has in the past legitimately interpreted the facts, while nourishing itself upon them, will teach us the normal way by which the sacred deposit develops, by which it will always adapt itself to the course of history.

II.   INCOMPLETE AND INCOMPATIBLE SOLUTIONS

Since neither facts nor ideas by themselves suffice for faith, should we look to the facts, or to the ideas, or to neither for the element capable of operating the synthesis? In order to discover what history can and must provide for dogma, what dogma can and must provide for history, we must ask: on what ground common to both does the exchange between them take place, and on what conditions is a fertile contact between them possible?

Recent discussions have yielded few methodical answers to these apparently elementary questions. They have been answered, if at all, indirectly and in practice, that is in a concealed manner, and in the course of solving other questions. Before they can be profitably examined they must be isolated from the more or less composite solutions in which they are involved. I have, therefore, no one in particular in mind: I have isolated certain abstract theses and presented them with a clarity and a rigour which they do not possess in reality. For a happy inconsequence and illogical compensations often correct, for the time being, the dangers of excessive tendencies. But, whatever may be said of their artificial and imaginary character, such theses are, little by little, taking shape and body; their influence, at first hidden and confused, becomes more and more marked, for the good reason that, unless one sees their logical structure clearly, one is not on one's guard against their long-term consequences.

However, in order to emphasize that we are dealing with abstract entities, and to establish the new state of old questions, the terms of which are defined anew by recent controversies, I shall make use of certain barbarous neologisms with a view to fixing attention and throwing into relief the exclusive character of each thesis. *Extrinsicism* and *historicism* offer two answers—each in their way incomplete, but equally dangerous to faith—to the essential problem now before the Christian conscience; they are opposite extremes, but of the same kind, based upon similar habits of mind, suffering from analogous philosophical lacunae, and aggravating one another by their conflict. Anyone desirous of subjecting his beliefs to reflective examination and accepting the critical conclusions to which it leads him and relying at the same time on one or other of these exclusive theses would risk losing his faith. How important, then, to realise plainly what they really are, and how essential to indicate where the saving solution lies!

1. *Extrinsicism*

How, from the point of view which I have now to describe, are we going to envisage the relation of facts to dogmas, and to the study of the scriptures, the rational justification of their value, a suitable type of commentary and, in a word, the determination of the Christian supernatural?

To some people the answer appears simple. All they ask of the facts is that they should serve as signs to the senses and as common-sense proofs. Once the signs have been supplied, an elementary argument deduces from them the divine character of the whole to which these signifying facts belong. Then, with the help of rational theses, they deduce the required universal conclusion from the premises, and take up an embattled position in the place to which history, it would seem, had yielded up the key, thanking her for her provisional services. From then on the place belongs to others, and she has only to take her leave.

Or rather history had never entered. For what was considered in the facts was not the facts for their own sakes or their original content, their real relation to the *milieu* in which they appeared, their position in the historical sequence; what was considered was their accidental, *extrinsic* and generic character; the aspect in which a phenomenon, it matters little what, appears miraculous or supernatural; a quality abstracted by spontaneous induction from a sensible perception, and set up as a notion which reason seizes upon and elaborates according to its absolute principles.[1] This means to say that a sign, a label, is simply detached from the facts and placarded at the entry to the dogmatic fortress. But it is noteworthy that this label remains external both to the events, which only support it arbitrarily, and to the ideas themselves, which accept it from

---

[1] It should be superfluous to note that I in no way deny the reality or the demonstrative force of signs and miracles: I am only criticizing the incomplete use which certain apologists make of them. They should not identify their way of interpreting and utilizing a proof with that proof itself, just when I am preparing to indicate and to preserve all its value.

outside, as an adventitious and empirical fact. From which it follows that the historical facts are merely a vehicle, the interest of which is limited to the apologetic use which can be made of them; for, whether *this* or *that* miracle is involved, provided it is *a* miracle, the argument remains the same. Moreover the argument itself only regards the supernatural as a sign, or a password, without having the right or the power or the desire to attain either the link which may exist between that miraculous character and the particular historical event invested with it, or the essential relationship which may exist between the facts and the ideas, or the connection which can and should be made between the given objective facts and our thought or our own lives.

Were this the place, I would point to the theory of knowledge on which this conception depends, and show how in its turn it appears to canonize that exclusive philosophy. It would then be seen that according to this thesis there is no knowledge which does not derive from sensation and that does not draw its whole matter from an external empirical fact: gross perceptions, as Leibnitz would have said, are the only gateway to the soul, the only initial ingredient of science. That being so, the supernatural itself can only be known, really known, in so far as it is originally offered under the guise of an external perception, so that the scientific knowledge which we might humanly acquire about it would never be greater than that which can be furnished by the given fact and its elaboration by the reason. Having entered the realm of the supernatural, the theologian will, no doubt, organize a science of Revelation. But here we are only concerned with the solidity of the bridge which leads there, so as to discover how much of our human science and our piled-up thought he can carry with him.

History, we said at the beginning, does not suffice where dogma is concerned, nor facts where faith is concerned. What, in the system which we are examining, is the source of the legitimate additional value which so inflates the brute facts of history? Can it come solely from grace? No, for short of falling into pure fideism, the act of faith must embrace the material of a human act. And what, in this instance, is that human act? It is restricted to furnishing the signs with the interpretation and the support of an argument which concludes from the miraculous to the divine.[1] Subsequently, no doubt, an appeal is made to complementary proofs; but they will only be confirmatory. As for the initial and principal impulse which should enable us to take the first step from the facts to dogma, it consists entirely in that rudimentary inference, the simplicity and clarity of which do not conceal its artificial and too exclusively, too immaturely, intellectual character. For after all, those who have the greatest faith in reason, in its scholarly and complex methods, in the richness of reality and in the profundity of the spiritual life, are just those who are most suspicious of abstract, scholastic ratiocination, particularly when it is a matter of planting in us and of justifying the total demands of a religion which lays claim to the whole man.

Thus the relation of the sign to the thing signified is extrinsic, the relation of the facts to the theology superimposed upon them is extrinsic, and extrinsic too is the link between our thought and our life and the truths proposed to us from outside. Such, in its naked poverty, is extrinsicism—it lacks the strength to make life circulate between faith and dogma or between dogma and faith, and allows them turn by turn to fall tyranically one upon the other.

And indeed, if the thesis is developed—disengaged from the correctives which prudence and evidence impose even upon the most intransigent theoreticians—what do we see happening, particularly where biblical criticism is concerned?

[1] The three points will then be arranged in sequence: the miraculous will be furnished by sensual perception; the divine disengaged by the work of reason, the supernatural defined by the facts of revelation authenticated by the divinely miraculous. But these elements remain external to one another and are only related, where we are concerned, by an argument, a purely intellectual structure, based solely on an empirical conclusion: as a result of which it is easy to see that the least weakness in the theory of perception, and in the reasoning required as a foundation, menaces its fragility. I am not maintaining that these theories are wrong, nor that the three elements do not exist, nor that the thread drawn tightly between them by the thesis I am analysing is not continuous: I am maintaining that these elements are linked together by something else in addition, and that that thread which may be sufficient for certain minds is not of a sufficiently strong texture to bring back all minds, as such, to the supernatural—and this, not just as a matter of practice, but in theory.

The moment one concludes globally from particular signs to the value of the whole, without considering the intrinsic nature of the affirmations made,[1] there is no more reason to modify a letter than to suppress a whole book, no more reason to modify the meaning of a line than to set aside the whole evidence of revelation. Since, from the point of view of the proof, the important thing is to establish *that* God has acted and spoken, not to examine *what* he said and did through human agencies; since all consideration of the historical or natural aspect of the facts is excluded from the argument on which the authority of the Bible is based, then the internal criticism of texts and the curiosity of historians seem futile or even sacrilegious, unless they are narrowly subordinated to the necessities of the thesis, and if they claim so much as provisional independence. The Bible is guaranteed *en bloc*, not by its content, but by the external seal of the divine: why bother to verify the details? It is full of absolute knowledge, ensconced in its eternal truth; why search for its human conditions or its relative meaning? The logical procedure of an exegete nourished on such thoughts is therefore to take the texts literally and to subject any critical study to the sovereign demand of a dogmatic ideology: the ageless facts are without local colour, vanish, as the result of a sort of perpetual docetism, into a light that casts no shadow, and disappear beneath the weight of the absolute by which they are crushed. As we saw, 'historical history' did not enter the fortress at the beginning; still less will it do so at the end.

The worst of it is that the thesis I have just sketched does not provide any means of accommodating itself to the facts, or any rule of interpretation: it cannot set bounds to itself. It is therefore from outside that it is controlled, and consequently grudgingly, because the control invariably resembles either a contradiction or a setback. Only the full weight of contrary evidence can stand up to the in-

---

[1] Need I observe, yet again, that I do not in any way throw doubt upon the absolute value and the total inspiration of the Bible, nor even upon the method which proceeds from that *de fide* thesis: I shall attempt to show *how* that global affirmation is in effect necessary and justifiable. May I beg the reader never to confuse the criticism of methods and justifications with the criticism of the truths themselves, the proofs of which it is my purpose to strengthen?

transigent absolutism of a thesis which, in its abstract purity, excludes obedience to experiment and suppleness of interpretation. Criticism will therefore be resisted with the help of forced distinctions; concessions will only be made in the last extremity, as though one were struggling against the attacks of an evil spirit. The impression given will be one of uninterrupted defeat, of the disillusioned obstinacy of men who imagined that they knew everything without having examined anything, of mystical ideologists claiming to impose their systems upon the concrete truth of history, and of men who end by taking refuge in an ostrich-like policy, shutting their eyes and not even allowing themselves to face too plainly the embarrassing literalness which they continue to teach the simple.

Is it possible, by this method, to accept the investigations of untrammelled history or to re-establish contact with authentically human facts? No doubt this seemed possible as long as the knowledge of the distant past remained so vague that the historian timidly left the last word to sweeping deductions and to large synthetic affirmations: what were a few little difficulties in matters of detail, a few *mendae*? The Scriptures *en bloc* appeared so solid that the imposing totality distracted attention from the tiny fissures which seemed here and there to reveal insignificant imperfections to the myopic eyes of a few scholars. But when, thanks to the discoveries of archaeology and philology, the past was resurrected—it had hitherto been defined by the requirements of ideology rather than by the exigencies of scientific observation—and intransigent deductions were confronted with facts which gave the lie to them, no longer on certain matters of detail, but on a whole aspect of the ordinary teaching which had been extracted from the Bible, then a dangerous crisis became inevitable.[1] Unable to discover an internal

---

[1] No doubt a philosophical criticism of extrinsicism might have revealed its inconsistencies and dangers: the incompleteness of certain forms of apologetic, which fail to analyse the reasons most likely to implant the faith in souls, has been pointed out a long time ago; they remain satisfied with such a purely formal argumentation that anyone who relied on it would risk seeing the *façade* collapse at the first shock. It required the visible and brutal warning of facts to reveal, if not to make intelligible to all, the profound crisis which it is our duty to face, not

principle of agreement in their ideology or a criterion of interpretation, some who were firmly anchored in their well-founded faith remained systematically hostile to everything which contradicted not only *the* faith but *their* faith; whilst others drifted haphazardly without knowing whether it was towards harbour or shipwreck, almost equally scandalized by the blindness of those who close their eyes to the facts, and by the importunate curiosity and the disturbing affirmations of those who expect too much light from them.

This preamble was necessary so that what I have now to say should be intelligible. For, in the very act of coming forward as the impartial expression of free and disinterested research, and still more so when it takes its stand in opposition to the old methods, historicism (and this brings me at last to the principal purpose of this study) cannot be fully understood except by reference to the contrasting thesis, the dangers of which it claims to parry, but which in many respects it only transposes, thus aggravating the evil by the remedy, and adding a good deal not only of pseudo-philosophy but of philosophy which is false.

2. Historicism

At first sight what could be more natural, more in conformity with a scientific habit of mind, and at the same time more compatible with the confidence of an unshakable faith, than to face up to the historical and philological facts of the biblical problem so as to allow honest independent study to produce an irresistible conviction in favour of the supernatural, incarnate in the long history of Revelation! If the supernatural is anywhere it is in the realities of history; so let us find it, where it is, as it is, obediently and with an imperturbable veneration for all the forms in which it has humbled itself: a folly and a scandal, perhaps, to a false science, but nourishment to the faith and the piety of those who do not prefer the complacent constructions of a system of thought, which is all the more human

---

only by receiving the directives and decisions of the only absolutely competent authority, but by trying to analyse their rational justification.

and subjective because it claims an absolute value, to the disconcerting inventions and humiliations of the divine.

As a result of searching the facts, not for their real being, but for a narrow ideology, everything has been compromised; living dogma has been imprisoned and swathed in bands which make it look like a corpse; history has been transformed into an allegory to which, subsequently, all the realism of the Christian's life has to be attached; but only a painted chain can be hung on a painted nail. Is it not legitimate, and indeed necessary, to adopt the opposite course: to consider the facts for their own sake, and, instead of looking for dogma and its abstract formula in history, to look for history and history alone even in regard to dogma, which will then come fully alive again? Could there be a finer and more decisive verification: the facts once more themselves, the corpus of the Scriptures exhumed from the sediment which obscured them, the sacred word untrammelled resounding once more through the world, an incredulous science hoist with its own petard, the sublime epic of God coming down to us through the generations, shown to us in a succession of progressive manifestations—that indeed is a project fit to awaken the enthusiasm of the scholar and the Christian. And it is because one has confidence in the conclusions of such an investigation that the most daring means become acceptable, that nothing is too audacious, and no sacrifice of mere detail too great. The role of the apologist is no longer to prepare a modest invitation and guarantee and placard it on the door of the palace of theology; from now on he will profit from the experience of mankind and the witness of history to render his tremendous testimony for the truth of the ever-present God, always acting in the world and in the Church, and to give his testimony from the very heart of the fortress.

It is perfectly true that history, like all sciences, has a consistency of its own and a relative autonomy (expressly recognized by the Vatican Council). Dogma does not disregard historical facts. One can do nothing without history and nothing against it. It even seems desirable, and nowadays almost indispensable, for the apologist to take up his position, together with those whom he is addressing, face to face with the facts, as though he neither believed nor knew anything of Christianity. But the question, however well framed, is still not the solution. And the difficulty here is only beginning to emerge. What attitude will the pure historian be led to take up in face of the Christian facts? Everything depends upon that. Can he legitimately ignore apologetic and dogmatic problems? And if he cannot, what method will he adopt in regard to these problems and what solutions? Thus we find ourselves back again at our initial difficulty without having advanced a single step: the Christian facts do not, by common consent, suffice for Christian beliefs; how then can one pass from the former to the latter? Some historians have claimed to practice free scientific enquiry and historical apologetics simultaneously and indivisibly; what then does their apologetic add to their history so as to augment the obscure meaning of the facts and to extract faith in the invisible supernatural from visible events? A moment ago the exclusively ideological sutures, while making the join, seemed too frail to sustain the new facts given by the moral and natural sciences; will the tissue of critical history be strong enough to bear the infinite weight of the ancient faith and the whole richness of catholic dogma?

Even if it were solely a matter of a specific problem peculiar to apologetics, and of the question of method peculiar to the relations between science and faith, there might be some cause for anxiety; for on what grounds, indeed, could one insist upon special precautions, and by what right could one impose limits upon history or, on the contrary, unaccustomed tasks, for the sake of either forbidding or prescribing conclusions falling short of or beyond its field of competence? But such is not the case. The human mind does not dispose of several ways of being reasonable and of ordering its thought. The critique which I am going to make of 'historicism' will be justified by the fact that I begin by adopting a purely rational point of view so as to dissipate certain confusions into which it seems to fall. It is only after showing on neutral ground its philosophical lacunae (A) that I shall indicate, as a consequence of its false principles or of their application, the inadequacy or the dangers of its apologetic (B).

A. We are asked to put our trust without prejudice or mental reserve in the testimony of history, as though it would produce an irresistibly strong proof of Christianity. But in the first place what are we to understand by this autonomy, and what is the normal relation of history with the other sciences? This preliminary question is an essential one; for the critical spirit does not consist solely in displaying sagacity in the detailed study of texts or in the interpretation of testimonies, in *criticizing our knowledge*; it consists in asking what a particular science or science in general can or cannot do, in a word it consists *in the critique of knowledge itself*. The scholar is only master in his own domain by virtue of a clear consciousness of its limits, of its entrances and exits, of its active and passive obligations.

Now, in what sense can one say that history is independent? Can one pretend that it is self-sufficient? Obviously not; it depends upon a number of other sciences, and no one denies it. Can one claim at least that, thanks to that assistance, it reaches doctrinal conclusions of which it remains, in the last resort, the judge, and which attain to the total reality? Once again, no; inevitably it remains dependent upon ulterior problems, upon sciences superior to it, which it can neither supplant nor replace except by a usurpation and by falsely proclaiming itself a sort of total metaphysics, a universal vision, a *Weltenschauung*: no one, it would seem, explicitly maintains that the historical synthesis sums up and dominates all the sciences, and that a speculative and dogmatic science is illusory and superfluous. So how are we to define the proper role of history and its relations with the connected sciences? It is here that the question is seen to be decisive, because it brings two conceptions of science to grips with one another, an ancient and a modern.

According to the Aristotelian doctrine, and to all those which can be affiliated to it, the sciences differ from one another as do different genera; they have their respective principles and their distinct objects; each one, master in its own house, freely pursues its task. There is no intelligible relation between the principles of the different sciences, for one does not go behind principles which are accepted on the evidence with which they appear; no legitimate transition from one genus to another is possible. Only the general principles of reason allow of a formal and extrinsic juxtaposition of these sciences and their results: each one of them adds its contingent of absolute truths to the sum total of knowledge; each one of them privately resolves a fraction of the problems raised by the study of things, and each therefore contributes a piece of reality itself; there is discontinuity in the work of the mind, contiguity in the objective results. For example, the historian purely as such performs his task behind his partition; he carries out his researches from his own point of view; and his labour finally furnishes a slice of real life and of absolute truth. Others must put up as best they can with his conclusions, which are what they are: so much the worse if they contradict other conclusions; for, if the facts are what they are said to be, they cannot be contradicted, and the historian is master in his own house and cannot be taken to task except by his peers. He has yielded up his fragment of ontology, and he owes neither more nor less. It is for the other scientists to carry out their tasks correctly; and the various pieces together will form a concert, like musicians who, without seeing or hearing one another, play the different parts of a symphony in proper time. On that view, the sciences appear to be independent in their researches and bound by their mutual results; they are obliged to find the necessary conclusions freely and in isolation, compelled as they are to agree with one another without having previous consultations; and this takes place, throughout, in a sphere of realist affirmations, which allow of no concessions, and provoke irreconcilable conflicts and contradictions.

The more recent conception of science and the sciences, however, is entirely different; and this conception, quite independently of the speculative justification which it possesses, seems to have demonstrated its soundness by its success. Just as algebra fertilized geometry, and mathematics physics, so the various scientific spheres are in perpetual communication. One must try to recapture the basic idea revealed to the critical mind under the all too often idolatrous names of determinism and universal solidarity; to the critical mind there is no question of affirming, from a metaphysical point of view, the subordination or fusion of beings in an absolute monism; it is simply a question, from a logical point of view, of grasping the unity of the problem of knowledge, and of understanding that the problem of existence cannot be asked except in relation to the total activity of the mind and of the combined data of the various sciences:

these sciences differ, therefore, less in respect of the diversity of their objects, which they help to make known in their ultimate reality, than in the diversity of methods and points of view opening on to an ulterior problem which they collaborate to define, to prepare and to posit rather than to resolve in its entirety; there is continuity and solidarity in the work of the mind; there is heterogeneity in the points of view and in the bearing of scientific affirmations; there is subordination of all the relative scientific data to the fundamental problems and the final solutions. Furthermore, none of the particular sciences claims to be sole mistress in its own house; none will remain in irreducible contradiction with its neighbour, because none of them produces anything ultimate, each having to compete with the other to furnish the data of that moral and religious metaphysical problem which it would be rash and precipitate to discuss fragmentarily or to solve piecemeal.

On what conditions can the critical mind, particularly where history is concerned, remain harmless, beneficial and, in a word, faithful to the genuine inspiration of which it is born? On condition that it keeps its researches perpetually dependent upon the ultimate questions which it has not the competence to decide by itself or, indeed, at all; for while the historian has, as it were, a word to say in everything concerning man, there is nothing on which he has the last word. What is, in fact, the object or rather the aspect which belongs to history, in the technical and contemporary sense of the word? Everything in the social life of mankind which can be verified or testified to, and everything which, with these facts as the basis of induction, is an explanation of the *fieri* of mankind, and a definition of the laws of its continuous and continual movement. The historian attempts first of all to become the perpetual contemporary of vanished ages and to picture them as might a universal witness, with the help of a detailed and synthetic view of the whole series which no partial or passing spectator could embrace; he then proposes to reintegrate scientifically, not the reality of life itself, but as intelligible an expression as possible of that reality and an explanation of the determinism which—to all appearances—links together the successive moments.

What, then, does the historian see; and what must he realize that he does not see from his own point of view ? What he sees is all that aspect under which humanity allows its inward invisible work to be grasped in observable manifestations—manifestations which modify one another mutually, continually undergoing the repercussion of facts upon man, even of those most remote from him, and forming no doubt a coherent whole, though without supplying a total and satisfying explanation of the smallest detail; no more should the apparent continuity of the cinematograph allow the spectator to forget the necessity of repeated interruptions. What the historian does not see, and what he must recognize as escaping him, is the spiritual reality, the activity of which is not wholly represented or exhausted by the historical phenomena (although the latter can be determined like a complete picture subsisting apart from the original). It remains true that the historian has to make the determinist explanation as intelligible and complete as possible—but it remains equally true that it is his duty to leave the issue open or even to open it as widely as possible to the realist explanation which lies always beneath.

It should never be supposed therefore that history by itself can know a fact which would be no more than a fact, and that would be the whole fact: each link in the chain, and the chain as a whole, involve the psychological and moral problems implied by the least action or testimony. It is easy enough to see why. Real history is composed of human lives; and human life is metaphysics in act. To claim to constitute the science of history without any speculative preoccupation, or even to suppose that the humblest details of history could be, in the strict sense of the word, a simple matter of observation, is to be influenced by prejudices on the pretext of attaining to an impossible neutrality—prejudices such as everyone inevitably has so long as he has not attained a conscious view of his own attitude of mind and subjected the postulates on which his researches are based to a methodical criticism. In default of an explicit philosophy, a man ordinarily has an unconscious one. And what one takes for simple observations of fact are often simply constructions. The observer, the narrator, is always more or less of a poet; for behind what he sees the witness puts an action and a soul so as to give the fact a meaning; behind the witness and his testimony, if they are really to enter history, the critic puts an interpretation, a relation, a synthesis; behind these critical data the historian inserts a general view and wider human preoccupations; which is to say that man with his beliefs, his metaphysical ideas, and his religious solutions conditions all the subordinate researches of science as much as he is conditioned by them.

Aristotle's remarks in this connection are as true as ever: 'If we must not philosophize, very well, we cannot avoid philosophizing about that.' Doubt is only methodical and scientific if it is provisional, if it leads to positive results, if, as in Descartes' case, it raises the whole problem in its entirety, if it allows one to verify results by one another, and to control facts and solutions alternately. Each science is therefore only a perspective opening on to others, controlling them and controlled by them, only a way of looking at that concrete reality in which alone the different lines of approach can be held together, an alternating rhythm of life and reflection, of action and thought, which enlighten, determine and prove one another mutually. So long as a science recognizes itself as an abstraction bound up with a thought and a life from which it borrows its material, it is useful and legitimate. But the moment it claims to isolate itself as an abstraction, the moment a science concludes from its independence within its own field of research to a sort of self-sufficiency, it becomes guilty of fraudulently converting a simple method of work into a negative and tyrannical doctrine. Willy-nilly it is led into the subtly crude illusion that because it is legitimate and necessary to divide the work of the mind, the divisions subsist in the reality.

No doubt the historian will sometimes be tempted to declare that he only wishes to remain modestly on his own ground, that one should be grateful to him for not trespassing on any reserved territory, and that so long as he respects and recognizes, as a man, the results furnished by other scholars in their isolated seclusion, he has perhaps the right to cultivate his own garden undisturbed. But I propose the following paradoxical answer to his systematic abstention: that this absolute reserve ends, without his wishing it or even knowing it, in a usurpation: the only way of remaining lawfully on one's own ground in such cases is to open all the doors and windows on to horizons other than one's own; never to lose sight of the essential truth that 'technical and critical history', in the precise and scientific sense of the words, is not 'real history', the substitute for the life of humanity, the totality of historical truths, and that between these two histories, of which one is a science and the other a life, one resulting from a phenomenological method and the other tending to represent genuine reality, there is an abyss.

The danger to which I am calling attention under the name of '*historicism*' lies in the alternation between 'real history' and 'scientific history' or the substitution of one for the other, the result of an infinitesimal oscillation which is constantly producing statements of an equivocal nature, both true and false at the same time, and makes the attentive reader see, as it were, double. At one moment he is in the realm of abstractions, and he is told that it would be presumption to solve dogmatic problems or to trespass on the domain of psychology and metaphysics—in a sense an irreproachable attitude. At the next moment (or indeed at the same moment) the affirmations of the moral or theological order, which equally claim to be historical interpretations of the facts, are set aside as impossible to discuss or even to conceive; and then it is no longer a question of a methodological critique or of scientific abstraction but of conclusions consistent and complete enough to occupy the whole field and to claim the right to formulate basic exclusions, just as a person suffering from strabism ends by totally eliminating the vision of the weaker eye from his field of consciousness to the advantage of the stronger.

We can now see the complicated mechanism which has produced this result. The mixture of two philosophies, of two ages of scientific thought, leads one unconsciously to superimpose the critical spirit (perfectly innocent of this abuse, which it has a perfect right to denounce as unfaithful to its principles) on a foundation of older conceptions (quite foreign to the distinctions and reserves of modern science); from which it follows that positive history is transformed into negative theology. It is therefore supremely important to analyse that subtle mixture and to isolate the elements whose combination masks and aggravates its noxious character.

What are, in fact, the theses borrowed from these two concep-

239

tions and from the two vocabularies of thought which are here confused? We shall see how easily, how almost inevitably, they corrupt each other.

The first thesis is adopted in so far as the observation of facts allows one to know the real truth about men and things, not by itself, no doubt, but as a result of an immediate induction and a spontaneous inference which should disturb no one; and this historical positivism appears to be *a* way and even *the* way of attaining to the reality of history. The second conception is adopted in so far as, according to it, only the matter of a testimony and the chain of facts linked together by a natural determinism can be the raw material of history. Now mix the two together and what does one get? The historical facts will be given the role of reality itself; and an ontology, purely phenomenological in character, will be extracted from a methodology and a phenomenology. A sort of dialectical evolutionism is deduced from this scientific determinism which claims to have penetrated the spiritual secret of the living chain of souls because it has verified the external joints of the links which are no more than its corpse. These objections will no doubt be answered with the energetic sincerity inspired by an intention quite contrary to such results—and as with the deceitful bird in the fable, though with more justification, there will always be some plausibility in the answers; but ultimately the ambiguities are unavoidable, as are indeed the theses which I am about to list summarily and characterize from a philosophical point of view before considering their application to the basic Christian problems.

1. Historicism tends to accept as reality 'historical' phenomena (in the critical sense of the word), or if not explicitly as reality or as the substitute for reality itself, at least as the measure of what can be scientifically known. Any other source will be considered 'extra-historical' (in the full, realist sense of the word); no account need be taken of such things, since one can never hope to know anything about real history except through these channels. This should be carefully noted and remembered when we come to the relationship between the historical Christ and the real Christ.

2. For that very reason historicism tends to mistake the external act, the expressive trait, the concrete image, for the object itself, and tends surreptitiously to substitute the fact for the actor, the testimony for the witness, the portrait for the person: a portrait which, like a mutoscope, can provide a composite effigy capable of producing a complete illusion of life, but never possesses life or real action, though in certain respects it derives from life and serves to fix the memory of it and to renew and prolong its influence. This should be carefully noted and remembered when we come to consider the relation of the historical Christ to his first witnesses.

3. Historicism tends, from then on, so as to explain the chain of events, only to register the effects of phenomena expressed, perceived or imagined, of representations, of effigies, in other words to consider not so much the initial operation of real beings as the influence of the idea which it has formed of them, without suspecting that, quite apart from what is distinctly perceived and intellectualized in the consciousness, actors and spectators have a thousand other hidden means of exercising their mutual efficacy. This should be carefully noted and remembered when we come to consider the relation between the Gospel and the Church.

4. Historicism, then, tends to look for the whole subject-matter of history in the *evolution* which unfolds the series of events under the pressure of the forces which compose our world, and for its form in the mechanical explanation of that kaleidoscope: as a result of that explanation, no doubt, and instead of submitting to the course of events as to a brute necessity, it makes it intelligible in detail and reveals a *logical development*, yet without being able to attain or demand an antecedent, concomitant and final cause, of which the whole series is simply *THE organic development*. This should be carefully noted and remembered when we come to consider the relation between Revelation and Tradition, the relations between the various 'moments' of the Church, and the notion of the Christian supernatural itself.

The time has come for examining the thesis of historicism in regard to Catholicism. Is it capable, not of enabling us to pass, but even of preparing our passage, from facts to faith? In order to judge it usefully it has seemed indispensable to analyse the mixed origins of this complex attitude. Many of those who reject its conclusions imagine that they can accept and praise its method without reservations. It was, no doubt, important to show that it was the root itself which needed attention if the fruit is to be good. If one limits the discussion to what is visible on the surface and does not probe to the subterranean complications of a composite philosophy, it becomes impossible to understand how the historian inspired by it is led, on the pretext of relying on facts alone, to the most dubious hypotheses, so as to avoid, *a priori* the only hypothesis which accounts for the facts themselves.

B. Let us disregard for a moment the hidden philosophical foundations and consider dispassionately the historical and apologetic structure which historicism erects, hoping to base it so solidly on the earth that it will enable us to reach the sky. Will the spectacle, as integral, impartial and exact as possible of the Christian facts be sufficient, by itself, to justify Christian beliefs—a justification all the stronger because it results, a by-product as it were, from the simple effort to determine their origins, progress and authentic meaning?

Clearly there is no question, in this programme, of disengaging an abstract and generic notion of the supernatural by means of arguments which would take us at once beyond historical science; nor is there any justification for formulating apologetic theses at each step; the truth of Christianity is not to be found in an idea extracted from a fact analysed in isolation, nor in the fragmentary interpretation of the successive moments of history, but in a view and appreciation of the whole, in the concrete realities, in the person of Christ and the Church which prolongs it. Instead of asking in ideological language: 'How can we move, at whatever point in the series, from the empirical data to the knowledge of a supernatural order?', the proposal is to rediscover the real Christ and to consider the gospel and the Church, its dogmas and sacraments, as things living a continuous life.

Thus, as a result of approaching the historical problem directly and in isolation, we are led to reorganize the field of apologetics in two ways: there is a change-over from the abstract to the concrete, and from expressive details to the whole in its totality. The critical historian need not, in fact, enquire which intellectual formulae correspond best to the realities which he proposes to describe to us; nor need he enquire what he would have thought or done had he lived in Palestine in about the year 40 of our era; for he cannot alter the fact that he is living in the XXth century and has to take account of both the obscurities and the enlightenment which result from the passage of time; his judgment bears upon the whole; and should he end up with certain apologetic conclusions, the issue before him will be the real and actual conditions of adhering to a real and actual Christianity—so far, nothing could be more reasonable, and even praiseworthy.

But here the difficulties start. One can only know the whole through the details. The movement of the human mind is an analysis between two syntheses: what then must we do to ensure that the first, divinatory, hypothetical synthesis which puts the questions to us and rouses our interest does not cripple the work of analysis and predetermine the final synthesis? For the critic always uses one part of the texts against another; and metaphysical questions are never entirely excluded from his mind, because they are antecedent, concomitant and subsequent to any positive research concerning man. So, far from asking the historian of Christianity in the course of his analysis for premature professions of faith and conclusions in respect of detail before considering his work as a whole, our whole effort must be to make sure that he respects the necessary conditions of criticism, preserves his independence of judgment, and asks all the necessary questions. Even if we limit ourselves to questions of method, without entering into the details of historical discussion, we cannot here examine how he joins all the links, even if only the most important ones in the sequence of the Christian centuries; it will be enough to consider three or four of the principal links carefully (A), thus preparing ourselves to undertake the fundamental criticism of this 'apologetics through history alone' (B).

A. What would be the natural reaction of a historian faced by the fact of Christ and the Catholic Church, if he had heard and believed no more of them than of Tarouth and the Varnian sect? He would try to fit the new facts into the pattern of events already known to him, and to explain them as far as possible by their circum-

stances. Nothing, certainly, could be more proper. On any hypothesis, Jesus was a man; and as such he took his place in the
sequence of secondary causes, involved in the world, speaking to his
contemporaries as he found them; in a word, clothed not in a
generic humanity but in a particular individuality, conditioned
apparently by antecedent history and by the whole civilization of
Israel, using a language already formed, with its particular intellectual resources and limitations, steeped in local colour: otherwise
his contemporaries would not have been able to understand him,
nor should we understand that he was outwardly like ourselves,
that he was a real historical person, and not the phantom or mental
construction which the misdirected zeal of the old docetists and the
new ideologists make of him. To appreciate his personality or his
work one cannot know too much about the *milieu* in which he was
rooted and which controlled his activity.

But one fact stands out in the course of such a study, and that is
the prodigious and lasting success of the Crucified. Now unless
we are content to say that this had to be so because it is so, and that
one only has to explain the effects to discover the cause in them,
we come up against the essential problem: faced by Christ and his
historical achievement, the historian cannot avoid asking: 'What
did he intend, what did he do, what is he in himself, and how are
his initial design and the tremendous consequences of Christianity
related?' And this is where we come across an ambiguity; for
without as a rule noticing it, we are presented at the very first step
with a decisive alternative which unconsciously governs all our
subsequent research. Have we no other means of attaining the
'real Christ' than the portrait drawn by his first witnesses, a
portrait which, in the technical sense of the word, might be called
the '*historic* Christ'? If we have not, then to judge his work and his
real intention we must limit ourselves to the idea formed, or at least
formulated and transmitted, only by those who have enabled us to
hear a direct echo of it in the earliest Christian literature; and then
it is the critic, the exegete, the philosopher who hold the keys of
theology. Or can we, in order to attain to the real Christ, profit
from the total effort of generations of believers, and, as it were, force
back to their source all the currents of life and of thought which

have since been directed upon the Gospels? In that case we must, look upon the understanding which his earliest followers had of his person and his work only as an expressive but necessarily rudimentary and summary picture of the Master whose words, example and influence they reported, though unable to exhaust their meaning, perceive their implications or transmit their whole secret to others: *non potestis portare;*[1] and in that case it will be necessary to look elsewhere, beyond the texts and beyond the testimony intellectualized by literary expression, for complementary sources and more authentic information.

Now if one were to commit oneself exclusively without reflection or reservations to one or other of these courses, the solution of this fundamental problem would be dependent upon that choice. Does Christianity proceed from what Christ was and still is, from what he willed and foresaw, from what he still does as well as from what he taught? Or does the Church stem only from what Christ contributed to the determinism of history, and from the repercussions of his actions on the machinery of facts and upon human consciousness? On the first hypothesis the prime question is the Christological problem; the question about the Saviour, his consciousness, his knowledge and his real power, is the soul of faith. On the second hypothesis these problems are accessory and, so to say, insoluble from the point of view of the scholar, who can only shrug his shoulders, leaving devotion, which always requires myths and symbols, to compose its 'pious fairy tale'. Who can fail to see the import of this alternative?

If we have only historical criticism to guide us, can we legitimately opt, I do not say *a priori* and definitively, but even provisionally, for one or other of these solutions? Above all, have we at present the right to exclude the first hypothesis in favour of the second, on the pretext that it is not scientific, or that it is possibly superfluous? We have not. Certainly an honest effort must be made with all possible circumspection to exhume from the texts the most direct impressions and the most authentic relics of the thought and life of Jesus. No doubt I shall be shown numerous passages in what are called the deepest strata of the synoptic gospels in which Jesus seems

[1] John XVI, 12.

to speak simply as a man of his time; no doubt it will be maintained that Messianism was the principal vehicle of his teaching, that the Good Tidings consisted primarily in the proximate advent of the Kingdom, that the horizon of his preaching seemed to be restricted, as was the outlook of those who received it, to short-term hopes. But does this mean to say that I must measure Christ by that first portrait, which after all is no more than a portrait? For I must remark that Jesus wrote nothing, so that we have not that direct testimony of his own thought which a man can leave behind him. The only way in which we can penetrate into his mind is through the *consciousness of his consciousness* on the part of simple men deeply involved in the prejudices of their restricted background, and better able, by reason of their lack of culture, to observe and to maintain the facts, to attach themselves wholeheartedly to a master and to undergo his personal ascendancy than to express ideas, to describe an interior life, or to explain their own faith. If it is true that spiritual problems, which the historian can never avoid, always escape him in some measure, what are we to say in this instance, when the extraordinary character of the texts unites the riches of an ardent faith and the inebriations of an unparalleled love with the forceful simplicity of a narrative? Let it not be objected that, if Christ had been fully conscious of his divinity and possessed a clear vision of the future, he would have uttered, like a man of genius who struggles to convey the whole secret of his soul, more decisive words, echoes of which would be audible in the gospels; that would be to forget that knowledge is not poured ready-made into minds like words into ears, and that the mystery of God could not be violated even by revelation itself; it would be a failure to realize that truth, even though divinely inspired, cannot commune with human thought except by becoming incarnate in the contingent forms which make it, little by little, assimilable; it would be to ignore this fact that, if the great man's duty is to express his little human secret, the dignity of God consists in revealing himself to the good will by effortless acts of power and of immeasurable goodness rather than by lucid declarations addressed to the intelligence; it would be to ignore the fact that what Jesus desired and obtained was not to be elucidated like a theological theme, but to be loved above all things.

And if he succeeded, if his work survived his death, if it was victorious over disappointments, that is because people did not only await that Parousia which was the goal of the ardent ambitions of the Jews, but had in their hearts what is essential in any spiritual movement: an invincible love, a devotion to the adored person of the Master.

At the very least, then, the question remains open: 'Did the early Church attach itself to the real Christ or the historic Christ?' Or rather no—it must be considered an established fact that if the direct influence of the habitual presence of any man creates an atmosphere of which even the most faithful witnesses cannot perpetuate the equivalent, then here more than anywhere the texts give an insufficient account of feelings and of actions; the personal and unexpressed influence of the Saviour inaugurated a tradition of devotion and adoration which Christian literature neither exhausts nor fully represents, even when closest to its source. To exclude the Christological problem from consideration, limiting oneself to the study of the repercussions occasioned by Christ upon human consciousness and upon the events of this world, is to immure him in the past, sealing him in his tomb beneath the sediments of history and to consider only the natural aspect of his work as real and effective; it would be to deprive him of the influence which every master communicates to his immediate disciples, although they themselves are incapable of transmitting it in their writings; and, by ignoring the effect of his presence perpetuated in forms which are partly refractory to history, one would exclude a *fortiori* the question of the properly supernatural mode of his mysterious person; one would thereby suppress the moral or ontological character of his acts by depriving them of the explicit intention and prevision which alone confer an absolute meaning upon his life, his death and his work. Is it clear now where this hypothesis leads if we follow it methodically to the end? If one accepts it, although one might continue to say that Christianity is founded *on* Christ as a cathedral is built on a geological foundation, one can no longer add that it was explicitly founded *by* Christ, because one no longer looks behind the historical facts for a substantial and active reality, that reality which, according to the other thesis, is called cosmothetic, redemptive, and even creative, so as to indicate the profound, permanent and substantial operation of the Word incarnate in the orders of nature and of grace.

But the critic who tacitly left aside the second alternative, even without explicitly adopting the first, would surely risk definitively adopting a system of explanations which eliminate the very spirit of Jesus. And if he continues his analysis and historical reconstructions with the texts for his sole material, could one really say that he was faithful to his rule—to the rule which requires him to envisage the whole before reaching decisive conclusions? No, one cannot behave even provisionally as though Christianity were founded upon testimonies and texts, on mere literary relics, on a portrait; for there may be, and indeed there certainly are, other strands linking us to Christ, another history formed of living relics, without which Christianity would be a religion of parchments and scribes, and in fact would not exist.

However, let us leave the first difficulty aside and suppose, if you like, that enthusiasm for the Good News suffices to explain the first faith in the message of Easter, the confident expectations of the glorious coming, the fervour of that heavenly novitiate. But there is a second step to be taken. Not only has Jesus disappeared, but those who knew him personally and told their story have passed on their recollections and their work to the zeal of the new faith and to the loving hope of the first Christian community. I see a new difficulty arising, an alternative as decisive as the first. If it is true that the apostolic generation lived in the desire and the certitude of the proximate return of Jesus, if that is what the immediate echo of the Master's preaching repeated as the essence of the primitive message, if the source of devotion to the Saviour and of submission to trials was the hope of a beatifying triumph, how did faith survive so immense a disillusionment? How was it purified, fortified and propagated with such rapidity and on such a disconcerting scale at the very moment when it appeared to have failed to fulfil the promises which appear to be the human cause of its early successes? To the historian faced by this paradoxical fact two radically divergent solutions now present themselves; and should he not consent to examine both, that could only be because he regarded the one as *a priori* chimerical or impossible, as though to make himself admit that the other must really be sufficient, however insufficient it might actually appear, so that once again an abstention amounts to an exclusion.

Can one explain the survival of Christianity after the failure of the promises which had been its first vehicle as a sort of substitution of feelings, a reorientation of hopes? What was expected was the Parousia; what came was the Church.[1] Shall it be said that if Christianity acclimatized itself to this valley of tears, to this land of exile, it was not so much the result of a direct impulse, foreseen, willed, always one and the same, as the result of a recoil, of the transformation of a hope too dear and too strong not to remain victorious in the midst of defeat? Is it enough to add that the disappointment was even useful in purifying the Christian soul of imperfections and mercenary ambitions? And if we conclude that the Church owes to this its power to serve truth and the spiritual life down the ages in this world of ours, in face of the ever-reviving appetite for domination and the temptation to relapse into millenarianism, then must we repeat *Felix error*! an error more true than the truth, since it allows the promotion of the same ideal of justice with the bait of the same ideal of happiness.

But is this satisfactorily established? Does not this explanation of an uncontested fact simply consist in proclaiming the fact as the explanation in itself in the name of the determinism of history—as though to understand what has happened were to know what produced it? The Church was born in blood and pain—but is it no more than a revised form of hope for joy? Ought we not, on the contrary, to say that the expectation of the Parousia was no more than a first imaginative synthesis indicating the point of insertion in the earth-bound minds of the witnesses of Christ, who were so slow to believe, a point of contact with these minds prepared by Jewish messianism, the prolongation of their patriotic desires, of their human longings, the outline of a metaphysic of man's supernatural destiny within the grasp of the fishermen of Lake Tiberias, the beginning of the transposition from a material sense to a spiritual one; for the Parousia seemed still to be, and yet no longer to be, of

[1] *Tr.* A quotation from Loisy.

this earth? Was it not also the providential way of infecting simple souls with the impulse, the enthusiasm, the absolute detachment, the inebriation of martyrdom? And, above all, was it not the concrete realization of the truth, like that which the expressive feasts of the liturgy teach us year by year, that the world is always on the point of ending for each one of us, and that what the goodness of God promises us is not some vague idealization but a fully and realist satisfaction, the material and spiritual transformation of the whole man and of the whole order of the universe? If the disillusionment of the second generation of Christians passed unnoticed, if indeed there was none, that is because there was always in the Good Tidings something else than the expectation of an Eldorado; always and essentially it contained a doctrine of sin and justification, a summons to penitence, to a spiritual life, to a faith consisting in an attachment to the very person of the Saviour, a need for moral purity and an impulse towards perfect happiness. And if the expectation of Christ's glorious Coming never flagged, perhaps it was because he was loved more than his glory, and because he was more truly present in the persecuted Church than if he had come suddenly on the clouds.

We can now see the importance of this new alternative, and the consequences of adopting the principles of historicism in the belief that we are opting for a provisional abstraction. For if one attempted, at this point, to make a final judgment, and if one admitted the historical adequacy of the view that the support of faith is not so much Christ in his concrete and messianic form as the reaction of men prompt to interpret a hope too beautiful and too powerful not to rise again from the ashes, we should still have to declare that the source of everything specifically Christian had been lost in a great movement of the human conscience, and to assume that to safeguard its confidence in Christ the Church had little by little substituted a different person: with the result that the worship of the faithful would no longer be directed upon what Christ was, or even what he said and thought and did, but upon a 'restored' image of him, constructed as a result of the disappointments of history, and by the aspirations of the human heart. To claim that the expectation of the Kingdom was the principal evangelical teaching is to deny Christ's full rights of paternity over the suffering pilgrims of this life. And there is something more. Even assuming that a human illusion served as the vehicle for God's work, the whole problem is to know whether, at the point of departure, there was a definite intention, a supernatural action, a providential design. If we are to say that the Church is not simply one chronological sequence among a host of others, actual or possible, but the development of the Gospel, it must be granted that the voice which preached the Kingdom of God inserted a *punctum movens* into the determinism of history, a word whose repercussion was so carefully calculated that the echo of it endures under a thousand harmonising forms. Have we really the right, in the name of historical science, to exclude even the possibility of an antecedent finality and of a unity of design in the historical plan? And, if so, could one still speak of it as a divine work?

But disregarding these difficulties, which after a thorough examination the critical mind would no doubt declare itself incompetent to solve without reservations or appeal, let us even assume for the sake of argument, in spite of the improbability involved, that the Church of the Martyrs and of the Catacombs could have been born of the dream of the Parousia. The resulting spectacle would be strange enough, and we should at once have to pass through a new crisis of growth, another difficulty infinitely more serious and more fundamental. In its infancy the Church did not only encounter the humble and slaves, who eagerly opened their hearts to their liberators, the unfortunate and the victims of life greedy for happiness and for earthly or heavenly revenge; she encountered also the whole Roman and Hellenic civilization, the philosophical and religious culture of the East and the West; now, she may have won over men's heart to her love, but is it conceivable she should have won over their minds to her folly? For in that astonishing enterprise too she succeeded, and has continued to do so for nineteen hundred years—a further improbability which the historian must take into account. And how is the Church to dominate and control the proud or subtle speculations to which she seemed so alien? And how would the Good Tidings of salvation become a metaphysic of the Incarnation and the Redemption, the recapitulation of the universe in Christ?

Here again the critic is faced with an alternative: for in effect only two irreconcilable hypotheses seem possible. On one view, dogma is simply the adaptation of Christian facts and feelings to the eternal themes of philosophical thought, which receives from them a special colouring but preserves its own movement and its own infinite plasticity; so that the doctrines which were the first interpretations of the Christian consciousness would remain as mutable as the systems and climates of human thought. In this case doctrinal definitions merely borrow a language from Christian facts in which to translate universal notions of religious morality in a metaphysical way. Or else dogma must be regarded as the concrete solution, as the incarnation in history of the ideal demands and the supreme *desiderata* of philosophy; so that far from expressing a simple idea, an intellectual interpretation, a superior systematization that remains always capable of working upon itself, dogmatic formulae will be confined to seeking in the historical facts for the fullness of unalterable truth, which they can never exhaust but on which they must always concentrate. In that case they are much more than a means of making ideas concrete; they have within them a factual reality to which their own progress is subordinated. So, on the one hand, the facts exist for the sake of the ideas; on the other, the ideas exist for the sake of the facts, for the *acts*, and gravitate around them. From the first point of view, one would have to regard the theories of St Paul or St John on the redemptive death of Christ and on the incarnation of the Word of God as artificial and provisional scaffoldings of the spiritual edifice. From the second point of view, one would have to say that, in disengaging the moral and metaphysical meaning of the acts and sufferings of the Saviour, such 'inventions' simply *rediscover* a substantial and antecedent reality and mark out the orientation of Christianity in a definitive way.

I can easily see why the critic, the historian or the philosopher, leans towards the first thesis; I can understand his astonishment at the very idea of an absolute incarnate in the relative, of the presence within the historical order of an activity capable of realizing the infinite; of a consciousness that remained human without ceasing to be divine; of a supernatural mystery fully contained at a point in time and place in the humblest forms of nature; of one risen from the dead who preserved the sensible appearance and reality of natural life. But if the *reality* of these facts is to be denied, then let it be denied by facts, if there are any, and let us not have the historian invoking or insinuating their *impossibility*; for one can never prove these facts impossible in the name of facts alone. And, speaking as a philosopher, I am prepared to say that there is no speculative reason against their possibility which could be decisive. A possibility does not depend upon positive science; and the philosophic proof of an impossibility is the most difficult of all.

Nor can it be claimed that the second thesis is utterly fantastic and without solid basis: for there is a difficulty here which must strike all historians of philosophy. How is it that men who did not think in philosophical terms were able, within a relatively short space of time, to invent doctrines which ended by converging and harmonizing so as to form a speculative and practical system more supple, more unified, more extensive than any other? One thing is attributed to John, another to Paul, something else to a third, but, if their views are as new and as original and as independent as we are told, then they had more genius than their master and without his help formed a school which is unparalled in its moral and intellectual homogeneity. There is something still more striking: while Gnosticism was lying in wait, ready to embroil Christians in ingeniously subtle theories which threatened the strong and rich simplicity of nascent doctrines, the prudence, moderation, balance and commonsense which refused to be carried away by the logic of the intellect seems more admirable even than the dialectical development of theology. And what is more wonderful still is that these dogmatic theses, originating from these various men, not only coincide with one another but with the facts (whether historical or fictional does not matter for the moment), and are so wedded to them that they fill even the most accidental features of Christ's life with a theology which is always in activity; indeed they coincide with our own lives, renewing our inward being by unprecedented new practices which experience immediately shows to be appropriate and beneficent: so that dogmas, the history of Christ and the life of man form a sort of indivisible whole: *mihi vivere Christus est.* In the name of all the knowledge which we have of the philosophical schools, moral doctrines or religious sects, it must really be granted that there is something here to explain. The historical anomaly remains rationally unaccountable even though we space out the discoveries in time, postpone the dates of uncertain texts, attribute certain documents to this or that author, overlook the anticipations and assume tendentious interpolations so as to make the cumulative effect more probable by first spacing them out and then linking them up together.

One could go on piling up difficulties of this kind, in the course of Christian history, for people who are too ready to say 'this happened, therefore it had to happen like that'; one must point out to them that the natural continuity of history does not prove that history itself can provide an explanation of it. The more one tries to tie up the facts in their determinism as though everything followed inevitably, the more patent the inadequacy of the explanations.[1]

[1] Historicism tends to make everything naturally coherent, and to reduce history to the intelligible determinism of phenomena; here, by comparison, are the conclusions of a historian free from philosophical prejudice: 'The supernatural character of the Church, the presence in it of a divine moderator, cannot be deduced with sufficient rigour from each of its triumphs taken separately. It might, indeed, have triumphed over the Jewish spirit and have imposed itself little by little on the Empire, appealing first of all to the good elements, attracting them by its morality and its hopes, then to larger numbers by the spectacle of its martyrs and the experience of its charity, and finally to the whole population through the infectious enthusiasm of its example and the support of authority: it might, admittedly, have freed itself from the parasitic growths of gnosticism, subjected prophets and philosophers to its authority, have constituted a dogma guided by sound commonsense and making full use of mystery. A human institution, led by enlightened and wise men, could have accomplished each of these things separately. But the whole taken together, victory in all these struggles simultaneously, its form preserved throughout a development vast in extent and very long in time, represents an impossibility, if one is to remain within the natural order. Even disregarding the initial impulse, the personality of the founder, and only taking into account the ecclesiastical history which begins with the apostles, one is led to recognize that they founded a more than human institution, that God was really in them, with them and that he is still with their work.'

B. But let us now leave aside detailed objections as well as the hypothetical and provisional interpretations of criticism, only retaining what is presented to us as a fact: 'In spite of all the reasons for its failure, the Catholic Church has survived for centuries; no demonstrable breach between its past and its present has occurred; and that factual continuity must be understood as a logical development, as an equilibrium which, though unstable, is invariably recaptured, as the progressive adaptation of Christian society to the mounting flux of humanity.' There unquestionably is the ground which the apologist-historian invites us to occupy. What act of faith is going to germinate in that soil?

To begin with, can one without ambiguity describe this proposed conclusion as *a fact*? For my part I confess to finding three different senses in the word, and I am afraid advantage might be taken of this so as to apply to one of them what is only true of another.

1. Is the 'fact', in this instance, the chronological succession and the real continuity of the Christian past and present? In that case it is a truism from which we can deduce nothing;

2. Is the 'fact' the intelligible continuity which links together the successive movements in the life of the Church in the eyes of science, just as they are united in the real history of ideas and events? But to establish this logical succession would require not so much a simple observation as an 'historical construction', and the analysis would depend upon a partially hypothetical synthesis;

3. Is the 'fact' in question the spiritual unity and the organic continuity of a single thought, of a single life, making the Church a single immortal being, as it were? In order to establish the truth of this it would be necessary to introduce a controlling idea into the heart of the facts, which is itself not a fact, and it alone could serve as a criterion to distinguish what was only *evolution*, that is to

---

(L. Duchesne: *Les origines chrétiennes*, p. 468.) It is true that these conclusions leave our problem intact, the problem of the relation of facts to faith and of facts to dogma; but at least they do not dispose of it, and even show how wide open it is. The attitude of the genuine critic in the course of his successive analyses will always be that of Gamaliel: *Si est ex hominibus consilium hoc, aut opus, dissolvetur.*

say the effect of external pressures or of interdependent influences, from what is vital development, that is to say continuous creation starting from a germ which transubstantiates its own nourishment. The fact that the chronological continuity of the Church is incontestable (and this applies to any Christian confession), and the fact that the dialectical continuity is established by criticism, are no proof that the 'results' either account for the spiritual continuity, or suffice to define it or dispense us from considering it. Even if we assume that the supernatural is in the facts, the facts do not cease to be natural; and empirical observations or historical constructions, under colour of scientific exactitude, are in danger of not finding it even when affirming its presence. Like an aeronaut without bearings, carried away by the winds, the critic who places himself wholly in the *fieri* is as incapable of judging the *esse* as the extrinsicist ideologue is incapable of understanding or of maintaining the *fieri*. Even if he believes that he has elucidated the past so as to understand the present and to calculate the graphs of the future, he is committed to the path on which history moves, without a criterion to determine its real direction or (*a fortiori*) to isolate a divine and absolute meaning. For, by interpreting everything *sub specie motus humani*, he easily persuades himself that religion can be reduced to the facts of history.

But let us now take the fact as it is given to us, with the ambiguity of meaning which seems to make it more plausible: has it of itself an apologetic meaning, and if so, what is it? There seem to be two possibilities: is it claimed that it is the totality of this astonishing spectacle which is supposed to produce faith, as a universal miracle which surpasses and obliterates all the particular miracles and obliges us to admit the divine origin of Christianity? Or is it claimed, on the contrary, that if the origin of the Christian movement is divine, everything that comes from that source, however distant or indirect the channels, is also divine?

Let us briefly examine these two interpretations which one cannot separate too sharply from one another, for this is no subtle distinction: if one adheres to the logic of historicism, it implies either an untenable claim to seize the supernatural in history and through history, or a complete abdication of criticism in the face of faith.

Does it suffice to say of the complete spectacle offered by the Church: 'Look and judge: there is no need for me to play the part of apologist when history does so'. It may well be that such a prospect is for the scholar, the equivalent and more, of the miraculous sign which everyone might find in the particular and accidental prodigy. One might add that this complete manifestation, this essential and permanent miracle, dispenses with the elementary reasoning which is required if each isolated sign is to stimulate faith; for it is no longer a matter of interpreting a fact or generalizing a character, but of affirming the presence of the divine in its universal development: the criterion which enables us to discern the authentic presence of God in Christian history is, it will be said, history itself. But no, the transition from facts to faith cannot be accomplished in this way. Such a claim is doubly contradictory.

Either, at each moment, at each crisis in the life of the Church, the exceptions to the ordinary laws governing human societies will have been excluded from the argument and set aside as a residue refractory to natural explanations; and in that case one could not say that history enabled us to cross the hiatus and fill in the gaps which it could, at the most, have indicated; *or*, regardless of the cost, one will have explained the coherence of the whole Christian development by excluding from the study of its successive moments not only any superhuman and supernatural element, but the question of the real relationship between them, as though the historical report embraced the whole reality of their mutual relations; and then so much logical continuity will have been established that everything will have seemed natural and no further problem remains. Thus, having eliminated the real, the metaphysical and the supernatural in every detail, there will be no need to look for it in the whole, since they are only hypotheses which can easily be dispensed with. So, when it is suggested that we should establish that the Church is simply the Gospel continued, let us beware, for the thesis, fine and fertile enough in the real, *lived* history of humanity, so true, equally in the eyes of determanist impartial criticism and determinist science, is disappointing and chimerical from the point of view of the historian-apologist, and if one were to push obstinately on with it, so dangerous that it almost automatically becomes subversive of all Christianity which is properly supernatural and of any positively divine revelation.

Must one, then, limit the conclusions of the 'historical apologetics' of Christianity to verifying the legitimacy of the link which unites the present forms of Catholic life to its original source? But in what respect will the source itself appear any more supernatural if all the natural explanations have been made to converge upon it and everything has been done to make them as satisfying as possible? By the very fact of having begun by eliminating the problems which may be called realistic, so as to concentrate on the determinist sequence and the chain of historical phenomena, it will be impossible to rediscover anything but a notion—more precise and extended, no doubt, though exclusively scientific and bereft of a religious character—of the complex dialectic which controlled the organization of Catholic dogma and discipline. And this kind of knowledge, which has for its sole object the external aspect and the intelligible form of Christian facts, can only extract an ideology from them, an ideology in which everything is reduced to an evolution of concepts, indefinitely sublimated, with no other ballast than indefinitely tractable texts.

So far from such a history's becoming *ipso facto* an apology, one can only say that, if the historian who limits himself to it is a believer, then it is without its support and in some respects in spite of it.[1] No

---

[1] Once again, I disclaim any personal applications that readers may be tempted to make of my words. I am studying abstract theses in their schematic form: at each bifurcation which I have indicated there are, in fact, cross-currents; and one can say that most exegetes mingle what I am trying to analyse and oppose as interlocked and incompatible theses. Any specific allusion would be a calumny. Indeed, one of those whose names has no doubt occurred to the reader has already said: 'The Christological problem presents itself not only to the intelligence of the critic, but to the conscience of the man, and the witness of history alone cannot solve it'. All that we provisionally ask, like him, is that 'the mystery of the consciousness of Christ should be respected by the historian'; for 'the texts do not allow of a psychological analysis of the notion of the Son of Man'. But other declarations must not be added so as to make assertions of belief which may have been real facts seem impossible, even though the historical method is incapable of testing them. What I am criticizing is the thesis of the water-tight compartment between history and dogma, and of the incommensurability of assertions of faith

doubt he will be able to claim that his faith is the magic wand that transmutes all that human lead into divine gold, and that the meaning of dogma emerges from the material facts for the spiritual man alone: but in that case his faith will be entirely divorced from his science; and that is what he is led to recognize when he declares that many gospel facts have no acceptable meaning except for those who already believe. Contrary to the project originally implied in his thesis, the facts, though better known and more accurately reconstructed, do not help to enlighten, strengthen and define his positive beliefs. Now, having shown the inadequacy of old attitudes and the failure of old arguments, one cannot fail to see that an attitude which proposes to reason a faith without reason is as unjust to reason as it is dangerous to faith. For where can this faith draw support and discover its direction? Like a kite without a string to secure it to the facts and without the compensating weight of ideas, it is in perpetual danger of finding itself suspended between heaven and earth, either dissolving into a mystical symbolism or falling back into scientific positivism.

Yet it is necessary to go still further; and in order to compel historicism towards the last bifurcation to which it is logically drawn, we must, while rehabilitating its intentions, demonstrate that the very sincerity of its faith may well result, for certain minds at least, in a greater threat to faith. For, faced by the spectacle of Christian history, we are told: 'What I call miraculous and divine is the marvellous repercussion of an initially almost imperceptible impulse, the infinitely amplified echo of an occurrence which, were it to happen today in Tibet or Turkestan, would probably escape our information services, the drama of Calvary which has produced among men such deep faith; for, in awakening the profoundest harmonies of the soul, Christ showed the goal of mankind's religious aspirations; and humanity, by proclaiming the divinity of Christ, has realized the best of truths: it is a permanent acquisition, and the curve traced by successive generations of Christians

---

and of truths of fact; and still more, of course, the thesis of an opposition between them which results in double-thinking.

Tr. The reference here is, of course, to Loisy.

will develop to infinity the impulse springing from the depths of its consciousness.' If that is to be called faith in the supernatural, not only is there no difference between the specifically Christian supernatural and the divine (a distinction which would then appear to be no more than a piece of ideological childishness, not a difference in nature but a difference in degree of concentration and intensity), but what is the divine itself? If one thinks that Christ's horizon was bounded by the eschatological illusions of his earliest interpreters, if one judges that Christianity emerged from an idea which required to be purified little by little by the fire of persecutions, by the hard lessons of facts and by philosophic thought, then the more one says that Christ is God, the more one makes God himself into an Unknown, not only mysterious to us but to itself, revealing itself to us, and perhaps even constituting itself, only through a *fieri* from which the ideas which we form of finality and personality remain excluded. And after having refused the Son of God any foreknowledge of his work, to attribute that work to him and call it absolutely divine is to put the Unknowable Unconscious in place of the Heavenly Father.

That is no doubt too verbal a deduction to be dangerous to even the driest of logicians. But, even on the most favourable interpretation, would the thesis of Christ's divinity leave the essentials of faith intact, if put forward by a historicism which remained quite consistent with certain of its principles? I quite recognize that in dealing with minds prompt to identify the supernatural with the signs which clearly manifest it to the senses, or with the definition which formulates it for the understanding, there is reason to insist that we ought not to look chiefly for intellectual satisfaction in our beliefs but that we should find there the mysterious gift of God and the meaning, always obscure in this world, of the real drama of our souls. But none the less it is a long step from that feeling of reserve to the thesis which forbids us to entrust our ignorance to the knowledge of the God-Man, to relate our ideal aspirations and our dogmatic formulae to clearly defined historical realities where they find their complete realization, to count less on the indirectly communicated teaching of the Master for whom we provide a field of action which makes him, though dead, live again in ourselves, than on the present real assistance of his grace which makes us, infirm though we are, live in him, the Saviour and life-giver. For if one says that we act through him and he through us, that his reign is without end, that not an iota of his teaching is lost, that dogma is only the translation of facts, it must equally be recognized that such expressions allow of two diametrically opposite meanings. And if one makes these expressions mean that the Christian facts have simply been a point of departure, a *viaticum*, a *via*, and not a point of return for Christian belief, its *veritas*, and that instead of striving to adapt themselves to the facts as their limits, these beliefs emerge from their swaddling clothes, moving away from the letter to mount up towards the spirit, then one could still no doubt speak of Christianity as a religious movement of the human consciousness; but at that point Christianity would be measured in terms of Religion, and not religion in terms of Christianity as its perfect reality, its *vita*.

Then the process of adaptation required of the Christian consciousness would no longer be a matter of *nuances*, of subtle changes, and gentle re-orientations, but one of harsh opposition, of a complete reversal. In fact, it involves, in the name of history, a revolution in the manner of defining the relations which obtain between Catholic dogma and the Christian fact, between the believer and the Church, between Christ and God: a radical transformation of the religious and philosophical spirit. And then the problem raised goes far beyond any confessional question; it affects the orientation of the spiritual life and the whole duty of humanity. It amounts to inquiring whether the divorce between what is known and what is believed is so complete that faith can only be saved by casting off all connections and taking refuge in the dualism of two incommensurable orders: on the one hand, a knowledge which is 'simply the residue of repeated perceptions', formulae expressing intellectual constructions out of empirical facts, a historical science which is only the concrete logic of becoming, a religious sense upholding and nourishing on its own substance a metaphysic of the unknowable where the unending *fieri* of a polymorphous evolution appears as the one and only absolute; on the other hand, a salutary mystery of faith, but humanly inaccessible, so that we have no means of ascertaining whether our expressions and our symbols more or less approximately represent it. Thus, in the place of the Dogmas of a *Sacred History* we shall be shown the holiness of historically salutary dogmas; faith in the beneficent Church will safeguard and justify faith in Christ the Saviour, so that there can be no conflict between scientific history, which is the only apologetic, and history according to faith, which is an edifying parable.

It is only at this point that we can see clearly the meaning of the whole process of transposition of which we have traced in a groping sort of way only certain stages. No doubt those who have undergone the influence of historicism will have accused me already of unfairness or incomprehension in the examination of these tendencies, because the detailed objections will seem to them false as resting on an antiquated notion of faith which, according to them, must be entirely transposed. In an incomplete form these views, they will say, have been and still are harmful; in their totality they are liberating and salutary. And the summary which they might well give of them, as though it were the last word of both criticism and philosophy, could be expressed in the following proposition: 'We must save faith from the attacks of historical science by suppressing Sacred History, that is to say by liberating dogma from the need for representing positive facts, or formulating ideas which are anchored in realities.'

This is not the place to give a final opinion; and I shall restrict myself here to the following two observations: no solution is offered to our initial problem except by suppressing one of its conflicting elements; and furthermore, no necessary and sufficient reason for such a transposition, or rather amputation, is advanced either by philosophy or by history. In order to appreciate this mental attitude equitably, it was necessary to link it, by some of the innumerable ties which envelop it, to its multiple origins. For it presupposes a whole conception of the relations of thought to its object, of truth to reality, of knowledge to action. Everywhere we find this thesis of 'segregated history' and of 'phenomenalist intellectualism' cropping up in one of its many varied forms: the determinism of facts is really self-explanatory, and historical phenomena provide a real and sufficient history. Thus, at the end of our investigation, we find ourselves again facing the very principles of historicism and, if we had not already analysed the basic equivocation on which it rests, it might easily be imagined that study, independent of any philosophy, and remaining on purely scientific ground, spontaneously rediscovers such doctrines; and there would be some danger of thinking that the coincidence confirmed both the methods and the results. But let us not forget that these modern methods by which people claim to be inspired have been adulterated by incompatible conceptions; and these hybrid theses, which appear to be rediscovered and confirmed spontaneously, have, in fact, already influenced people's thought: so that it is neither the genuinely philosophical nor the truly critical conceptions which are responsible for the conclusions towards which we are led in their name. It is important to know this so as not to be influenced by their prestige, and equally so as not to react unjustly against them.

But, my dear Sir, the problem which we raised at the beginning of this study is still far from being solved and seems more disconcerting than ever. One cannot hope to remedy the lacunae of extrinsicism by showing up the inadequacies of historicism. You see what a strange position we are now in. A moment ago, when we were treating history dogmatically, the human history of the Bible was virtually done away with, a barricade had been erected against independent criticism, and all that happened was that a rope-ladder was let down from above, to be withdrawn at will, and, though it appeared to lead from the facts to dogma, in fact it stretched from dogma to facts. At least lightly-burdened minds, agile or docile or audacious spirits, could reach faith by this means—not to speak of those who have never risked a step or a look outside the holy city. But now, lo and behold, when criticism is called in to help, after promising us a grand staircase, the ground floor has been so effectively occupied that there is no room to go up higher; dogma is respectfully left at the door, or rather on the upper floor. Once it has been acknowledged that access to dogma could only be gained by history, history closes all the doors, even depriving dogma of Sacred History, so that there should no longer be two different histories, one according to science and one according to faith. You must admit that the position is embarrassing: is it the case that the powers which we proposed to reconcile, and whose synthesis seemed vital to faith, cannot come to an understanding except by the extermination of either the one or of the other? Of course not. If the faith of the believer remains unshakable, if the Church passes infallibly through these conflicts, the reason is that it has, in fact, other means besides texts and ideas or arguments by which to direct its controlling and moderating activity. Surely it must be obvious that there is a philosophical gap to fill, a lacuna not in Catholic life or in the practice of the Church but in the theoretical justification which is commonly given of it? But what is it exactly, and how shall we remedy it? On the answer to this question, it would seem, must depend the solution to the crisis.

III. THE VITAL ROLE AND THE PHILOSOPHICAL BASIS OF TRADITION

What great need have the foregoing analyses revealed to us? The need for an intermediary between history and dogma, the necessity for a link between them which would bring about the synthesis and maintain solidarity without compromising their relative independence. And that synthetic principle must have an original force, and a foundation of its own; for neither facts nor ideas nor reasoning have really succeeded in extricating us from the circle in which we were enclosed by the initial question: 'How is it that the Bible legitimately supports and guarantees the Church, and the Church legitimately supports and interprets the Bible?' This means that the Church does not rest entirely on the Scriptures, and that the History in which Catholicism obliges us to believe is not only the history which the historian can establish; and conversely that scientific history cannot claim of itself to measure the meaning of dogmas, their value and their implications. From this it manifestly follows that only a principle distinct from texts and formulae can relate, harmonize and organize them.

This vivifying power is known to everyone. It is a commonplace to say that the Church rests on 'Scripture AND Tradition'. But what is it precisely? What is its function? What rational justification can be offered for it? How is it that it is linked, on the one hand, to historical facts without being absorbed into history, and that it is bound up, on the other hand, with speculative doctrines though it is not completely absorbed in them; that it causes them to adhere together while still occupying its own distinct place between them? How comes it that, while the capital importance of Tradition is conceded in principle, the role which is granted to it in the theory of dogma and in discussions on exegetical method is yet quite a minor one? The reason is that the accepted notion of Tradition is so interwoven with the theses which I have just criticized that between them they make it unrecognizable. And that distortion of essential truth is not the least strange or the least dangerous thing about the present crisis: truth is invoked on either hand, but the fragmentary aspects which each thesis displays are so presented that the fragmented truths, instead of being joined together and completed, seem to be exclusive of one another.

Our first task is, therefore, to free Tradition from the wrappings which disfigure and hide it, to set out the complete idea of it, to describe its vital role and its fecundity. It will then be necessary to discover the source of its strength, and by virtue of what right it knows history in some respects otherwise and better than the critical historian, and dogma otherwise and better than the speculative theologian. After revealing the philosophical foundation, it will be easy to point out the value of such a solution for our present problems.

1. The usual idea evoked by the word Tradition is that of a transmission, principally by word of mouth, of historical facts, received truths, accepted teachings, hallowed practices and ancient customs. Is that, however, the whole content, is it even, where Catholicism is concerned, the essential content of the notion?

If that were so, there would be grounds for thinking that it would not resist analysis; and this would perhaps explain why the theoretical justification of Tradition is commonly confined to generalities which cannot be concretely verified; and also why the authority of Tradition is invoked over difficulties of detail, when precise or apposite arguments are not available. For in fact if it simply reports *de ore in aurem* what the first audiences did not write down, if it simply answers to a need for the esoteric or to a 'discipline of the secret', if even today its object is to teach us what the texts could have transmitted to us, simply supplementing the lacunae, their laconic form, and their failure to mention the commonest customs of the time, which are the least noticed, then how can one fail to see how little authority and how little usefulness it has? The interval of time which separates us from the sources, the inventive inaccuracy of popular recollection, the growing tendency of humanity to put down in writing all its reminiscences and all fine shades of meaning, the uprootedness of modern life with its consequent loss of continuity, the habit of committing everything to black and white (a sort of paper memory), surely all this results in the progressive erosion of traditions and the exhaustion of Tradition itself?

In contradistinction to the Scriptures, which relate the immediate testimony of the apostolic age, the name of Tradition is specifically reserved for the immense echo of oral Revelation in early Christian literature and in the works of the Fathers, because their writings serve to fix a recollection which may go back to the earliest times, though without having been preserved in the New Testament. Again, a text which reveals an ancient custom or a state of mind anterior to its spontaneous or reflective expression in writing serves as a vehicle for what is called 'a tradition'; but after all, however varied the objects transmitted, or the organs of transmission, *sive voce, sive scripto, sive praxi*, those who cling to this point of view and speak of Tradition with the greatest respect and in the greatest detail, always seem subject to a double presupposition: tradition only reports things explicitly said, expressly prescribed or deliberately performed by men in whom we are interested only for their conscious ideas, and in the form in which they themselves expressed them; it furnishes nothing which cannot or could not be translated into written language, nothing which is not directly and integrally convertible into intellectual expression: so that as we complete our collection of all that former centuries, even without noticing it, confided to memory—rather like students of folklore noting down folk-songs—Tradition, it would seem, becomes superfluous, and recedes before the progress of reflective analysis, written codification and scientific co-ordination.

Now these consequences are manifestly contrary to the spirit which inspires the Church, to the esteem in which she holds Tradition, and to the permanent and unchanging confidence which she places in it. And if these consequences can be logically deduced from a conception of tradition as essentially the oral transmission of what has been distinctly thought and could have been written down in the past, it must be that the conception itself is incomplete and defective. One only has to reflect for a moment on the role played by Tradition in the Church to see that it includes something altogether different from the transmission of the spoken word or of ancient custom. And, to state at once the full extent of the thesis I want to justify, I would say that Tradition's powers of conservation are equalled by its powers of conquest: that it discovers and formulates truths on which the past lived, though unable as yet to evaluate or define them explicitly, that it enriches our intellectual patrimony by putting the total deposit little by little into currency and making it bear fruit.

Contrary to the vulgar notion, but in conformity with the constant practice of the Church, we must say that Tradition is not a simple substitute for a written teaching. It has a different purpose; it does not proceed solely from it and it does not end by becoming identified with it. It preserves not so much the intellectual aspect of the past as its living reality. Even where we have the Scriptures, it always has something to add, and what passes little by little into writing and definitions is derived from it. It relies, no doubt, on texts, but at the same time it relies primarily on something else, on an experience always in act which enables it to remain in some respects master of the texts instead of being strictly subservient to them. In brief, whenever the testimony of Tradition has to be invoked to resolve one of the crises of growth in the spiritual life of Christians, it presents the conscious mind with elements previously held back in the depths of faith and practised, rather than expressed, systematized or reflected upon. This power of conservation and preservation also instructs and initiates. Turned lovingly towards the past where its treasure lies, it moves towards the future, where it conquers and illuminates. It has a humble sense of faithfully *recovering* even what it thus discovers. It does not have to innovate because it possesses its God and its all; but it has always to teach something new because it transforms what is implicit and 'enjoyed' into something explicit and known. So that whoever lives and thinks as a Christian really works for this, whether it be the saint who perpetuates Jesus among us, the scholar who goes back to the pure sources of Revelation, or the philosopher who strives to open the way to the future, and to prepare for the unending birth of the Spirit of newness. And so the various members contribute to the health of the body under the direction of the head which alone concerts and stimulates progress, in the unity of a consciousness which is divinely assisted.

However paradoxical it may sound, one can therefore maintain that Tradition anticipates and illuminates the future and is disposed to do so by the effort which it makes to remain faithful to the past. It is the guardian of the initial gift in so far as this has not been entirely formulated nor even expressly understood, although it is always fully possessed and employed; it frees us from the very Scriptures on which it never ceases to rely with devout respect: it helps us reach the real Christ whom no literary portrait could exhaust or replace, without being confined to the texts. Thus the Gospel itself appears as part of the deposit, not as the whole deposit, for, however divine the text, we cannot legitimately rest all dogma and all faith on that alone.[1] Something in the Church escapes scientific examination; and it is the Church which, without rejecting or neglecting the contributions of exegesis and of history, nevertheless controls them, because in the very tradition which constitutes her, she possesses another means of knowing her author, of partici-

---

[1] It is only right at this point to recall the special character of the Gospels: the inspired text contains something more than a text can normally furnish and, if I may so express it, an anticipated and already miraculously realized Tradition containing more of the revealed reality. If this question were the object of this study, it would be necessary to isolate that character, throwing into relief the fullness of a text which the historian has not after all the right to mutilate simply because it seems paradoxical to him. And by means of an analysis more conscious of all the elements of the problem, and by a more objective criticism, one would have been led, in the name of the texts themselves, to react against certain systematic interpretations.

pating in his life, of linking facts to dogma, and of justifying both the capital and the interest of her teaching.

Two corollaries follow from the role of tradition thus conceived. The Church is a proof of itself: *index sui est;* for it supplies the verification of what it believes and teaches in its age-old experience and its continuous practice. One can, in fact, make use of an argument, too often reduced to mere rhetoric, in this esoteric sense: the truth of Catholicism is not demonstrated simply by the miracle of an institution's surviving so many disasters, nor by the beauty of its achievement; it has within it a power of self-justification which is independent of historical proofs or moral probabilities; and it is important not to reduce that internal criterion to an extrinsic and accessory argument. Furthermore, it is clear that, in order that we may pass from facts to dogma, even the most exact analysis of the texts and the effort of individual thought are not sufficient. The mediation of collective life, and the slow progressive labour of the Christian tradition, are essential. Here again we find the esoteric meaning of such formulae as the following: 'Faith in dogma presupposes a living faith', an altogether false expression if taken to mean that the personal belief of each believer is not justified by explicit reasons, but profoundly true if it reminds us that the intellectual expression of Christian dogma was worked out in the matrix of a believing society, that it cannot be brought to life and further developed except by a living faith, and that in order to understand a dogma fully one must bear within one the fullness of the Tradition which has brought it to light. In this way the difficulty which held us up at the outset seems to be resolved: the active principle of the synthesis lies neither in the facts alone, nor in the ideas alone, but in the Tradition which embraces within it the facts of history, the effort of reason and the accumulated experiences of the faithful.

All the same, it may sound strange to say that after more than nineteen centuries of Christianity we still have a method—and not a purely mystical one—of attaining the real Christ, of determining what he wanted, of developing what he has made, of explaining the meaning of the supernatural gifts which he brought. The historian will, no doubt, ridicule the 'extra-historical' means of penetrating the consciousness of Jesus[1] and of constituting the Sacred History of Revelation without the *placet* of criticism. A philosopher, or perhaps even a theologian, will protest against the unreasonable hope of discerning men's authentic thoughts when they have not formally expressed them and would have been incapable of understanding the formulae in which they are now enclosed as those which most closely conform to their beliefs. As against those who see in Tradition nothing but a fixed deposit and those who regard it as an accumulation of superimposed novelties, it behoves us to discover its rational basis; it does not work in the dark, without principles of discrimination, without rules, simply by instinct. One cannot therefore say that it is 'in the final analysis' that one appeals to Tradition, in default of other arguments and to get round awkward corners by falling back on authority where rational grounds are wanting. On the contrary, we shall see that, to conserve the past and to prepare the future, Tradition adopts reasonable and even rational processes whose laws can be made clear and whose organon can be established. Thus we are no longer exposed to the objections of those who would tie us to a bed of Procrustes, mutilating us and forbidding us growth, or of those who see only the Protean metamorphoses of an indefinite evolution where they should see a development governed and unified by the internal finality of an organism.

2. Tradition extends further than Scripture. Even in regard to what Scripture tells us, it possesses a special virtue and a distinct competence; and it does not rely only on oral transmission to lead us deeper and deeper into the reality revealed, and to the Revealer himself who constitutes it in its entirety. But what is the human foundation for that extension of our knowledge? What rational guarantee, what philosophical justification can be invoked against the fantasies of private judgment and extravagant intuitions or deductions? However supernatural its object and its mode of action, there must be some natural basis on which Tradition may work. The best way of bringing it to light will be to consider how the Church in fact proceeds.

[1] *Tr.* Loisy had indeed done so in the exchange of letters which preceded the writing of *History and Dogma*.

She does not proceed by way of research nor does she appeal primarily to science. However attentive she may be to the results of criticism, or concerned to steep herself in the pure sources of her origin, she knows that she will not have to revise or reform essential teaching in the light of any discovery.

She does not proceed dialectically, like a philosophy which is built up by the analysis and synthesis of balanced concepts. She adapts herself to the diverse forms of intellectual culture; she borrows the language she needs from philosophical systems so as to confer upon her doctrine the degree of precision required by a given state of civilization; but she is the slave of no system; even the most fully worked-out formulae, those most closely bound up with a philosophical terminology, Aristotle's for example, the Church considers only as provisional in their scientific form.[1] So that the Church preserves its sovereign autonomy *vis-à-vis* the human doctrines which it uses, which it appears to obey and which in reality it turns to its own account.

Nor does she proceed by a sort of empirical mysticism, without the means of justifying her decisions, even when the motives which she reveals are neither the only ones nor the most essential. She speaks with an independent authority; but she speaks to the intelligence as much as to obedience, claiming the rights of reason because she wishes to teach a communicable truth. She need take no account of human contingencies, and, while she is not concerned to be adroit, opportune or timely, she uses any human means so as to be understood and so as to discover in men the point of contact

[1] The formulae serve to determine precisely the sense which the Church wished to express. That meaning is a definite acquisition; but the formulae remain mutable on condition that the new expression, retaining the full meaning comprised in the old language, is more completely adapted to the progress of Christian knowledge. Thus in physics the hypothesis of an electric fluid is a discarded language, though the facts and the laws it served to make known are not discarded; and the theory of a potential, which differs entirely from it as a formula, expresses the same facts, the same laws, and others as well. The fact that Latin is the official language of the Church does not mean that it is superior to other idioms or that it possesses some magic virtue; any more than the peripatetic terminology of most definitions can tie down knowledge, although it serves to tie down meaning.

prepared for her action. So her supernatural wisdom is always enlightened; she surrounds herself with precautions and makes use of natural means. And that is no doubt what is meant by saying that the *Magisterium* is guided in its infallible teaching not by revelation, nor even by inspiration, but by 'assistance'. Assistance implies a simple negative help; that is, God requires man to use all the resources of science and reflection as though to hide his regulative action behind the natural means.

But, since the Tradition of the Church presupposes to some extent a normal use of natural activity, since, in consequence, it allows of rational justification, where shall we look for the secret of this work and the principle of this explanation? Doubtless they could never be discovered by a doctrine which had no feeling for those elements contained in the moral and religious life which are not unconscious and irrational, but subconscious and unreasoned, which are provisionally and partially irreducible to explicit thought. But where a philosophy of action is concerned it is an entirely different matter: for this studies the various regular, methodically determinable ways by which a clear and formulated knowledge succeeds in expressing, more and more fully, the profound realities on which it feeds. If Tradition had no other purpose than to transmit what had been thought and formally expressed, or even if there were nothing in the spiritual life of man which could be preserved apart from reflective ideas, then it would obviously be confined to struggling against the ravages of time and of human forgetfulness. But is it beyond comprehension that there should be another deposit to be preserved, other than expressed and understood thoughts, and other ways of preserving it than by the didactic precision of an oral teaching? That can easily be discovered by asking not only how Christ's words have been remembered, but also how he has left us the means of legitimately supplementing what he did not say. We shall see that, man being what he is and supernatural Revelation being what it is, it is hardly conceivable that it should have been otherwise.

Certain things which we have heard as children, and which perhaps struck us by their very obscurity, sometimes come back to us much later in the light of experience and reflection. They were preserved in us by a memory always at work which is not purely intellectual, since we end, as the result of a sort of rumination, by grasping what had first of all escaped us.[1] That is why the direct witness, the immediate disciple of a Master, who can say 'I myself heard his own words', can at any moment unearth an unpublished impression, a new comment, distinct from the written testimonies. The ears of the spirit hear more slowly than the ears of the flesh. It may no doubt be legitimately affirmed that the Fourth Gospel could not, except by a miracle, have been written, even by St John, immediately after the Ascension; as indeed is suggested by the text describing in an expressive phrase the labour of discovering an already distant past, that return to full consciousness of what had never entered it completely, *Spiritus suggeret vobis omnia quaecumque dixero vobis* (John xIV, 26). Thus we see that even things which have been said may still need to be insinuated in a new and more intimate way.[2]

And it is in these ways too that those things which were not said, because they could not be made clear to the Jews of the first century, by that rudimentary intelligence without, which neither perception nor reminiscence is possible, still reach, and will continue to reach the Christian consciousness: *Adhuc multa habeo vobis dicere sed non potestis portare modo* (John xVI, 12). Now what is the human means, the normal and natural intermediary of such a suggestion? *Servate mandata . . . Si quis diliget me, sermonem meum servabit . . . et ad eum veniemus et mansionem apud eum faciemus.* (John xIV, 23).

A man can carry out completely what he cannot entirely understand, and in doing it he keeps alive within him the consciousness of

[1] *Et ipsi (parentes) non intellexerunt verbum quod locutus est ad eos . . . Et mater eius conservabat omnia haec in corde suo* (Luke III, 50.) I am not concerned to ask whether these texts are 'historical' or not; I only maintain that they express a profound psychology and describe real experiences, teaching us by a method which, though neither that of Aristotle nor of Richard Simon, seems no less legitimate and fertile.

[2] The normal concern of a human master, and *a fortiori* of a disciple, is fidelity *ne varietur*. This proclamation of future and unforeseen growth, of unheard of suggestions, even if attributed to the author of the Fourth Gospel, is not, of course, discoverable in any ancient philosophical or religious text, intellectual in character and purely human in origin.

a reality which is still half hidden from him. 'To keep' the word of God means in the first place to do it, to put it into practice; and the deposit of Tradition, which the infidelities of the memory and the narrow limits of the intelligence would inevitably deform if it were handed to us in a purely intellectual form, cannot be transmitted in its entirety, indeed, cannot be used and developed, unless it is confided to the practical obedience of love. Faithful action is the Ark of the Covenant where the confidences of God are found, the Tabernacle where he perpetuates his presence and his teaching. If the essential truth of Catholicism is the incarnation of dogmatic ideas in historical facts, one must add reciprocally that the miracle of the Christian life is that from acts at first perhaps difficult, obscure and enforced, one rises to the light through a practical verification of speculative truths. *Lex voluntatis, lux veritatis.* So we see that since the beginning of Christianity the love of Christ has served as a vehicle for a doctrine which literature does not relate in its entirety, and that by putting his law and his spirit into practice the Church has been continuously enriched ever since. Moreover, faced by intellectual novelties, or exegetical hypotheses, there is an autonomous principle of discernment in the total experience of the Church: in taking account of ideas and of facts, traditional faith also takes account of proven ways, of practice confirmed by the fruits of sanctity, of the enlightenment gained through piety, prayer and mortification. That testimony is not the only one, no doubt, but it has its own inalienable value because it is based at the same time on the collective age-old action of the most human of men and on God's action in them. Now according to the very exigencies of the scientific method, which only surrenders to evidence and prudently resists till it is impossible to doubt, nothing can modify Tradition which does not, when put to the test, reveal itself as compatible with it and favourable to its progress; so that, though fundamentally stimulating, it shows itself in the main as a moderating, curbing influence in regard to the diverse intellectual elements of the Christian faith.

And not only is this true in fact, and good that it should be so; but also, knowing what we know about man, and admitting what faith obliges us to admit about Catholicism, we must say that it could not be otherwise. For certain precise consequences follow from the hypothesis of a positive Revelation, that is to say from the presence of an eternal truth in a local, temporal and contingent form; and that is really the specific character, the ἅπαξ of Christianity. A truly supernatural teaching is only viable and conceivable if the initial gift is a seed capable of progressive and continual growth. The divine and human Word of Christ did not fix itself in immobility. Jesus wrote only in the sand and impressed his words only on the air: his living teaching comes to mobile and inconstant minds. The human translation of it, however literal it may be, leaves it incomplete and motionless, or rather it only reaches us in so far as it passed first through the minds of men of a particular race and century. It can only be understood and assimilated, little by little, if nourished by the sources of the moral life and by the suggestions of the invisible Spirit present in every age and in every civilization. So far is 'development' from being heterodox, as so many believers fear, that it is the static idea of tradition, *fixism*, which is the virtual heresy—whether the static conception is that of the historian who claims to seize the truth of Revelation in its earliest version, or that of the speculative theologian, ready to confine infinite reality in a completed synthesis, as though at some given moment in history the spirit of man had exhausted God's spirit. To reach Christ, if he is really the Word incarnate, to justify dogmas if they express the absolute, it is useless simply to retrace the course of historical determinism and to squeeze out the sense of the primitive texts; for this is to look for the last word in the first echo, to decide *a priori* the whole question of the supernatural character of that initial testimony and to decide it in an irremediably negative manner. Only a progressive and synthetic movement can lead us from the effects produced to their cause, can trace all the rays of light in the Christian consciousness over the centuries to their source, and through its unending progress imitate the infinite riches of God, revealed and always hidden, hidden and always revealed. In that profound sense, when it is a question of finding the supernatural in Sacred History and in dogma, the Gospel is nothing without the Church, the teaching of Scripture is nothing without the Christian life, exegesis is nothing without Tradition—the Catholic Tradition which is now seen to be not a limitative and retrograde force, but a power of development and expansion. Careful not to hide its talent safely away, and faithful to the injunction to make it bear fruit, Tradition is less concerned to conserve than to discover: it will only attain the α at the ω.

Two objections may be made to this. Regardless of the fact that the complaints are contradictory, people object on the one hand that such a method misconceives the necessary role of definitive thought, of stable definitions, demonstrable and communicable formulae, and so is lacking in precision, leaving to the individual fantasy and to subjective illusions a scope which it is impossible to limit; it is objected on the other hand that what is required in order to solve the initial problem is not a method of explaining how dogmas arise through the collective work of Christian thought and religious authority, but a method personal to each individual of linking together facts and beliefs, history and doctrine. It is worth pausing a moment before those two difficulties; they will prove illuminating.

To look behind distinct perceptions, reflective thoughts, and formal reasoning towards the many sources of the spiritual life is not to misconceive the necessary role of thought, the validity of the reason, the salutary firmness of the formulae in which its work is crystallized. There is no idea so false, none more infected by the worst kind of subjectivism, than the belief that there is no ordered reality in subjective life, and that our moral activity, once freed from the framework of a purely intellectual reflection, escapes all laws which are scientifically determinable.[1] The extrinsicist seemed to be saying: 'Here is a stone; I have established that God's order

[1] There are no grounds for saying 'dogmatic development was lacking in method' because it did not obey the laws of classical logic. There is another dialectic besides that, and I have tried elsewhere to indicate the *Elementary Principle of a Logic of the moral life* (*Bibliothèque du Congrès de Philosophie*, II, 51–85). As for those who still think that syllogistic logic is the first and last word of human reason, let them consult the labours of M. Peano and his school, as they have been recently summarized by M. Couturat in the *Revue de Métaphysique* (15th Jan. 1904, especially pp. 45–50) before contesting the incomplete, artificial, partially false and irrational character of this logic. It will then perhaps be seen that there is some danger in taking the peripatetic horizon for the bounds of the world and of thought.

requires you to take it.' I am quite ready to do so, but should I be unreasonable and disrespectful towards God if I showed that it was not a stone, if, profiting by accumulated experience and from the progress of chemistry, I analysed the object and studied its effects, the better to utilize its virtues?

If the moral method on which Tradition tacitly relies lacks precision, how can we explain the competence acquired through asceticism, that skill in the discernment of spirits and in spiritual direction which is found in individuals, and how *a fortiori* shall we explain the holy society, the summary of collective experience? Nothing is more reliable than the light shed by the orderly and repeated performances of Christian practices. To believe that each one constitutes in isolation his own fundamental theology, that the consideration of miracles and the effort of the individual reason provides an adequate apologetic, is surely just another form of 'subjectivism', and the Church has always protested against it. She declares that she alone is competent to discern miracles because the senses, science and philosophy cannot be relied upon here; for, if miracles serve to prove doctrine, doctrine also serves to establish miracles. So we must realize both what the Church does, and her *reason* for doing so.

Let us have no more talk of a purely individual, purely intellectual criterion for linking facts with beliefs: if we faced texts and facts by ourselves alone, we could no more extract dogmas from them, although they are there, than we could recognize a plant from its seed-pod alone. By explaining how dogmatic definitions are engendered, *mediante praxi fidelium et traditione Ecclesiae*, the objections which arise from a misunderstanding of this will be set on one side, and each individual reason, each human life, will be helped to rediscover within itself, where it might otherwise remain imperceptible, some outline of the complete task which justifies the Church's real and actual teaching. Without the Church, the faithful could not detect the true hand of God in the Bible and in souls; but, unless each believer brought his little contribution to the common life, the organism would not be fully alive and spiritual. The infallible *Magisterium* is the higher and really supernatural guarantee of a function which has its natural foundation in the concert of all the powers of each Christian and of all Christianity: *viribus unitis docet discendo et discit docendo semper*. Divine assistance ensures the normal, indefectible exercise of this essential function.

Let us now look back at the ground covered. Consider, on the one side, extrinsicism, in which some people perhaps saw the pure expression of the 'traditional' thesis—a thesis that neglects the role of Tradition! How strange to find the acme of orthodoxy in assertions such as these: 'The Church does not search for the truth; she has nothing to learn; a Church which still has something to discover is not the Church to which Jesus Christ has taught all that he learnt from his Father'. So the sacred deposit of faith is simply an aerolith, to be preserved in a glass case safe from a sacrilegious curiosity which, if allowed to analyse it, would only discover in it elements which are identical with those of mere earthly bodies! Now that we have understood both the psychological impossibility and the theological error of such opinions we may remark upon the particular irony of the fact that these zealots, so ready to point to Protestant infiltrations and to the danger of subjectivism, adopt an attitude like that of the early Reformers, who also, reacting against the Church's development and refractory to her living authority, claimed in their rigid intellectualism to attach themselves to the original letter of the text and to discover in it, by their reason alone, the reason of their faith.

Consider, on the other side, historicism, in which some believed themselves to have found the pure spirit of science, the true meaning of tradition, of its plastic power and its transforming activity. There is no question now of a sacred stone, handed down from one generation to the next, each limiting itself to proving that it has fallen from heaven as the unique foundation for the spiritual edifice or as that edifice itself. But, while ridiculing the narrowness of an almost materialist conception of religion, does one cure it by substituting as a basis for the temple of souls all the sediment accumulated by centuries of human thought? And by failing to recognize that dogmas are not so much the result of a dialectical exercise upon the texts as the expression of a perpetuated and experienced reality, one would have lost, if not all sense of that historical continuity which maintains profound analogies throughout apparent differences, at least the realization of that unity of life and thought which is always present and always supernaturally identical. What can one say of all these heterogeneous strata except that they bury Christ beneath a heap of rubble which is supposed to be fertile but has only the fertility of dead leaves?

3. To conclude this hasty sketch, it must suffice, in the first place, to set out the answer to the problem of method with which we started, and then to note that it contains, perhaps, the means of resolving the fundamental questions raised by the opposing theses themselves in the course of their conflict.

A. Dogmas cannot be rationally justified either by history alone, by the most ingenious application of dialectics to the texts, or by the efforts of the individual; but all these forces contribute, and they converge in Tradition, the authority of which, divinely assisted, is the organ of infallible expression. As the dogmas of Catholicism were extracted in their present defined forms only by that immense labour which, up to a point, is accomplished by natural, ordered and discoverable means, the synthesis of facts and beliefs can be rationally justified only *in concreto* by the study of the complex genesis which controlled it. And if that conclusion is true of phylogenesis, it is true also of ontogenesis; which means to say that the processes of individual faith are a microcosm of the faith of the Church; it is no more the result of a pure knowledge of facts or of an objective demonstration than the faith of the Church. In a sense already explained, and without misconceiving the legitimate role of discursive thought, it would be true to say that one goes from faith to dogma rather than from dogma to faith.[1] Any apologetic which began with the factual and rational proofs or with objective credibility immediately, in isolation and exclusively would provoke more resistance than useful results in minds accustomed to critical methods and psychological analysis. Since it does not conform to

[1] This assertion may still, despite everything, disturb some minds; but it is, after all, no more disconcerting than the following: in digging a tunnel, even in the most crumbling sand, excavation always precedes consolidation. The fixity of arguments and definitions, in the moving depths of our life and in the obscurities of our passage to God, is simply part of the unavoidable masonry required in order to keep the road open and to permit further excavations which, in their turn, will need fresh supports.

the concrete exercise of thought and the real history of faith, it is hardly surprising if it fails to find a theoretical link between faith and dogma, dogma and faith, when it claims to restrict itself to elements which, by themselves, were incapable of linking them in practice.

Attached as she is to texts and facts and definitions, the Church has a vital tradition which is a perpetually renewed and controlled commentary on them, and so is not literally dependent on them. She preserves the old meanings scrupulously, but always so as to disentangle the spiritual intention. She need have no fear of contradicting herself because the ascetic method which has always supported the speculative method is such that even the greatest intellectual innovations leave the spirit which inspires the Church untouched. She has lived long enough for a consciousness of her orientation, of her strength and of her divine guest, to allow her in the face of certain exigencies, arising from archaeology or from philosophy or certain unforeseen evidences, to find within herself the stability she needs. The more she clings to the reality of divine history, to which she strives to conform herself, the more she liberates herself from the figurative representations and the pictures in particular colours with which the first generation described it. The power confided to her, which by her long fidelity and by her very trials she has always merited, is not the authority of a museum custodian or a Keeper of Archives or of a Janissary of the Seraglio; she has the dignity and the authority of a spouse: *viva conjux, dimidium Christi vivi.* Her intrinsic proofs do not, of course, dispense her from using others, but they regulate their use—which is not an automatic one—and, by widening her scope, ensure her greater flexibility and greater freedom of movement. Instead of being dependent upon details, the Church proceeds synthetically and, according to the thesis *de fide* of the total inspiration of the Scriptures, she proceeds from the whole to particular solutions. Sole judge in the last resort of what is real in the immense parable addressed to the child-creatures which we are in this world, she can regard what other times took literally as figurative because the divine reality of the Bridegroom is sufficient for her and everything else is but a symbol and a preparation. Fully conscious of the power of her Tradition, she can dispense with scaffoldings which were provisionally required to shelter the growth of her work or useful for her spiritual edification but which may have to be cleared away, not to overturn the building but to reveal proportions hitherto unobserved and its granite consistency. Since there are parables in the New Testament, why should the Old Testament be exclusively and literally historical? The time has come when we shall be no more disconcerted by the conclusions of criticism about Tobias, Daniel, Job, or Noah than we should be edified by pious attempts to find the tomb of the Prodigal Son or to accumulate, as was attempted not so long ago, 'a super-abundance of proofs about the geographical site of Eden'. What remains unshakable is the truth of these prodigious facts: the purity of faith miraculously aroused and preserved in the one Lord and Creator, the prophetic fervour of the expectation of the Messiah, the divinely disconcerting realization of the Saviour's great promise and of man's great hope. Thus the Bible appears as the instrument through which we hear the voice of the Holy Spirit sounding more and more power-fully till, in the end, with the Gospel as its centre, it reaches all the races of mankind and every century of time. Catholicism owes its increasing correspondence with its own idea, its power to hold or recapture the minds of men, to its consciousness of being the culmination of man's religious life. For while its mission is to preserve and propagate the gift of Revelation, which is always something limited, it does not forget the universal gift of the Redemption, which is the divine reality, the absolute term, to which revealed knowledge refers, though this is not identical with it. And to draw men to the body of the Church it becomes more than ever necessary to open to them her soul.

Thus a fuller realization of the traditional basis of the Church results at the same time in a greater freedom, a greater breadth and precision. By finding in herself a solid support, she preserves her sovereign authority in regard to Scripture, but in such a way as to leave the Scriptures their own physiognomy and their original spon-taneity. She is free to see the facts as contemporaries saw them, and not as the deductive mind imagines them, or as modern thought would like them to be, and this effort for precision and fidelity becomes the source of a renewal; for with the help of the past she liberates the future from the unconscious limitations and illusions of the present.[1] As she becomes increasingly aware of the diversity of God's approaches to man, and defines the expression of revealed truth more rigorously, she takes a broader view of the extension of the redemptive goodness. She discovers within herself what the incomplete theses which we have had to criticize could not provide: a means of setting limits to the exigencies of history or the deductions of theology, and a means of self-development. Finally, after having fought for so long against various forms of a dissolving *latitudinarianism*, she will realize, in the plenitude of her power, and in her need for self-expansion, that to be too broadminded and to minimize Revelation is not the only way of departing from orthodoxy, that it is equally possible to be too narrowminded and to restrict the Redemption: that is also a heresy, and one which has been the least effective in breaking up Christian society.

B. After these considerations of method we should glance, in conclusion, at the basic doctrinal questions involved. The ordinary believer is not called upon, of course, to deliver absolute judgments: but, faced by the alternatives which nowadays present themselves, he can and must say how, in his view, the practical solutions supplied by living faith lead to doctrinal ones.

Can there be an ultimate divorce between the conclusions of history and ecclesiastical definitions or religious practices, so that critical science, speculative theology and moral practice evolve in isolation? Or is it a question of accepting them in their real inter-

[1] If the nature of this study allowed of it, it would have been well to insist on this double aspect: the doctrine which ensures the relative independence of the Church and the Scriptures also co-ordinates them, instead of binding them so tightly together that they cannot move without harming one another. It is because it must take the initiative that the Church is not content to offer the world a rough-hewn deposit: she encourages and practises an intellectual probity which listens to all the witnesses and accepts enlightenment from all sources. It is obvious that, in fact, the solidarity of the sciences safeguards their legitimate autonomy and so relieves us of this sort of sophism which caused so many men to lose their faith: 'They were right not to make any concessions, since a single admission of error ruins the edifice of absolute truth' (Renan, *Souvenirs*, p. 292).

dependence so as to discover their several contributions, their relative autonomy and their compensating action on one another: so that their legitimate independence, which is the condition of their co-operation, derives from their very solidarity, and that to isolate the study of facts or of Christian theology from the science of Christian life would be to tear out the heart of the bride and to expect her to go on living, and living for the bridegroom?

Was the work of Christ just a means of stimulating the religious consciousness; is Christian truth only a *truth*, operating only when known, expressible as an ideal which benefits only those who know it and only in so far as they discover its lessons through their own initiative? Or is it a reality, an end no less than a means, corresponding, through the Incarnation, to a metaphysical function, while answering, through the Redemption, to moral and substantial exigencies and applicable in certain conditions even to those who are ignorant of its efficacy?

Does the supernatural consist, as the extrinsicist thesis implies, in a notional relationship determined and imposed by God, there being no link between natural and supernatural but only an ideal juxtaposition of heterogeneous and even impenetrable elements which only the obedience of our minds can bring together? In that case the supernatural subsists only if it remain extrinsic to the natural, and if it is proposed to us from outside, its whole value residing in the fact that it is *above* nature. Or can it be reduced, as the historicist thesis implies, to being no more than another name for the divine or for a sort of concentration of it in nature itself, so that, if it is not entirely confused with nature, that is because after all one must have a word for the phase at present reached by our religious aristocracy? In short, should it be regarded more or less as an intellectual privilege which only exists as such, in opposition to, and as external to, the common state? Or is it a love-relationship which insinuates a new order into the normal order—where man is and can only be *servus Dei*—one in which the slave can become the friend, the brother, and even *tanquam Deus Dei;* so that, through this relationship, through grace, all men are made to feel, if not the spirit of adoption lost by the first fault, at least a profound sense of unrest, a mysterious hunger of the soul? This is an order, a state, all the more freely infused into nature because it cannot be confused with nature. For the 'state of nature' is a pure abstraction which does not exist and never has existed; in studying the nature of man as it actually is, we do not get to know the 'state of nature' any more than we can abstract, in our lives, the radical and universal penetration of something which will always prevent us from finding our equilibrium in the merely human order.[1]

Behind all these alternatives there is only one problem, that of the relation between man and God in Christ, and consequently of the relation of Christ to each one of us. No partial solution can satisfy us in the exposed position in which the present disputes have placed us; and it cannot be concealed that several of the old answers need to be gone into more fully, deepened and extended beyond mere ideology into the domain of psychology, history and metaphysics. The problem of Christ's own consciousness is, in certain respects, unexplored territory; and it is very difficult not to abolish either the humanity or the divinity in the inner unity of his mysterious person. For it is not enough to juxtapose mechanically the human nature and the divine nature as abstract and static entities attached by an equally abstract notion, that of his personality. The educated believer can no longer fail to ask himself what is the finite element which marks the human knowledge of Jesus with its limitative character, so that it does not lose itself in the ocean of the knowledge of the Word; how is it possible for his words and attitudes not to have been sometimes a pretence; how, in fine, did there subsist in him something of that mixture of light and shadow which seems to be the condition of all human consciousness ?

We must not say that such curiosity is idle: it can never be a matter of indifference, either to the human heart or the philosophic

---

[1] I do not wish to be saddled with a confusion between the *supernatural life*, as formed in us by baptism and habitual grace, and the antecedent *supernatural state* in which man is placed so as to be able to realize this life of grace. I do not overlook the conditions of personal access to salvation or the infinite difference which separates the spiritual life from spiritual death. But what has often been ignored is the fact that previously to habitual grace there is another grace, a first vocation, a state which results from the loss of the initial gift, but which contains a need and an aptitude for recovering it.

reason or the life of society, whether or not 'the mystery of Jesus' in the soul of a Pascal or a St Theresa of Avila is only a pious fairy-tale. Has devotion fed upon a dream for all these centuries, a dream from which it will one day awaken, by believing in the personal intuition of the Saviour in each human soul, in his living presence, in the reality of his grace, of our own action in his Passion and of his Passion in ourselves? If Christ is more than a prophet, if he is God, no degree of subtlety avails: the consciousness of his divinity is less able to desert him than the consciousness of our humanity can desert us, and the consciousness of his humanity embraces our human consciousness. For if, even in being God, Jesus remains man, first of all he suffered, living the life of the senses, learning by direct and laborious experience; but then at the same time the vessel of his humanity was shaped and expanded by the divine forces which he poured into it increasingly in a progress (intensive, not extensive) which assumes the finite into the infinite. His prayers and solitary vigils are like the labour of our spiritual birth; they are the perfect holocaust of his humanity to his Father. And above all his experimental knowledge is the term of a comparison which makes him sympathize physically with us. His divine knowledge serves only to put that infinite sympathy into action, according to circumstances, to make his human imagination realize, in all their acute reality, our sufferings, our ignorances, our weaknesses, so as to penetrate his whole being with the indelible mark of a complete humanity, which is the Passion itself. He is the universal stigmatic marked by all our human miseries: *aliter per carnem, aliter per divinitatem*, as St Bernard says, *idem eadem cognoscens*. And therefore tears, distresses, agonies, all become genuine and substantially true, humanly and divinely real. For if his human consciousness is not absorbed by the light of the Word, then it is because all our humanities serve as a screen for his humanity; because, if we exist through him, he exists, in a sense, through us; because he is literally the Son of Man, and if the creation finds its consistency in Christ's knowledge and his loving will, Christ's singular reality as a contingent being consists in the universal fulfilment of all life and of every being that was created in him. Far from having to degrade his divinity or diminish his humanity in order to preserve them intact, perhaps if we become more deeply conscious of their reality and their intimacy we shall find the secret of their unity in him and of their supernatural union with ourselves.

At the outset we were faced by two antagonistic and even irreconcilable attitudes, each full of dangers and difficulties; two theses incapable of limiting or correcting themselves or of supporting and completing one another. And yet each of them contributed truths which cannot and must not be ignored. That, in a word, is the crisis. If, then, it is conceded that a conception of Tradition obtained with the help of a philosophy of action provides us with the light which we need, the means of reconciling these opposite theses and of giving life to opposed methods, perhaps it will also be recognized that a similar solution could be applied to analogous conflicts, even if such an enterprise provoked contradictory accusations which indicate rather its complex equilibrium than any departure from orthodoxy. As against those who offer us a Christianity so divine that there is nothing human, living or moving about it, and those who involve it so deeply in historical contingencies and make it so dependent upon natural factors that it retains nothing but a diffused sort of divinity, one must show it to be both more concrete and more universal, more divine and more human, than words can express. Because there is a living unity in Christianity, because it is the whole of man, the various sciences can only split it up by a provisional abstraction. A separate dogmatic theology, a separate exegesis, a separate history, necessarily remain incomplete: a conception which isolates the sciences without making them autonomous must be replaced by a view which grants them their autonomy all the more readily because it never allows them to be isolated.

One realizes through the practice of Christianity that its dogmas are rooted in reality. One has no right to set the facts on one side and the theological data on the other without going back to the sources of life and of action, finding the indivisible synthesis; the facts and definitions are simply faithful translations of it into different languages. The link between facts and beliefs can never be rationally justified by scholarship or dialectics, as though each human reason separately performed its dogmatic task. To succeed in that justification one must consider not only the efforts of each man, but the consensus of all who live the same life and share in the same love. That is why definitions of doctrine are not so much innovations as the authentic recognition of collective anticipations and of collective certifications. Christian practice nourishes man's knowledge of the divine and bears within its action what is progressively discerned by the theologian's initiative. The synthesis of dogma and facts is scientifically effected because there is a synthesis of thought and grace in the life of the believer, a union of man and God, reproducing in the individual consciousness the history of Christianity itself. And while it is true that Christian knowledge does not disdain the support of history (for the facts in this instance are both the redemptive reality and the revelatory message), history cannot, without leading to the shipwreck of faith, disregard Christian knowledge, by which I mean the results methodically acquired by the collective experience of Christ verified and realized in us. It can no longer be held that the part which it plays in the inner life of each Christian is simply a matter of individual psychology: as long as it is not clearly realized that in addition to dogmatic theology and exegesis there is a knowledge, a real science of action, capable of extracting, for the benefit of an experimental and progressive theology, the lessons which life draws from history, there will always be recurrent conflicts or interferences or mutual ostracism. The Church has an age-old experience of that science, although the theology of it has not been worked out; and that is why she alone is competent to form in souls the authentic Christ. And when she proposes the God-Man for our adoration no one can legitimately make out, by whatever indirect suggestion, that she is guilty of a substitution of persons.

BIBLIOGRAPHY

BIBLIOGRAPHY

THE PRINCIPAL WORKS OF MAURICE BLONDEL IN
THEIR CHRONOLOGICAL ORDER

Abbreviations
in text

L'Action   *L'Action. Essai d'une critique de la vie et d'une science de la*
pratique. Paris, Alcan, 1893. Three versions appeared:
The thesis, xxv-433 pages; the printed version, xxv-
495 pages, put on sale without Blondel's permission,
and this gave him the opportunity of recalling it and
of re-casting the last section, beginning at page 401,
and of adding 42 pages. This last version has been
republished as the first volume of *Premiers Écrits* by the
Presses Universitaires de France (P.U.F.), 1950.

De Vinculo substantiali et de Substantia composita apud
Leibnitium. Lutetiae Parisiorum, Alcan, 1893. 79 pages.
The Latin thesis. Privately printed. (A French version
appeared in 1930: *Une énigme historique: le 'Vinculum*
substantiae', Beauchesne.)

Volume II of *Premiers Écrits* includes:

Lettre   1. *Lettre sur les exigences de la pensée contemporaine en*
or Letter   *matière d'apologétique et sur la méthode de la philosophie*
dans l'étude du problème religieux.

2. *L'Illusion idéaliste.*

3. *Principe élémentaire d'une logique de la vie morale.*

History and   4. *Histoire et Dogme. Les lacunes philosophiques de*
Dogma   *l'exégèse moderne.*

5. *De la valeur historique du dogme.*

Semaine   *La Semaine Sociale de Bordeaux et le Monophorisme* (pseudonym Testis), Paris, Bloud et Gay, 1910; (the articles
published in *Annales de Philosophie Chrétienne,* 1909-
1910.)

BIBLIOGRAPHY

Le procès de l'intelligence (in collaboration with Paul Archambault), Paris, Bloud et Gay, 1921 (three articles published in *La Nouvelle Journée*).

Le problème de la mystique, in Cahier No. 3 of *La Nouvelle Journée*, Paris, Bloud et Gay, 1925.

L'Itinéraire   *L'Itinéraire philosophique de Maurice Blondel.* Attributed to Frederic Lefèvre, but written by Blondel. Paris, Spes, 1928.

Le Problème de la Philosophie Catholique. In Cahier No. 20 of *La Nouvelle Journée*, Paris, Bloud et Gay, 1932.

The Trilogy
1. *La Pensée*, 2 vols., Paris, Alcan, 1934.
2. *L'Être et les êtres*, Paris, Alcan, 1935.
3. *L'Action*, 2 vols., Paris, Alcan, 1936 and 1937.

La philosophie et l'esprit chrétien, 2 vols., 1944 and 1946.

Exigences   *Exigences philosophiques du christianisme*, Paris, Presses Universitaires de France, 1950.

Études Blondeliennes, 3 vols., includes:

Vol. I: *Une soutenance de thèse*, by Blondel.

Vol. II: Notes for a second edition of *L'Action* (1893). Studies by Archambault, Jacques Paliard, Jean Lacroix, Emil Bréhier.

Vol. III: *Dialogues sur la Pensée*, by Blondel.

LETTERS AND CORRESPONDENCE

Bl-Val Corr.   *Maurice Blondel and Auguste Valensin*, 1899-1912, 2 vols., Paris, Aubier, 1957. Containing voluminous notes, quotations from other correspondents and from Blondel's letters. No editor named.

Au Coeur   *Au Coeur de la Crise Moderniste. Le Dossier d'une controverse.* Letters of Blondel, Henri Bremond, Fr. von Hügel, Alfred Loisy. Presented by René Marlé, Paris, Aubier, 1960. Also contains valuable notes and references.

Corr-Phil.   *Correspondance Philosophique*, Maurice Blondel-Lucien Laberthonnière, presented by Claude Tresmontant, Paris, Editions du Seuil, 1961.

L.P.   *Lettres Philosophiques de Maurice Blondel:* Letters to E. Boutroux, V. Delbos, L. Brunschwicg, J. Wehrlé, Henri Bremond, Ed. Le Roy, etc., Paris, Aubier, 1961.

BIBLIOGRAPHY

Archives de Philosophie (January-March, 1961) contains the memoranda exchanged between Maurice Blondel and P. Teilhard de Chardin, presented by Henri de Lubac, and a study of the last chapter of *L'Action* (1893) by H. Bouillard, which includes some early drafts of the text.

C.I.   *Carnets Intimes*, 1883-1894. Les Éditions du Cerf, 1961.

BOOKS AND ARTICLES ON BLONDEL'S WORK REFERRED TO IN THE INTRODUCTION

BORNE, ETIENNE, *Passion de la vérité*, Arthème Fayard, 1962.

BOUILLARD, HENRI, *Blondel et le Christianisme*, Paris, Editions du Seuil, 1961.

CARTIER, ALBERT, *Existence et Vérité*, Philosophie blondélienne et problématique existentielle, Paris, Presses Universitaires de France, 1955.

DUMÉRY, HENRI, *Blondel et la religion*, essai critique sur la Lettre de 1896, Paris, Presses Universitaires de France. 1954; *Raison et Religion dans la Philosophie de l'action*, Editions du Seuil, 1964.

ÉCOLE, JEAN, *La métaphysique de l'être dans la philosophie de Maurice Blondel*, Louvain, 1959.

HENRICI, PETER, *Hegel und Blondel*, Verlag Berchmanskolleg, 1958.

LACROIX, JEAN, *Maurice Blondel*, Presses Universitaires de France, 1963.

NÉDONCELLE, MAURICE, *Existe-t-il une Philosophie Chrétienne?* Paris, Arthème Fayard. Translated into English: *Is there a Christian Philosophy?* London, Burns and Oates, 1960.

NICOLAS, J. H., O.P., 'The Centenary of Maurice Blondel,' *Revue Thomiste*, July-September, 1962.

POULAT, ÉMILE, *Histoire, Dogme et critique dans la Crise moderniste*, Paris, Casterman, 1962.

TRESMONTANT, CLAUDE, *La métaphysique de Maurice Blondel*, Paris, Editions du Seuil, 1963.

TROUILLARD, JEAN, 'Pluralité spirituelle et Unité normative selon Blondel,' *Archives de Philosophie*, January-March. 1961.

INDEX

INDEX

Action, L': presented as Blondel's thesis, 40-3; the context of his thought in it, 45-57; his refusal to reprint it, 58; some principles of his thought in it, 80-97; mentioned, 13, 14, 25, 67

Action française: founded as a reaction to public decadence, 27-8; an alliance between Positivism and Catholicism, 29; supported by Pius X, 29-30; its appeal to conservatism, 30-1; support of theologians, 31; Blondel's reasons for intervening, 31-3; mentioned, 17, 19, 25

Acton, Lord, 24

Americanism, 18, 25

Annales de Philosophie Chrétienne, 59-61

Archambault, Paul, 39, 78

Aristotle, 173-4, 238

Aubert, R., 82*n*

Ballanche Pierre, 24

Barrès, Maurice, 27, 54

Battifol Mgr P., 217

Bauer, B., 48

Baunard, Mgr, 133*n*

Bayle, Pierre, 214

Benedict XV, 26, 122

Bergson, Henri, 17, 52, 82

Besse, Dom, 31

Billot, Cardinal, 31

Biran, Maine de, 47, 48, 59

Blondel, Claude, 34

Blondel, Henri, 34

Blondel, Maurice (1861-1949): his influence, 13-19; family background and childhood, 34-5; entry to the École Normale, 35-6; *agrégation* (1886), 36, 38; development of his thought expressed in the *Carnets Intimes*, 36-8; appointed to the University of Aix, 38-9, 43; at the Collège Stanislas, 39; interest in the social Catholics and opposition to *Action française*, 39-40; presents his thesis *L'Action* (1893), 40; which is accepted after opposition, 40-3; his formulation of his life's task, 43-5; meets Rose Royer (1894), 45; the context of *L'Action*, 45-57; refusal to reprint it, 58; installs Laberthonnière as editor of *Annales de Philosophie Chrétienne* (1905), 59; correspondence and relations with him, 60-7; loss of sight (1926), 68; *L'Itinéraire* and the Trilogy, 67-9; *Letter on Apologetics*, 119-208; *History and Dogma*, 211-87

Some principles of his thought: his relevance, 80-2; the logic of Action, 82-5; the option, 85-90; the 'proof' of God's existence, 90-4; questions of terminology, 94-7

Disputed questions: the natural and the supernatural, 98-105; the notion of Christian philosophy, 105-112; the interpretation of his thought, 112-16

Blondel, Thérèse, 34

Boissard, Adéodat, 39

Bonald, Louis Gabriel de, 24, 30

Borne, Etienne: influenced by Blondel, 14; on his method, 16, 115; on the study of Blondel, 78-9

Bossuet, J.-B., the clash with Fénelon and its effects, 20, 22-4

Bouillard, Père Henri: on Blondel's influence, 13-14, 15, 16; comments on his work, 83, 90-1, 92, 94, 98-105, 107; 134n, 155n, 158n, 166n, 181n

Boutroux, Emile, 35, 40, 59

Bréhier, Emile, 106

Bremond, Henri, 22-3, 48, 60, 70, 213, 217

Broglie, Abbé de, 133n, 140

Brunetière, F., 60

Brunschwicg, Léon, 56

Burckhardt, Jacob, 214

Canet, Louis, 66n

Carnets Intimes, Blondel's early thought in, 36-8

Cartier, Père Albert, 14, 52, 53, 77, 82, 104n

Caussade, Père J. P. de, 22

Chardin, Pierre Teilhard de, 50, 75, 89

Chateaubriand, François de, 24, 51, 136

Claudel, Paul, 17; analyses the Catholic crisis, 21-2, 23; his Animus and Anima, 70-1

Clérissac, Père Humbert, 31

Combes, Emile, 26

Comte, Auguste, 29

Consalvi, Hercules, 24

Cousin, Victor, 149n

Croce, Benedetto, 73

Daudet, Léon, 31

Debussy, Claude, 17

Delbos, Victor, influenced by Blondel, 14; on Blondel and Hegel, 16-17; with Blondel at the École Normale, 36; mentioned, 49, 56, 64, 109

Denis, Père Charles, 123

Déroulède, Paul, 27

Des Bosses, Père, 46

Descartes, René, 189n, 238

d'Hulst, Mgr, 211

Dimier, Louis, 29

Drey, Sebastian, 47

Dreyfus affair, 17, 27

Duchesne, Mgr Louis, 17, 217

Duméry, Henri, 111, 112-14, 120

École, Jean, 114-15

Esprit chrétien, L', 68, 73-4, 211, 221n

Être et les êtres, L', 67, 68, 71-3

Eucken, Rudolf, 56

Fénelon, F. de la Motte, the clash with Bossuet and its effects, 20, 22-4

Fessard, Père Gaston, 14, 16

Fonsegrive, George (Yves le Querdec), 141, 143-5, 216-17

Garrigou-Lagrange, Père, 31, 64

Gayraud, Abbé Hyppolite, 42, 212

Gentile, G., 73

Gide, André, 17

Gilson, Etienne, 60, 74, 108-10

Goyau, Georges, 48, 60, 217

Graves de communi, 25

Guesde, Jules, 27

Guitton, Jean, 62

Harnack, A. von, 25
Hefele, Karl-Josef von, 47
Hegel, 16-17, 48, 49, 53
Heidegger, 72
Henrici, Dr Peter, 16, 115
Herr, Lucien, 36, 42
History and Dogma: Introductory Note, 211-17; text, 219-87; mentioned, 14, 19, 25, 51
Houtin, Albert, 211
Huby, Père, 63
Hügel, Friedrich von, 38, 42, 56-7, 211, 217
Humani generis, encyclical, 103
Huvelin, Abbé, 43

Itinéraire philosophique de Maurice Blondel, 67-79

James, William, 14, 56, 60
Janet, Paul, 40-2, 56
Jansenism, 20, 23
Janvier, Père, 31
Jaurès, Jean, 27
Jousse, Marcel, 69

Kant, Immanuel, 47, 53
Kierkegaard, S. A., 38, 48-9, 52-5, 70, 72, 75
Kuhn, F., 47

Laberthonnière, Père Lucien: his career and position, 58-9; editor of *Annales de Philosophie chrétienne*, 59; his works placed on the Index, 59; his aggressiveness, 59-60; correspon-
dence and growing differences with Blondel, 60-7, 75-6; mentioned, 48, 56, 75, 78
La Bruyère, 23*n*
Lachelier, 116
Lacordère, J.-B., 59
Lacroix, Jean, 14
Lagrange, Père M.-J., 211
Lamentabili, decree, 25
Lasson, Adolf, 14, 56
Lavelle, Louis, 14, 82
Lavoisier, 68
Lefèvre, Frédéric, 67
Le Floch, Père, 31
Leibnitz, 46, 50, 78
Leo XIII, 20, 25, 26, 124, 192
Le Senne, René, 14, 82
Letter on Apologetics: prefatory note, 119-24; text, 125-208; mentioned, 19, 25, 51
Lévy-Bruhl, 69
Loisy, A. F., 17, 25, 51, 211-12, 217, 259*n*, 270*n*
Lorin, Henri, 39, 43
Lubac, Père Henri de, 14, 104, 106-9
Luther, Martin, 175

Maistre, 24, 30
Malevez, L., 104*n*
Marcel, Gabriel, 14, 82
Maréchal, Père, 62
Maritain, Jacques, 13, 31, 64, 108-9
Marlé, Père René, 14, 216
Massis, Henri, 31
Mathieu, Cardinal, 217
Matisse, 17
Maurras, Charles, his work for *Action française*, 27-31; on Pascal, 49
Mehl, Roger, 115

Mercier, Cardinal, 15, 61-2
Merleau-Ponty, 82
Merry del Val, Cardinal, 30
Mignot, Archbishop, 60
Möhler, J. A., 47
Montalembert, Comte C. R. Forbes de, 24
Montauban Lycée, 38
Mourret, F. Abbe, 212, 216-17

Nantes, Edict of, revocation, 20, 23, 24
Napoleon III, 24
Nédoncelle, Mgr Maurice, 110-12, 115
Newman, Cardinal, 61, 213
Nicolas, Père J. H., 98-105
Nietzsche, F., 52

Ollé-Laprune, M., 33, 135-6, 140, 142*n*, 154*n*
Ossa, Manuel, 89

Pascal, 47, 48-9, 59, 73, 78, 207
Pascendi, encyclical, 25, 62
Peano, M., 276*n*
Péguy, Charles, 17, 18, 40, 67
Pensée, La, 67, 68, 69-71
Pératé, André, 15, 36
Perraud, Cardinal, 124
Pius VI, 24
Pius IX, 25, 30
Pius X, 25, 26, 29-30
Pius XI, 31
Poincaré, Raymond, 43
Problème de la mystique, Le, 67
Problème de la philosophie Catholique, Le, 67, 102*n*, 120-1

Procès de l'intelligence, Le, 67
Proust, Marcel, 17
Providentissimus Deus, encyclical, 211

Querdec, *see* Fonsegrive
Quietism, 20, 22-4

Rahner, Karl, 103-4
Ravel, M., 17
Reardon, Rev. B. M. G., 81
Renan, Ernest, 54, 282*n*
Renaudin, P., 39
Rerum novarum, 26
Riet, Georges van, 105*n*
Rivière, Jacques, 212
Rolland-Gosselin, Père, 31
Rouault, G., 17
Rousselot, Père, 63
Royer, Rose (Mme Maurice Blondel), 45

Sabatier, Alfred, 29
Sangnier, Marc, 39
Sanson, Père, 59, 66
Sartre, J.-B., 82
Schelling, F. W. von, 48, 49
Schleiermacher, F., 48
Schwalm, Père, 42, 56
Segond, Joseph, 215
Semaine Sociale de Bordeaux et le Monophorisme, 19, 26
Semaines Sociales, character of, 39
Sillon, Le, 18, 26, 39
Simon, Richard, 214
Solages, Mgr de, 108
Stanislas, Collège, 39
Staudenmaier, Franz Anton, 47

Stendhal, 23n

Taille, Maurice de la, 31
Taine, 28, 52
Tizac, H. d'Ardenne de, 69
Tresmontant, Claude, 16, 54, 58n, 78, 114
Trouillard, Père Jean, 115
Tübingen theologians, 47-8
Turinaz, Mgr, 59
Tyrrell, G., 42, 57

Valensin, Père Auguste, 40, 50, 96
Valéry, Paul, 71-2
Vaugeois, 27
Venard, M., 217
Vermeil, Edmond, 48
Veuillot, Louis, 24, 30
Vico, G. B., 214
Vigouroux, F., 217

Wehrlé, Johannes, 36, 56, 211-12, 216, 217

CPSIA information can be obtained
at www.ICGtesting.com
Printed in the USA
FSHW022001300120
66673FS

9 780802 808196